CYBERPSYCHOLOGY AND NEW MEDIA

D1434426

Cyberpsychology is the study of human interactions with the Internet, mobile computing and telephony, games consoles, virtual reality, artificial intelligence and other contemporary electronic technologies. The field has grown substantially over the past few years, and this book surveys how researchers are tackling the impact of new technology on human behaviour and how people interact with this technology.

Examining topics as diverse as online dating, social networking, online communications, artificial intelligence, health-information seeking behaviour, education online, online therapies and cybercrime, *Cyberpsychology and New Media* provides an in-depth overview of this burgeoning field and allows those with little previous knowledge to gain an appreciation of the diversity of the research being undertaken in the area.

Arranged thematically and structured for accessibility, *Cyberpsychology and New Media* will be essential reading for researchers and students in social psychology and cyberpsychology, and in communication and media studies.

Andrew Power is Head of the Faculty of Film, Art, and Creative Technologies, at the Institute of Art, Design, and Technology in Dun Laoghaire, Ireland. Prior to this Andrew spent many years in the ICT industry working for a number of multinational corporations. Originally trained as an engineer, Andrew holds an MA from the University of Dublin, an MBA from the University of Strathclyde and a doctorate in Governance from Queens University Belfast. Andrew's research interests include social networking, governance and the psychology of online crime.

Gráinne Kirwan is a lecturer in psychology in IADT, teaching on both the BSc (Hons) in Applied Psychology and the MSc in Cyberpsychology. She lectures on topics such as forensic psychology, cyberpsychology, computer-mediated communication and the psychology of virtual reality and artificial intelligence. She holds a PhD in Criminology as well as an MSc in Applied Forensic Psychology, a Postgraduate Certificate in Third Level Learning and Teaching, and an MLitt in Psychology.

CYBERPSYCHOLOGY AND NEW MEDIA

A thematic reader

Edited by
Andrew Power and
Gráinne Kirwan

Psychology Press
Taylor & Francis Group

LONDON AND NEW YORK

First published 2014
by Psychology Press
27 Church Road, Hove, East Sussex BN3 2FA

Simultaneously published in the USA and Canada
by Psychology Press
711 Third Avenue, New York, NY 10017

Psychology Press is an imprint of the Taylor & Francis Group, an informa business

British Library Cataloguing in Publication Data
A catalogue record for this book is available from the British Library

Library of Congress Cataloging in Publication Data
Power, Andrew, 1965 –
Cyberpsychology and new media: a thematic reader/Andrew Power and
Grainne Kirwan.
  pages cm
  1. Internet users – Psychology. 2. Internet – Psychological aspects.
  3. Internet – Social aspects. 4. Cyberspace – Psychological aspects.
  5. Psychology – Computer network resources.
  I. Kirwan, Grainne, 1978 – II. Title.
  HM1017.P69 2014
  302.23'1 – dc23   2013012645

ISBN: 978-1-84872-165-4 (hbk)
ISBN: 978-1-84872-166-1 (pbk)
ISBN: 978-0-20379-661-0 (ebk)

Typeset in Bembo and Stone Sans
by Florence Production Ltd, Stoodleigh, Devon, UK

Dedicated to the past and present students and staff of
the Faculty of Film, Art and Creative Technologies in IADT
for their inspiration, enthusiasm and innovation.

CONTENTS

FIGURES

TABLES

CONTRIBUTORS

Hannah Barton holds an MA in Psychology from University College Cork and is currently the coordinator of the MSc in Cyberpsychology. She has been lecturing in personality and social psychology in Applied Psychology and Cyberpsychology in IADT for the past twelve years. Her research has included altruism and positive psychology, mobile learning (podcasting), and group dynamics in both online and offline settings.

Ellen Brady has a BA and an MLitt in Psychology from University College Dublin, and is completing a Medical Research Council funded PhD at the University of Manchester. Her current work is examining the online social networks of chronically ill patients, and she has done previous research on mothers' and fathers' use of parenting websites. Her research interests include online social support, Internet forums and the ethics of online research.

Irene Connolly holds an MLitt and a PhD in Educational Psychology from Trinity College Dublin, specialising in the area of bullying. Other research has focused on learning, the use of technology in the classroom and learning difficulties. She lectures in developmental and educational psychology on the BSc (Hons) in Applied Psychology at IADT. Irene is a member of the Psychological Society of Ireland (PSI) and a former panel psychologist for the National Educational Psychological Service (NEPS).

Cliona Flood holds a BSc in Psychology from the Open University and an MSc in Work and Organizational Psychology from Dublin City University. She is a lecturer in IADT, teaching perception and ergonomics, organizational psychology and abnormal psychology on the BSc (Hons) in Applied Psychology. She has also been involved on the MSc in Cyberpsychology, supervising theses and lecturing.

Cliona is the Peer Assisted Learning coordinator at IADT. Her research interests include counselling in the online environment, podcasting as a teaching tool and the first year experience.

John Greaney is a Lecturer in Psychology at IADT. He holds a BSc (Hons) in Mathematics and Psychology and PhD in Psychology (both from the University of Birmingham). Prior to joining IADT, John worked for the Royal National Institute for the Blind in the UK and held lecturing positions at the universities of Birmingham and Manchester. These were followed by spells in industry working for Hewlett Packard and Frontend.

Olivia Hurley holds an MSc and PhD from University College Dublin in her specialty research and teaching area of sport psychology. She is a lecturer on the BSc (Hons) in Applied Psychology in IADT. Olivia is a member of the panel of sport psychologists for the Irish Institute of Sport and is also a member of PSI and BASES. She has acted as a reviewer for the *Irish Journal of Psychology* and the *International Review of Sport and Exercise Psychology* and has published research on the psychology of sports injuries.

Gráinne Kirwan is a lecturer in psychology in IADT, teaching on both the BSc (Hons) in Applied Psychology and the MSc in Cyberpsychology. She lectures on topics including forensic psychology, cyberpsychology, computer-mediated communication and the psychology of virtual reality and artificial intelligence. She holds a PhD in Criminology as well as an MSc in Applied Forensic Psychology, a Postgraduate Certificate in Third Level Learning and Teaching, and an MLitt in Psychology by Research.

Marion Palmer is Head of the Department of Technology and Psychology at IADT and chair of the Institute's Teaching and Learning Committee. Marion has worked on the MSc in Cyberpsychology since its inception with a particular focus on educational cyberpsychology. She holds a doctorate in education from Queen's University Belfast. Marion was a national NAIRTL Award of Teaching Excellence winner in 2011.

Andrew Power is Head of the Faculty of Film, Art, and Creative Technologies, at the Institute of Art, Design, and Technology in Dun Laoghaire, Ireland. Prior to this Andrew spent many years in the ICT industry working for a number of multinational corporations. Originally trained as an engineer, Andrew holds an MA from the University of Dublin, an MBA from the University of Strathclyde and a doctorate in Governance from Queens University Belfast. Andrew's research interests include social networking, governance and the psychology of online crime.

Brendan Rooney holds a PhD from University College Dublin and lectures on the MSc in Cyberpsychology as well as the undergraduate BSc (Hons) in Applied

Psychology in IADT. He is also currently Chair of the Psychological Society of Ireland's Special Interest Group for Media, Art and Cyberpsychology. Brendan's research interests include the psychological processes of cognitive and emotional engagement with virtual or fictional worlds.

The following contributors are all graduates of the MSc in Cyberpsychology at IADT and co-authored chapters along with the academic writing team. Each chapter was based on their original research work. These graduates are: Mary Aiken, Sinéad Cochrane, Eily Coghlan, Genevieve Dalton, Nicola Fox Hamilton, Graham Gilbert, Kostas Mavropalias, Phelim May, Donna McCabe, Dean McDonnell, Mary O'Brien, Richard O'Connell, Andy Osborn, Kelly Price, Karen Reilly, Mark Siggins and Rory Tierney.

PREFACE

Andrew Power and Gráinne Kirwan

This book sets out to describe a wide range of research projects in the psychology of new media. It takes as its starting point – and its source for much of the research – the MSc in Cyberpsychology taught in the Institute of Art, Design and Technology (IADT) in Dublin, Ireland. IADT is a vibrant third-level institution, thriving on new ideas and originality. Specialising in creativity and innovation, programmes embrace the opportunities and challenges of the digital age.

In 2005 staff at IADT began the development of an MSc in Cyberpsychology. The programme grew out of the existing undergraduate BSc (Hons) in Applied Psychology, which for many years had explored human computer interaction and the development of an information society. Cyberpsychology is about human–computer interaction, how technology impacts on our behaviour and our psychological state. Cyberpsychology looks at issues of design and usage and seeks to make complex systems more intuitive and easy to use. In addition to looking at how the Internet affects humans, there is a considerable body of research that examines how other technologies can influence us, for example the application of virtual reality (VR) and artificial intelligence (AI) to psychological settings, such as therapy and education.

In 2005 cyberpsychology was still a relatively new field within applied psychology. However, its emphasis on the study of human interactions with the Internet, mobile computing, mobile phones, games consoles, virtual reality and artificial intelligence was a good fit with IADT's existing research and teaching in applied psychology.

The MSc in Cyberpsychology is a ground-breaking taught programme, unique in both Ireland and the world at the time of launch although in the intervening period a number of universities have offered similar programmes. The programme provides graduates with an in-depth understanding of how humans interact with technology and in online environments. The course is wide-ranging, encompassing a variety of perspectives and sub-disciplines within cyberpsychology.

After a number of years teaching this programme it occurred to the editors that there was a body of work that had been developed by successive graduating students of the MSc in Cyberpsychology that was current, relevant and pioneering. It was decided to bring together the academic team who had supervised these theses and, with the cooperation of the graduates themselves, produce an edited volume of the best of this work from the last five years.

Structure of the book

Following a general introduction in Chapter 1 (which defines the discipline of cyberpsychology), the research studies described in the book are divided into four main themes. These are 'Communication', 'Personality and Internet Use', 'Internet Interventions and Therapies' and 'Internet and Education'. Finally, Chapter 19 explores the contribution of the research in this volume to the field of cyberpsychology and considers how cyberpsychology might respond to future technological advances.

ACKNOWLEDGEMENTS

The editors would like to acknowledge and express their gratitude to the many people who made this publication possible.

In the first instance we would like to thank Mr Jim Devine and Dr Annie Doona, past and current presidents of the Institute of Art, Design and Technology (IADT) in Dun Laoghaire, Ireland. Without their support and vision, the innovative programmes in new fields that this work draws on would not have developed. We would also like to acknowledge the role of Dr Marion Palmer, Head of Department of Technology and Psychology at IADT, for her advice and mentoring during the development of the MSc in Cyberpsychology.

We would like to thank our many colleagues who contributed chapters to this book and who worked with graduates of the programme to develop their research. They gave their advice generously, and we are honoured to work with such talented and knowledgeable individuals.

We would like to thank the editorial team in Psychology Press. In particular, we would like to thank Michael Fenton, Michael Strang and Sharla Plant for their assistance in bringing this work into print. Their patience and advice has been greatly appreciated. We would also like to thank Vodafone Ireland for their permission to use the screenshots in Figures 7.1, 7.2 and 7.3.

As always, we would like to thank our families and friends for their good-humoured understanding of our absences at social occasions due to our incessant tapping away at keyboards. We'd love to promise that we'll stop writing, but we can't!

Finally, we would like to thank the students past, present and future who contribute to the development of this subject through their curiosity, hard work and talent. It is a privilege to teach them, and to watch them push the boundaries of the field in both academia and industry.

PART I

Introduction

1

WHAT IS CYBERPSYCHOLOGY?

Gráinne Kirwan and Andrew Power

Chapter summary

Cyberpsychology is a relatively new field within applied psychology, although there are now several journals and texts examining the area. As an area of research, it assesses how we interact with others using technology, how our behaviour is influenced by technology and how our psychological states can be affected by technologies. The most commonly studied technology in cyberpsychology research is the Internet, although the area considers human interactions with many devices, including mobile phones, games consoles, virtual reality and artificial intelligence. This chapter provides a brief overview of some areas of research in cyberpsychology, including computer-mediated communication, impression management, online groups, disruptive behaviour, forensic cyberpsychology, clinical cyberpsychology and the psychology of virtual reality and artificial intelligence.

Introduction

We are living in a world where technology and communications are advancing at a phenomenal rate. Within a generation we have progressed from a time when the only communications device in the home was a traditional landline telephone to an era where a small handheld device, which can be carried around the globe, can replace a person's calendar, watch, maps, music player, camera and computer. This same device can also provide access to the Internet, and many forms of text, audio, picture and video communications. These communications can be (and are) conducted with family, friends, colleagues, acquaintances and, frequently, complete strangers.

Cyberpsychology examines how we interact with others using technology, how our behaviour is influenced by such technology, and how our psychological states can be affected by such technologies. It also considers how technology can be designed so that it best complements human capabilities and weaknesses, and provides guidance on how systems can be developed that are intuitive and easy to use. While much of cyberpsychology focuses on how the Internet affects humans, there is a considerable body of research that examines how other technologies can influence us. Much of this research examines the application of virtual reality (VR) and artificial intelligence (AI) to psychological settings, such as therapy and education. Because of this, a brief outline of the types of research conducted in these areas will be examined below, in addition to an overview of the psychology of online behaviours.

While still a relatively young field, cyberpsychology has been studied for some time. Several peer-reviewed journals focus on psychological and societal implications of new technologies. These include *Cyberpsychology, Behaviour and Social Networking* (formerly *Cyberpsychology & Behaviour,* published since 1998), *Computers in Human Behaviour* (published since 1985) and *New Media & Society* (published since 1999). There have also been several general texts and readers examining the area, including Amichai-Hamburger's *The Social Net* (2013), Barak's *Psychological Aspects of Cyberspace* (2008), Joinson *et al.*'s *The Oxford Handbook of Internet Psychology* (2007) and Gackenbach's *Psychology and the Internet* (2007).

Cyberpsychology is a diverse field, and it is impossible to describe all the relevant theories and research in a single chapter. As a result, a very brief overview of a selection of areas of research within cyberpsychology will be presented here, and the reader is encouraged to consult the books and journals listed above, the references cited in this chapter, and the relevant chapters of this book to learn about the topics in more depth. The chapter will first examine the area of Computer Mediated Communication (CMC), before considering some aspects of how social psychology can be applied to Internet behaviours – specifically in relation to impression management, online groups and disruptive behaviour. The subject of forensic cyberpsychology will be examined, identifying the key types of cybercrime and some examples of how psychology can improve our understanding of such offences. A brief overview will be provided of the application of clinical psychology to online settings, with particular focus on excessive Internet use and therapeutic interventions in online environments. The final sections of the chapter will examine the psychological applications of virtual reality and artificial intelligence.

Computer Mediated Communication (CMC)

Our online communications are becoming more frequent and use a variety of mechanisms. Within this volume alone, research is presented regarding the use of blogs (Chapter 2), social network sites (Chapters 3, 11, 12 and 18), mobile communications (Chapter 4), online dating websites (Chapter 5), virtual worlds (Chapter 8), informative websites (Chapter 6), online educational materials (Chapter 16), online recommendation sites (Chapter 9) and wikis (Chapter 17). Early online communication was wholly text-based, and users experienced the Internet as a 'lean medium', devoid of many of the additional communicative cues found in other interactions, such as tone of voice, facial expressions and body language. To compensate for this, Internet users quickly developed methods of demonstrating emotional responses online. These included emoticons (or 'smileys'), abbreviations, acronyms, paralanguage and punctuation (such as use of upper case, excessive use of question and exclamation marks, and speech acts). Linguistics online is a fascinating area of research, and considerable work in this area has been done by David Crystal (see, for example, Crystal, 2006, 2008, 2011), Naomi Baron (see, for example, Baron, 2008, 2010; Baron and af Segerstad, 2010) and Chris Fullwood (see, for example, Fullwood *et al.*, 2009, 2011; Orchard and Fullwood, 2010). One of the commonly cited worries of parents and teachers is that the use of abbreviations and acronyms online and in texting is having a negative impact on literacy. The evidence regarding this is mixed (see, for example, Bushnell *et al.*, 2011; Drouin, 2011; Crystal, 2006, 2008; Plester *et al.*, 2009), with some studies showing increased literacy and spelling ability among those children who use 'text-speak'.

There has also been considerable research focus on emotional expression online (see, for example, Derks *et al.*, 2007a, 2007b, 2008). Both Derks *et al.* (2008) and Kato *et al.* (2009) found that emoticons are more widely used to depict positive rather than negative emotions. It has also been noted that computer mediated communication can result in heightened levels of affection and emotion between individuals – a phenomenon known as 'hyperpersonal communication' (Walther, 1996, 2007). This can result in increased personal disclosures and perceived intimacy when communication occurs online (see, for example, Jiang *et al.*, 2011), which may pose particular advantages and disadvantages for different types of communication. Chapters 13 and 15 in this volume both consider the potential of computer mediated communication in therapeutic settings, which might possibly be enhanced by these disclosures. Hyperpersonal communication arises because of several factors, including the ability of the communicator to edit their messages to create specific impressions through engaging in selective self-presentation. Such impression management is considered in more detail below.

Impression management

In many social activities, we adjust our behaviour in order to modify or create a certain impression of ourselves in the eyes of our companions. In classes, we might attempt to appear as attentive as possible, perhaps even asking what we hope are intelligent-sounding questions, to impress our classmates or lecturer. In a job interview, we dress well, act in a polite manner, and attempt to make ourselves appear to be the ideal employee. On a first date, we choose a nice outfit, emphasise our positive qualities, and try not to talk too much about our former relationships or embarrassing habits. Online, we engage in similar impression management techniques. In some online contexts, such as gaming or some online bulletin boards, we may not know the other users who we interact with. In these cases we can choose to present any impression we wish – we can portray ourselves as more attractive, or taller, or even of the opposite gender (see, for example, Chapter 8 in this volume) with little risk of being found out. Aspects of impression management that are normally far beyond our control in face-to-face interactions can be managed online (Chester and Bretherton, 2007).

There may be other occasions when we have the option of using such extreme impression management but we choose not to. For example, if we use an online dating service, we are often interacting with strangers, so we could portray ourselves in whatever manner we like. However, we are less likely to do so because we may be hoping to meet a long-term partner on such a website, and if we engage in such deception, we are likely to be discovered as soon as we meet our potential partner offline. Nevertheless, there is still some evidence for some impression management in online dating – for example, Hancock and Toma (2009) found that about one-third of online dating photographs were judged as inaccurate representations of the person, with female photographs generally being less accurate than those of males, and common tactics being the use of older or retouched photographs. Chapter 5 in this volume considers our self-portrayal in online dating services in more detail.

A third type of online interaction may result in minimal impression management. The rise in the popularity of social networking sites (SNS) has meant that users are increasingly communicating online with people that they already know in offline contexts. In these cases, there is little advantage to engaging in extensive impression management – our online contacts already know us. However, we may still engage in some impression management, particularly in relation to managing others' impressions of our sociability. Underwood et al. (2011) found that some SNS users did engage in deceptive behaviour designed to self-promote the individual. It should also be remembered that it is not just our own actions online that affect others' impressions of us – Walther et al. (2008) found that the postings of online associates, and even their physical attractiveness, can affect how third parties view a profile owner. Nevertheless, our online groups can have many positive influences on our lives.

Online groups

We are all part of many different groups, such as our classmates, colleagues, family and several groups of friends, perhaps. We may also be part of other groups, such as voluntary organisations or sports groups. The chances are that we are also part of groups online – perhaps we are members of groups on social networking sites or an online community of enthusiasts for a certain hobby or collectable. We have many motivations for joining groups: sometimes it is for social support; sometimes it is to alleviate loneliness; sometimes it is to provide a social outlet; and sometimes it might be to reinforce our specific beliefs or attitudes.

Online groups may be particularly important for those who have rare or unusual interests or those who are facing a predicament that they wish to receive guidance on. They may also be particularly important for those who feel extreme levels of social anxiety or loneliness. Groups online can also be different to offline groups – it may be more difficult to clearly identify a leadership structure, and the communication mechanisms outlined above might result in unusual interpersonal relationships.

A positive aspect of online groups involves the greater social capital available to members. Social capital refers to the resources available to a person due to their network of relationships. For example, you may know several individuals who could be of assistance to you in different ways – such as a plumber, a doctor, an electrician or an accountant. Authors such as Putnam (1995) had noted a decline in social capital, describing the declining vibrancy of American civil society as evidenced by the reduced participation in community based groups. It is possible that our online interactions, particularly on social networking sites, allow us to maintain contact with a larger group of people than we would otherwise be able to (Donath and boyd, 2004), thus increasing social capital again. Our ties with this group might be looser than those we have with our smaller number of close friends, but we may still be able to draw on their resources when we need to (Ellison et al., 2007). Nevertheless, time spent using social media does not necessarily correspond to having a larger offline network, or to feeling emotionally closer to offline network members (Pollet et al., 2011).

A particular type of online group involves social activities in online games. Massively Multiplayer Online Role Playing Games (MMORPGs) can attract millions of players. In some of these games, players must cooperate in order to achieve certain tasks, so it had been thought that online groups in such games might be very important. However, Ducheneaut et al. (2006) found that the prevalence and extent of social activities in MMORPGs might be overestimated, particularly in the early stages of the game. Chapter 8 in this volume considers one aspect of MMORPGs – specifically 'gender-bending'.

Disruptive behaviour

Not all online behaviour is positive – there are several types of disruptive online behaviours, including spamming, hate speech, trolling, flaming and disruptive behaviour in online virtual worlds. Psychology can provide insights into some of these behaviours.

Flaming ('hostile and aggressive interactions via text-based computer-mediated-communication' – O'Sullivan and Flanagin, 2003) has existed for a long part of the history of the Internet, and has been studied by many researchers. Derks et al. (2007b) noted that flaming seems to be relatively rare and is an extreme form of negative emotional expression. That is not to say that the absence of flaming means that no negative emotions are felt or expressed. In a similar manner to offline communications, it is likely that upset and anger are felt far more often than a transcript would demonstrate – users are likely to keep their emotional responses in check on many occasions. It is also possible that communications can be misinterpreted. O'Sullivan and Flanagin (2003) suggested a framework of flaming, describing how some communications could be interpreted as a flame by a recipient and/or third party when they were not intended as such by the sender. Similarly, flames sent may be misinterpreted as 'innocent' remarks by recipients or third parties.

Disruptive behaviour can also occur in online virtual worlds, such as the MMORPGs mentioned above or virtual communities. Kirwan (2009) and Power and Kirwan (2011) consider these behaviours in detail. In some cases, the disruptive behaviour in virtual worlds equates to offline criminal behaviour (for example, if there is theft of virtual items that have real world value). 'Griefing', the intentional harassment of other players in an online role-playing game, is another example of disruptive behaviour. Many forms of griefing are not illegal but might result in penalties or disqualification if the actions are severe enough. Still other disruptive behaviours in online virtual worlds can involve assaults, and there have been several examples of such attacks and their effects on victims (see, for example, Kirwan, 2009; Power and Kirwan, 2012). These assaults do not necessarily equate to criminal events offline, but can still result in upset or other harm to the victim.

In addition to disruptive online behaviour, there are also many types of cybercrime for which psychology can provide some insights.

Forensic cyberpsychology

There are three main types of cybercrime, of which crimes in online virtual worlds is one (Power, 2010). Other cybercrimes comprise crimes that previously existed offline but are now greatly facilitated by the Internet, such as fraud, copyright infringement, distribution of child pornography, stalking and identity theft (see Chapters 10 and 11 in this volume for more detailed discussion of phishing and identity theft). The final type of cybercrime comprises those that could not have existed prior to the existence of computers and/or the Internet, such as malware development and hacking.

Forensic psychology can provide insights into such cybercrimes (Kirwan and Power, 2011, 2013). Criminological and psychological theories can help to determine why cybercrimes exist, and why an individual may choose to engage in cybercriminal activity. For example, social learning theory and reduced self-control have been proposed as potential explanations for engagement in digital piracy. The psychology of cybercrime also examines potential methods of deterrence, as well as the effects of such crimes on victims. Psychology can provide insights into the behaviour of victims and potential victims – see Chapter 12 for research considering Protection Motivation Theory and online behaviour.

Clinical cyberpsychology

As we spend more time online, there have been growing concerns that we are becoming dependent on the Internet, possibly to the extent of it becoming an 'addiction' (Beard, 2008; Block, 2008). There are conflicting views as to whether 'Internet addiction' should be classified as a psychological disorder (see, for example,

Block, 2008; Pies, 2009), with the American Psychiatric Association suggesting that 'Internet Use Disorder' may be included in the fifth edition of the *Diagnostic and Statistical Manual* (*DSM-5* – to be released in 2013), but that further research is required (American Psychiatric Association, 2012). Symptoms of such a disorder could include 'preoccupation with Internet gaming', 'Use of the Internet gaming to escape or relieve a dysphoric mood', 'continued excessive Internet use despite knowledge of negative psychosocial problems' and 'withdrawal symptoms when Internet is taken away'. Many of these proposed criteria refer specifically to gaming, but there have been arguments that other types of online addiction exist, including auction site addiction, cybersex addiction, and compulsive surfing. Chapter 14 in this volume considers 'cyberchondria' – searching for medical information online, often in pursuit of a diagnosis. Specific treatments have been proposed for Internet addiction (see, for example, Young, 2011; Young and de Abreu, 2010).

It is also possible that our online lives may aid our mental health. There has been a growing interest in the provision of online psychological therapy (see, for example, Suler, 2004; Bell, 2007; Jones and Stokes, 2009; Chapters 13 and 15 in this volume). There are several potential advantages to such therapy – it removes the need for the client to travel to the therapist's office, it is easier to schedule therapeutic sessions, and the client may find it easier to disclose intimate information (in accordance with hyperpersonal communication as discussed above). However, such therapies also need to be carefully managed – for example, there can be security issues, and the online medium may mean that a therapist misses some non-verbal cues, even if voice and video communication media are utilised. However, cyberpsychology considers not only how psychotherapy can be mediated via technology but also how technology can enhance the therapeutic process – most notably through the use of virtual reality.

The psychology of virtual reality

As well as studying online behaviours, cyberpsychology examines interactions with other technologies, such as mobile phones, games consoles, tablet computers and virtual reality. The most common type of virtual reality equipment involves head-mounted displays, but other types of display and interface devices also exist. Virtual reality can be used for many purposes, including gaming, architecture, engineering and data visualisation. From a psychological perspective, the most common uses of virtual reality are education and psychotherapy. In education, complex or theoretical concepts, such as particle physics or mathematical constructs, can be visualised and interacted with (see Oloruntegbe and Alam, 2010, for an overview of the use of virtual environments in science education). Virtual reality can also be used in training of medical procedures, military personnel and specialist equipment users (see, for example, Roy *et al.*, 2006; Tichon, 2007; Van Dongen *et al.*, 2011; Keller, 2011).

The use of virtual reality to augment psychotherapies has been the focus of considerable research. Much of this has focused on the use of virtual reality in the treatment of anxiety disorders, such as phobias and post-traumatic-stress-disorder (see, for example, Meyerbröker and Emmelkamp, 2011; Safir *et al.*, 2012; Pelissolo *et al.*, 2012; Reger *et al.*, 2011), although some other therapeutic interventions have been attempted, such as treatment of some addictions. In general, virtual reality treatments do not modify underlying therapeutic principles, and they are almost always designed to be conducted by (rather than replace) a human psychotherapist. Another technology that could potentially be used for psychotherapy is artificial intelligence.

The psychology of artificial intelligence

While artificial intelligence (AI) is often associated with science fiction, many aspects of our interactions with modern technology involve AI to a certain extent. This includes the behaviours of Non-Player Characters (NPCs) in computer games, as well as user assistive devices and software, such as those becoming popular in voice-controlled smartphones and artificial intelligence in search engines. Because of a phenomenon known as the 'AI effect' we tend to underestimate advances in artificial intelligence, feeling that the advances made to date are not really indicative of 'real intelligence'. Indeed, it is difficult to even define the point at which true AI is achieved. A commonly cited standard involves the 'Turing test', which a computer is deemed to have passed if it can hold a conversation indistinguishable from that of a human. However, some 'artificially intelligent' beings portrayed in science fiction would seem to fail such a test (Kirwan and Rooney, 2012), and there is some debate about whether the Turing test is an appropriate test of artificial intelligence (Nilsson, 2006; Legg and Hutter, 2006; Shieber, 2007).

There are several interesting psychological applications of AI, including allowing cognitive scientists to explore and test theories of human decision making, perception and other cognitive processes. AI can also be applied to educational settings, customer service (see, for example, Chapter 7), sales, companionship and entertainment. The possibility of using artificially intelligent 'chat bots' (computer programmes designed to carry out a human-like conversation with a user) in psychotherapy has also been explored, though mostly in theory (see, for example, Suler, 2004; Hudlicka *et al.*, 2008; Chapter 15 in this volume). While such therapy bots might have many advantages (such as a flawless memory for detail), they also raise many questions regarding ethical therapeutic interventions, including queries regarding the type of problems that such a therapy might be suited for, and the failsafes that would need to be put in place to ensure that deteriorating clients, or those who are potentially at risk of self-harm or suicide, would be diverted to a human therapist. Psychotherapeutic interventions provided by artificially intelligent agents have not yet undergone tests to compare them to interventions provided by appropriately trained therapists, and so it is uncertain how clients would react to such a situation. Nevertheless, chat bots could still add value to another aspect of psychotherapy – specifically training of therapists. For example, Gutierrez-Maldonado *et al.* (2008) used a combination of virtual reality and artificial intelligence to simulate diagnostic interviews with virtual clients. Trainee psychotherapists interviewed these virtual clients and the trainees' ability to make an accurate diagnosis was assessed. The advantages of such a system are that it can be easily monitored by supervisors and can be repeated as often as required, while no real patient is ever put at risk or inconvenienced.

Conclusion

This chapter has provided an overview of cyberpsychological research and applications, although the depth and breadth of coverage of material has been necessarily superficial. Many aspects of the areas described above have not been considered (for example, when studying online groups, other phenomena such as group formation, dissolution, productivity, group dynamics, in-group/out-group behaviours and leadership, among many other topics, could also be examined). There are also other sub-topics within cyberpsychology that have not been considered here. For example, consumer cyberpsychology (which examines topics such as consumer trust, advertising, purchasing behaviour, and so on), health cyberpsychology (examining how individuals use technology to promote healthy lifestyles or to seek information on medical conditions, among other areas) and human-computer interaction (a broad subject examining how users interact with technologies using a variety of interfaces) are also important components of cyberpsychological research. Many of these topics are considered in more depth in the chapters that follow, and the interested reader can also consult the journals and texts listed at the beginning of this chapter for further sources of research and theory in these areas. The diversity and innovativeness of cyberpsychological research is part of what makes it an exciting and absorbing area to work in, and the chapters that follow describe some of the research being conducted in this area.

References

American Psychiatric Association (2012). DSM-5 Development – Internet Use Disorder. Retrieved from: www.dsm5.org/ProposedRevisions/Pages/proposedrevision.aspx?rid =57.

Amichai-Hamburger, Y. (2013). *The Social Net: Understanding our online behaviour* (2nd edn). Oxford: Oxford University Press.

Barak, A. (2008). *Psychological Aspects of Cyberspace*. New York: Cambridge University Press.

Baron, N. (2008). *Always On: Language in an online and mobile world*. New York: Oxford University Press.

Baron, N. (2010). Discourse structures in instant messaging: The case of utterance breaks. *Language@Internet*, vol. 7, article 4.

Baron, N. and af Segerstad, Y.H. (2010). Cross-cultural patterns in mobile-phone use: Public space and reachability in Sweden, the USA and Japan. *New Media and Society*, 12, 13–34.

Beard, K.W. (2008). Internet addiction in children and adolescents. In C.B. Yarnall (ed.) *Computer Science Research Trends* (pp. 59–70). New York: Nova Science.

Bell, V. (2007). Online information, extreme communities and Internet therapy: Is the Internet good for our mental health? *Journal of Mental Health*, 16, 445–457.

Block, J.J. (2008). Issues for DSM-5: Internet addiction. *American Journal of Psychiatry*, 165, 306–307.

Bushnell, C., Kemp, N. and Martin, F. (2011). Text-messaging practices and links to general spelling skill: A study of Australian children. *Australian Journal of Educational and Developmental Psychology*, 11, 27–38.

Chester, A. and Bretherton, D. (2007). Impression management and identity online. In A. Joinson, K. McKenna, T. Postmes, and U.D. Reips (eds) *The Oxford Handbook Of Internet Psychology* (pp. 223–236). Oxford: Oxford University Press.

Crystal, D. (2006). *Language and the Internet* (2nd edn). Cambridge: Cambridge University Press.

Crystal, D. (2008). *Txting: The gr8 db8*. Oxford: Oxford University Press.

Crystal, D. (2011). *Internet Linguistics: A student guide*. Abingdon: Routledge.

Derks, D., Bos, A.E.R. and von Grumbkow, J. (2007a). Emoticons and social interaction on the Internet: The importance of social context. *Computers in Human Behaviour*, 23, 842–849.

Derks, D., Fischer, A.H. and Bos, A.E.R. (2007b). The role of emotion in computer-mediated communication: A review. *Computers in Human Behaviour*, 24, 766–785.

Derks, D., Bos, A.E.R. and von Grumbkow, J. (2008). Emoticons in computer mediated communication: Social motives and social context. *Cyberpsychology and Behaviour*, 11, 99–101.

Donath, J. and boyd, D. (2004). Public displays of connection. *BT Technology Journal*, 22, 71–82.

Drouin, M.A. (2011). College students' text messaging, use of textese and literacy skills. *Journal of Computer Assisted Learning*, 27, 67–75. doi: 10.1111/j.1365-2729.2010.00399.x.

Ducheneaut, N., Yee, N., Nickell, E. and Moore, R.J. (2006). 'Alone together?' Exploring the social dynamics of massively multiplayer online games. In *Proceedings of the ACM conference on Human Factors in Computing Systems (CHI 2006)* (pp. 407–416). New York: ACM.

Ellison, N.B., Steinfield, C. and Lampe, C. (2007). The benefits of Facebook 'friends': Social capital and college students' use of online social network sites. *Journal of Computer-Mediated Communication*, 12 (4), article 1. Available at: http://jcmc.indiana.edu/vol12/issue4/ellison.html.

Fullwood, C., Sheehan, N., and Nicholls, W. (2009). Blog function revisited: A content analysis of MySpace blogs. *CyberPsychology and Behaviour*, 12, 685–689.

Fullwood, C., Evans, L. and Morris, N. (2011). Linguistic androgyny on MySpace. *Journal of Language and Social Psychology*, 30 (1), 114–124.

Gackenbach, J. (2007). *Psychology and the Internet: Intrapersonal, interpersonal and transpersonal implications* (2nd edn). Burlington, MA: Academic Press.

Gutierrez-Maldonado, J., Alsina, I., Ferrer, M. and Aguilar, A. (2008). Virtual reality and artificial intelligence to train abilities of diagnosis in psychology and psychiatry. In J. Luca and E. Weippl (eds) *Proceedings of World Conference on Educational Multimedia, Hypermedia and Telecommunications 2008* (pp. 5871–5876). Chesapeake, VA: AACE.

Hancock, J.T. and Toma, C.L. (2009). Putting your best face forward: The accuracy of online dating photographs. *Journal of Communication*, 59, 367–386.

Hudlicka, E., Lisetti, C., Hodge, D., Paiva, A., Rizzo, A. and Wagner, E. (2008). Panel on 'Artificial Agents for Psychotherapy'. Association for the Advancement of Artificial Intelligence. Retrieved from: www.aaai.org/Papers/Symposia/Spring/2008/SS-08-04/SS08-04-011.pdf.

Jiang, C.L., Bazarova, N.N. and Hancock, J.T. (2011). The disclosure-intimacy link in computer-mediated communication: An attributional extension of the hyperpersonal model. *Human Communication Research*, 37, 58–77.

Joinson, A., McKenna, K., Postmes, T. and Reips, U.D. (2007). *The Oxford Handbook of Internet Psychology*. Oxford: Oxford University Press.

Jones, G. and Stokes, A. (2009). *Online Counselling: A handbook for practitioners*. Basingstoke: Palgrave Macmillan.

Kato, S., Kato, Y. and Scott, D. (2009). Relationships between emotional states and emoticons in mobile phone email communication in Japan. *International Journal on E-Learning*, 8, 385–401.

Keller, J. (2011). SRI International to develop prototype virtual-reality training system for Marine Corps infantry. *Military and Aerospace Electronics*, 22, 6.

Kirwan, G. (2009). Presence and the victims of crime in online virtual worlds. Proceedings of Presence 2009. The 12th Annual International Workshop on Presence. Los Angeles, 11–13 November.

Kirwan, G. and Power, A. (2011). *The Psychology of Cyber Crime: Concepts and principles*. Hershey, PA: Information Science Reference.

Kirwan, G. and Rooney, B. (2012). The judgement of emotion and intellectual ability in character dialogue of *Blade Runner* and *Star Trek: The Next Generation*. In C. Dowd (Chair), Turing Arts Symposium 2012. Symposium conducted at the meeting of the Society for the Study of Artificial Intelligence and Simulation of Behaviour (AISB) and International Association for Computing and Philosophy (IACAP) World Congress 2012 – Alan Turing, Birmingham. Proceedings available at http://events.cs.bham.ac.uk/turing12/proceedings/05.pdf.

Kirwan, G. and Power, A. (2013). *Cybercrime: Characteristics and behaviours of online offenders*. Cambridge: Cambridge University Press.

Legg, S. and Hutter, M. (2006). A formal measure of machine intelligence. Proceedings of the 15th Annual Machine Learning Conference of Belgium and The Netherlands (Benelearn 2006), 73–80.

Meyerbröker, K. and Emmelkamp, P.M.G. (2011). Virtual reality exposure therapy for anxiety disorders: The state of the art. In S. Brahnam and L. Jain (eds) *Advanced Computational Intelligence Paradigms in Healthcare: 6. Virtual reality in psychotherapy, rehabilitation and assessment* (pp. 47–62). Berlin: Springer.

Nilsson, N.J. (2006). Human level artificial intelligence? Be serious! *AI Magazine*, 26, 68–75.

Oloruntegbe, K.O. and Alam, G.M. (2010). Evaluation of 3D environments and virtual realities in science teaching and learning: The need to go beyond perception referents. *Scientific Research and Essays*, 5, 948–954.

Orchard, L.J. and Fullwood, C. (2010). Current perspectives on personality and Internet use. *Social Science Computer Review*, 28 (2), 155–169.

O'Sullivan, P.B. and Flanagin, A.J. (2003). Reconceptualising 'flaming' and other problematic messages. *New Media & Society*, 5, 69–94.

Pelissolo, A., Zaoui, M., Aguayo, G., Yao, S.N., Roche, S., Ecochard, R., Gueyffier, F., Pull, C., Berthoz, A., Jouvent, R. and Cottraux, J. (2012). Virtual reality exposure therapy versus cognitive behaviour therapy for panic disorder with agoraphobia: A randomised comparison study. *Journal of CyberTherapy and Rehabilitation*, 5, 35–43.

Pies, R. (2009). Should DSM-5 designate 'Internet Addiction' a mental disorder? *Psychiatry*, 6, 31–37.

Plester, B., Wood, C. and Joshi, P. (2009). Exploring the relationship between children's knowledge of text message abbreviations and school literacy outcomes. *British Journal of Developmental Psychology*, 27, 145–161.

Pollet, T.V., Roberts, S.G.B. and Dunbar, R.I.M. (2011). Use of social network sites and instant messaging does not lead to increased offline social network size, or to emotionally closer relationships with offline network members. *Cyberpsychology, Behaviour and Social Networking*, 14, 253–258.

Power, A. (2010). The online public or cybercitizen. *SCRIPTed: A Journal of Law, Technology and Society*, 7 (1), 185–195. Retrieved from: www.law.ed.ac.uk/ahrc/script-ed/vol7-1/power.pdf.

Power, A. and Kirwan, G. (2011). Ethics and legal aspects of virtual worlds. In A. Dudley, J. Braman and G. Vincenti (eds) *Investigating Cyber Law and Cyber Ethics: Issues, impacts and practices* (Chapter 7). Hershey, PA: Information Science Reference.

Power, A. and Kirwan, G. (2012). Trust, ethics and legal aspects of social computing. In G. Dodig-Crnkovic, A. Rotolo, G. Sartor, J. Simon and C. Smith (Chairs), *Social Turn – Social Computing – Social Cognition – Social Networks and Multi-agent Systems*. Symposium conducted at the meeting of the Society for the Study of Artificial Intelligence and Simulation of Behaviour (AISB) and International Association for Computing and Philosophy (IACAP) World Congress 2012 – Alan Turing 2012, Birmingham.

Putnam, R. (1995). Bowling alone: America's declining social capital. *Journal of Democracy*, 6, 65–78.

Reger, G.M., Holloway, K.M., Candy, C., Rothbaum, B.O., Difede, J., Rizzo, A.A. and Gahm, G.A. (2011). Effectiveness of virtual reality exposure therapy for active duty soldiers in a military mental health clinic. *Journal of Traumatic Stress*, 24, 93–96.

Roy, M.J., Sticha, D.L., Kraus, P.L. and Olsen, D.E. (2006). Simulation and virtual reality in medical education and therapy: A protocol. *Cyberpsychology and Behaviour*, 9, 245–247.

Safir, M.P., Wallach, H.S. and Bar-Zvi, M. (2012). Virtual reality cognitive-behaviour therapy for public speaking anxiety: One year follow-up. *Behaviour Modification*, 36, 235–246.

Shieber, S. (2007). The Turing Test as interactive proof. *Noûs*, 41, 686–713.

Suler, J. (2004). Psychotherapy in Cyberspace: A five dimensional model of online and computer mediated psychotherapy. Retrieved from: www-usr.rider.edu/~suler/psycyber/therapy.html

Tichon, J.G. (2007). Using presence to improve a virtual training environment. *Cyberpsychology and Behaviour*, 10, 781–787.

Underwood, J.D.M., Kerlin, L. and Farrington-Flint, L. (2011). The lies we tell and what they say about us: Using behavioural characteristics to explain Facebook activity. *Computers in Human Behaviour*, 27, 1621–1626.

Van Dongen, K.W., Ahlberg, G., Bonavina, L., Carter, F.J., Grancharov, T.P., Hyltander, A., Schijven, M.P., Stefani, A., van der Zee, D.C. and Broeders, I.A.M.J. (2011). European consensus on a competency-based virtual reality training program for basic endoscopic surgical psychomotor skills. *Surgical Endoscopy*, 25, 166–171.

Walther, J.B. (1996). Computer-mediated communication: Impersonal, interpersonal and hyperpersonal interaction. *Communication Research*, 23, 3–43.

Walther, J.B. (2007). Selective self-presentation in computer-mediated communication: Hyperpersonal dimensions of technology, language and cognition. *Computers in Human Behaviour*, 23, 2538–2557.

Walther, J.B., Van Der Heide, B., Kim, S.Y., Westerman, D. and Tong, S.T. (2008). The role of friends' behaviour on evaluations of individuals' Facebook profiles: Are we known by the company we keep? *Human Communication Research*, 34, 28–49.

Young, K.S. (2011). CBT-IA: The first treatment model for Internet addiction. *Journal of Cognitive Psychotherapy*, 25, 304–312.

Young, K.S. and de Abreu, C.N. (2010). *Internet Addiction: A handbook and guide to evaluation and treatment*. Hoboken, NJ: John Wiley & Sons.

PART II

Communication

The growth of Web 2.0 technologies and the proliferation of social networking and mobile telephony in particular have had a profound effect on how we communicate. Web 2.0 refers to cumulative changes in the ways software developers and end-users interact with the Web. The creative process by which humans interact with technology is changing and developing at an increasingly rapid pace. Web 2.0 is associated with web applications that facilitate interactive information sharing, interoperability, user-centred design and collaboration. Examples include web-based communities, hosted services, web applications, social-networking sites, video-sharing sites, wikis and blogs. A Web 2.0 application allows its users to interact with other users or to change content. This change is significant because these new media are pervasive, user friendly, non-technical, platform independent and focused on collaboration and interaction. They are pervasive in that young and old have found applications to suit their needs. They are user friendly in that the software and its features are expected to be intuitive; if it has to be learnt, it will not be used. They are non-technical in that no prior technical or programming knowledge is required for use – increasingly the creation as well as the use of new applications is within the capabilities of the novice user. They are platform independent not just between manufacturers of equipment – applications are equally available on computers, mobile phones, tablet computers and every conceivable device. Finally, they are different because their focus is not on using the software in isolation to perform some task (such as word processing): rather, their focus is on collaboration and interaction. Users of new media are communicating, interacting, collaborating and working in groups. Often this is so subliminal as to be invisible to users, but when online they are now part of a community of users and contributing to the nature of the experience of all the others.

The chapters brought together in this section look at blogging, Facebook usage, technology separation anxiety, online dating and gendered web design. Chapter 2 investigates the attitudes to blogging in both bloggers and non-bloggers. It examines issues of identity, privacy, motivation and social capital. Chapter 3 investigates the motivations and personality traits that influence people's Facebook usage. Examining the distinction between older and younger users and male and female users, it seeks to establish whether personality factors influence Facebook usage. Chapter 4 investigates people's dependence on their mobile phones, their willingness to be separated from their mobile phones and the perceived anxiety associated with this separation. The study provides an insight into the unwillingness of people to be separated from their mobile phones. Chapter 5 compares the profiles of American and Irish men on online dating sites to establish if cultural differences result in differences in how profile authors write about themselves, specifically in relation to honesty and trustworthiness. Chapter 6 investigates how the graphic design of science, technology, engineering and mathematics (STEM) websites is perceived by female students, how these perceptions might influence their motivations to pursue careers in STEM, and whether designing science websites in a more female-orientated manner might encourage greater female participation in STEM careers.

2

BLOGS

A study into current uses and perceptions in society

Sinéad Cochrane and Hannah Barton

Chapter summary

This chapter investigates attitudes and perceptions regarding blogs in both bloggers and non-bloggers. The research was conducted online and it was found that non-bloggers are more concerned than bloggers about the persistent nature of the Internet. No differences were found between the groups regarding online privacy. The research found that a majority of bloggers publish online using their real name, with their primary motivation to blog being the ability to articulate their ideas through writing. Bloggers tend to consider their blogging as a form of journalism. This research found that blogging can increase social capital and has limited negative effect on bloggers' lives.

Introduction and background

Blogs are described as 'frequently updated websites where content (text, pictures, sound files, etc.) is posted on a regular basis and displayed in reverse chronological order' (Schmidt, 2007, p. 1) and feature archive functionality. Blogs often consist of regular, date-stamped articles that represent a time-line (Kirchhoff *et al.*, 2007) and are primarily used for 'personally oriented written communication' (Kirchhoff *et al.*, 2007, p. 3) where the author publishes information about themselves or about topics of interest to them (Baker and Moore, 2008). Blogs are unlike web pages in that they are effortless, requiring little or no technical ability, and can be published online for free. They also differ from web pages due to the temporally ordered nature of blog entries and the informal writing techniques employed by most bloggers (Kirchhoff *et al.*, 2007).

The popularity of blogs

Blogs are popular because of their flexibility and interactive components, which differentiate them from more traditional print or digital publication formats (Herring *et al.*, 2005) and give the audience the ability to immediately respond and therefore gratify different needs from those met by other online resources (Kaye, 2007). Blog users enjoy expressing their opinions, and there is a perception that bloggers present information in ways that are not found elsewhere (Kaye, 2007). Researchers have identified convenience, checking information found in other media, information seeking and a sense of community as the four main reasons why Internet users frequent blogs (Johnson *et al.*, 2007).

The social aspects of blogging

Many bloggers rate the effectiveness of their writing on the number of links to their blog (Marlow, 2004). Through comments, links to other blogs and other online sources, many blogs form clustered networks of interconnectivity (Schmidt, 2007). This is referred to as the blogosphere. 'The structure of the blogosphere can be seen as a combination of a network of information and a network of people' (Kirchhoff *et al.*, 2007, p. 3). These networks are often formed out of a commonality, such as interests, political outlook or geography. As a result, diverse social networks and online communities can develop, demonstrating the strength of acquaintances or 'weak ties'. This suggests that blogging has the potential to increase social capital. Social capital can be described as the resources accumulated through the relationships among people (Coleman, 1988). What facilitates social capital is the network of social relationships, trust among members and the norms of behaviour (Blanchard, 2004). The Internet supports social networks, helping to build social capital (Raine *et al.*, 2006). Having access to individuals outside one's usual close circle can provide access to non-redundant information, resulting in benefits such as employment connections (Granovetter, 1973).

Weak ties are typical of relationships among casual acquaintances and are important for sharing information, making contacts and increasing awareness about new ideas (Wellman and Gulia, 1999). Weak tie relationships focus on information exchange and debate (Granovetter, 1973). Claims have been made that online weak ties are of poorer quality than strong ties already established offline (Kraut *et al.*, 1998). However, research by Ando and Sakamoto (2008) found that online friendships, weak ties, were psychologically beneficial. Strong tie relationships can and do initiate online and can successfully move offline (Whitty and Joinson, 2008).

What motivates blogging?

There are many possible motivations for blogging. It can be ego gratifying and behaviourally empowering, and authorship/ownership of a blog can give individuals a sense of autonomy that is intrinsically motivating (Sundar *et al.*, 2007). Blogs can be used to plan and organise ideas, or to help process emotionally difficult situations, allowing the author to engage in emotional expression and cathartic venting (Baker and Moore, 2008). Blogging has been compared to keeping a journal or diary, which is known to be therapeutic in nature, the difference being that blogs offer the presence of peer commentary (Baker and Moore, 2008). Bloggers are motivated by a desire to publish, to provide information to others, to present information on their interests and refine their thinking (Loftus, 2006). This research seeks to build on these findings and investigate the personal and professional motivations of bloggers. Personal motivations could include life-documentation, the expression of deeply felt emotions, and the forming of connections with likeminded people. Professional motivations could include providing commentary and opinions, sharing knowledge and experience, and articulating ideas through writing and self-promotion.

The self and blogging

Research has found that people are likely to disclose more information about themselves online in comparison to face-to-face encounters (Whitty and Joinson, 2008). How much someone self-discloses online is, however, dependent on the space online and the audience (Whitty and Joinson, 2008). Truthful self-disclosure online is also linked to an individual's perceptions of the situation, the goals of the disclosure, factors related to the interactional dynamic (who they are disclosing to) and their privacy concerns (Whitty and Joinson, 2008), if any. There are many possible positive psychological benefits for bloggers that write about and talk about their problems online. Research by Ko and Kuo found that self-disclosure by bloggers had a significant effect on their perception of social integration and social capital, which in turn promoted their subjective well-being. They suggest that self-disclosure through blogging could promote the creation of intimate relationships and that the social capital built through blogging may improve a blogger's social contact, interpersonal communication and overall quality of life (Ko and Kuo, 2009).

Identity and anonymity online

Anonymity online is often cited as the explanation for the high levels of self-disclosure online (Sobel, 2000) as it can help individuals to explore their identity, reduce shyness and encourage interactions with others online (Whitty and Carr, 2006). However, Whitty and Joinson (2008) suggest that the readers of blogs are usually already known to the blogger – they are not strangers. Joinson and Paine (2007) argue that increased surveillance of online activities makes anonymity an invalid explanation for high levels of self-disclosure, and that trust, control, costs and benefits are other factors that must be considered with regard to the disinhibitory effect of the Internet.

Credibility in blogging

'Bloggers are communicators whose potential to influence is derived from their credibility (i.e., expertise on a subject or perception of being trustworthy, unbiased and independent)' (Kaid and Postelnicu, 2007, p. 152). Internet users may perceive blogs as being more credible because they are viewed as being independent from corporate controlled media (Johnson et al., 2007). However, previous research has found conflicting results concerning how much trust the public puts in blogs (Johnson et al., 2007). The more that an individual relies on a source, the higher credibility they attribute to it (Johnson and Kaye, 2000). This could suggest that frequent users of blogs would rate them as highly credible sources, and this research will query that. To best gauge media credibility the following variables are measured: believability, fairness, accuracy and depth of information (Johnson et al., 2007).

Deception and trust online

The Internet offers individuals the freedom of truthful self-disclosure but also allows users to 'engage in creative self-presentation, misrepresentation and outright lies' (Whitty and Joinson, 2008, p. 55). Feature based theory suggests that three dimensions must be considered when examining deception: whether the medium is synchronous, recordless and distributed (Hancock et al., 2004). Hanock et al. (2004) proposed that individuals were less likely to lie in a recordable medium. Because of the archiving feature of blogging, this could suggest that bloggers are less likely to lie on their blogs in comparison to other online channels, such as synchronous chat. However, with regard to blogging there are issues of identity concealment to consider – while deceptive, they are sometimes necessary to preserve the bloggers' privacy (Utz, 2005).

The Internet poses unique information privacy threats. Advances in processing power, storage capacity and wider communication connectivity mean that information can be efficiently and cheaply collected, stored and exchanged (Sparck-Jones, 2003). Once information is recorded online it rarely disappears. It has permanence, and the individual the information belongs to may have no power to decide what happens to it (Sparck-Jones, 2003).

The overall aim of this research is to explore the perceptions, attitudes and behaviours of bloggers and non-blogging Internet users. Perceptions of the credibility of blogs were investigated. Attitudes to the issues surrounding blogging – trust, honesty, liability, privacy and permanence – were explored. This paper also summarises findings on writers' behaviours with regard to identity, motivations and socialisation

The current study

This was a correlation study using an online survey. Cluster sampling was applied to gather participants, and a snowball technique was used that allowed respondents to forward the survey to fellow blog readers and writers. The survey consisted of 18 standard questions, and either 19 additional questions (37 questions in total) or 4 additional questions (22 questions in total) depending on whether the participant was a blogger or someone who read blogs without contributing to a blog themselves (non-bloggers). The independent variable was whether the participant was the author of a blog or not. The main dependent variables included levels of concern and ratings of credibility. Other variables investigated included the effect of blog writing on the social/academic/personal lives of bloggers and whether bloggers with personal motivations were more likely to publish under a pseudonym.

There was a sample size of 422 participants in total. Of these, 275 (65.2 per cent) of the participants were male and 147 (34.8 per cent) were female. The ages of participants ranged from 18 to 86. Bloggers comprised 244 (57.8 per cent) of the sample, with 178 respondents engaging in reading (but not writing) of blogs. The majority of participants (60.7 per cent) indicated that they read blogs more than once a day, with a further 16.4 per cent reading blogs once a day.

Summary of findings

The key findings of this research related to credibility, deception and liability of content, privacy and permanence, motivations and effects of blogging.

Credibility

The majority of participants (84.8 per cent) indicated that they had attempted to double-check information found on blogs at least once. When asked to assess the credibility of blogs, bloggers assigned a mean score of 13.38 ($SD = 2.743$), while non-bloggers assigned a mean score of 12.64 ($SD = 2.999$).

Deception and liability of content

The vast majority (86.96 per cent) of blog writers indicated that they actively attempt to verify information before posting it to their blog. However, 12.93 per cent indicated that they had lied on their blog. Reasons given for these lies included the maintenance of anonymity (22.58 per cent of lying bloggers) and the embellishment of stories or for obvious fiction or satire (35.48 per cent of lying bloggers). The majority of the sample (87.56 per cent) indicated that they believed that it was possible for a legal action to be taken against a blogger because of what they had published, although this belief was slightly less prevalent among bloggers than among non-bloggers.

Bloggers were asked how liable they considered themselves to be for content posted to their blogs, considering both the blog itself and the comments of other users on blog posts. A minority (7.39 per cent) indicated that they thought they were not at all liable, with 36.52 per cent indicating that they were slightly liable and 56.09 per cent indicating that they believed themselves to be completely liable. When asked about how concerned they were about the possible misuse of information on their blogs, 38.26 per cent of bloggers indicated they were 'concerned' and 10 per cent indicated they were 'very concerned'.

Privacy and permanence

Only a minority (39.49 per cent) of bloggers used a pseudonym, with most using their real name. The overall mean score of rates of concern with regard to privacy online was 3.66 (out of a possible maximum of 5). Most (65.8 per cent) of the total sample indicated they were 'concerned' or 'very concerned' about online privacy. The mean score of rates of concern with regard to privacy issues online in the non-bloggers group was 3.69 (SD = .069; again out of a maximum of 5), and in the bloggers group the mean score was 3.64 (SD = .064). The overall mean score for the persistent nature of the Internet was 3.39 (n = 422), with 52.37 per cent of the total participant sample indicating that they were 'concerned' or 'very concerned' about online permanence. The mean score of rates of concern with regard to the persistent nature of the Internet in the non-bloggers group was 3.54 (SD = .957) and in the bloggers group this was 3.28 (SD = 1.056).

Motivations for blog writing

Various motivations were cited for blog writing. Personally oriented motivations included 'To document my life' (10.43 per cent), 'To express deeply felt emotions' (1.3 per cent), and 'To meet and connect with likeminded people' (5.65 per cent). In total, 21.74 per cent of bloggers indicated that they had personally oriented motivations for blogging. Professionally oriented motivations were cited by 78.22 per cent of bloggers, including 'To provide commentary and opinions' (21.74 per cent), 'To share my knowledge and experience' (1.74 per cent), 'To articulate ideas through writing' (36.96 per cent) and 'To promote myself online' (8.26 per cent).

Effects of blogging

Writing a blog was found to have a slightly positive effect on the social lives of bloggers (mean = 3.745), with 81.3 per cent of bloggers having made online friends because of their blogging, and 62.07 per cent meeting people offline because of blogging. Furthermore, 28.45 per cent of bloggers made close friends because of their blogging. Less than 1 per cent (.87 per cent) indicated that blogging had a negative effect, with 55.4 per cent indicating that blogging had a positive or very positive effect for them. Bloggers were asked what impact blog writing had on their professional lives, with 69.47 per cent indicating that it had a positive or very positive effect. Only 3.52 per cent indicated that blogging had a negative or very negative effect on their professional lives.

The negative effects mentioned by bloggers included personal and legal threats. These fell into several categories: 17.39 per cent of the negative effects experienced by bloggers were personal; 39.13 per cent related to flaming; 15.22 per cent were in the form of legal threats; 19.57 per cent were issues regarding companies or organisations; and 8.7 per cent involved other issues. A minority of bloggers (10.92 per cent) had experienced having their blog content illegitimately sourced by the traditional media. Of this, 29.17 per cent included photos or images and 58.33 per cent included written content.

Interpretation

This study showed that there is a high readership level of blogs. Both bloggers and non-bloggers were found to have similar levels of concern regarding online privacy. Bloggers were less concerned than non-bloggers regarding online permanence, and these results are similar to those found in previous studies (Viégas, 2005).

Blogging was found to have a positive effect on social lives, particularly in the development of weak tie relationships, although strong tie relationship formation was also noted, in line with Whitty and Joinson (2008). Despite socialisation not being a popular primary motivation for blogging, it is seemingly a by-product of writing a blog. This suggests blogging has the potential to positively affect the social lives of bloggers, especially with regard to weak ties that are psychologically and intellectually beneficial (Wellman and Gulia, 1999).

Bloggers rated the credibility of blogs slightly higher than the non-bloggers did, indicating that bloggers consider blogs as more credible as forms of media in comparison to the non-bloggers. This could suggest that a higher level of interaction with the medium increases perceptions of its credibility. Bloggers that used their real name to publish their blog were more likely to cite professional reasons as their primary motivation for blogging, and the majority of bloggers indicated that they used their real name online. However, a minority of bloggers indicated that they had lied at least once on their blog, often describing the maintenance of their anonymity as the reason for doing so. Interestingly, bloggers who used a pseudonym did not differ in their levels of concern for privacy or permanence online in comparison to those that blogged using their real name. A large majority of both the bloggers and non-bloggers believed it was possible for legal action to be taken against a blogger because of what they had published online.

The findings of this study suggest that the major appeals of blogging are to improve writing skills and self-expression through sharing their points of view. These two most popular motivations were categorised as professionally orientated, distinguishing them from personally orientated motivations such as 'To document my life' and 'To express deeply felt emotions'. Only a minority of bloggers listed personally orientated motivations as their primary motivation for blogging, suggesting that they were more interested in writing and publishing than discussing their personal lives and self-expression. This differs from the traditional concepts of personal blogs having characteristics in common with conventional diaries and that they are actually much more topical in nature. This suggests that researchers in future should perhaps consider motivations over categorisation as a way to investigate blogging behaviour. Although only a small number of bloggers indicated that socialising was a primary motivation, many listed it as an additional motivation. A substantial minority of bloggers had experienced minor personal or legal issues because of their blogging.

Conclusion

This study has highlighted interesting findings regarding the motivations, privacy awareness, credibility and positive and negative effects of blogging on the blogger. It highlights an increase in shared intellectual capital as well as an increase in social capital.

References

Ando, R. and Sakamoto, A. (2008). The effect of cyber-friends on loneliness and social anxiety: Differences between high and low self-evaluated physical attractiveness groups. *Computers in Human Behaviour*, 24 (3), 993–1009.

Baker, J.R. and Moore, S.M. (2008). Distress, coping, and blogging: Comparing new Myspace users by their intention to blog. *CyberPsychology and Behaviour*, 11 (1), 81–85.

Blanchard, A. (2004). The effects of dispersed virtual communities on face-to-face social capital. In M. Huysman and V. Wolf (eds) *Social Capital and Information Technology* (pp. 53–73). London: MIT Press.

Coleman, J.S. (1988). Social capital in the creation of human capital. *American Journal of Sociology*, 94, 95–120.

Granovetter, M. (1973). The strength of weak ties. *American Journal of Sociology*, 78, 1360–1380.

Hancock, J.T., Thom-Santeilli, J. and Richie, T. (2004). Deception and design: The impact of communication technologies on lying behaviour. *Proceedings of the Conference on Computer Human Interaction* (pp. 130–136). New York: ACM Press.

Herring, S.C., Scheidt, L.A., Bonus, S. and Wright, E. (2005). Weblogs as a bridging genre. *Information, Technology and People*, 18 (2), 142–171.

Johnson, T.J. and Kaye, B.K. (2000). Using is believing: The influence of reliance on the credibility of online political information among politically interested Internet users. *Journalism and Mass Communication Quarterly*, 77 (4), 865–879.

Johnson, T.J., Kaye, B.K., Bichard, S.L. and Wong, W.J. (2007). Every blog has its day: Politically-interested Internet users' perceptions of blog credibility. *Journal of Computer-Mediated Communication*, 13 (1). Retrieved from: http://jcmc.indiana.edu/vol13/issue1/johnson.html

Joinson, A.N. and Paine, C.B. (2007). Self disclosure, privacy and the Internet. In A.N. Joinson, K. McKenna, T. Postmes, and U.D. Reips (eds) *Oxford Handbook of Internet Psychology* (pp. 237–252). Oxford: Oxford University Press.

Kaid, L.L. and Postelnicu, M. (2007). Credibility of political messages on the Internet. In M. Treymane (ed.) *Blogging, Citizenship, and the Future of Media* (pp. 149–164). London: Routledge.

Kaye, K.B. (2007). Blog use motivations: An exploratory study. In M. Treymane (ed.) *Blogging, Citizenship, and the Future of Media* (pp. 127–148). London: Routledge.

Kirchhoff, L., Bruns, A. and Nicolai, T. (2007). *Investigating the impact of the blogosphere: Using PageRank to determine the distribution of attention*. Retrieved from: www.alexandria.unisg.ch/EXPORT/DL/38960.pdf.

Ko, H.C. and Kuo, F.Y. (2009). Can blogging enhance subjective well-being through self-disclosure? *CyberPsychology and Behaviour*, 12 (1), 75–79.

Kraut, R., Patterson, M., Lundmark, V., Kiesler, S., Mukopadhyay, T. and Sherlies, W. (1998). Internet paradox: A social technology that reduces social involvement and psychological well-being? *American Psychologist*, 53, 1017–1031.

Loftus, M. (2006). The Irish blogosphere: Who is blogging and what motivates them to do so? Dissertation submitted for MSc in Internet Systems. Dublin: Dublin City University.

Marlow, C. (2004). Audience, structure and authority in the weblog community. Presented at the International Communication Association Conference, May, 2004, New Orleans, LA. Retrieved from: http://web.media.mit.edu/~cameron/cv/pubs/04-01.pdf.

Rainie, L., Horrigan, J., Wellman, B. and Boase, J. (2006). The strength of Internet ties: Pew American and Life Project. Retrieved from: www.pewinternet.org/Reports/2006/The-Strength-of-Internet-Ties.aspx.

Sparck-Jones, K. (2003). Privacy: What's different now? *Interdisciplinary Science Reviews*, 28, 287–292.

Schmidt, J. (2007). Blogging practices: An analytical framework. *Journal of Computer-Mediated Communication*, 12(4), 1409–1427.

Sobel, D.L. (2000). The process that 'John Doe' is due: Addressing the legal challenge to Internet anonymity. *Virginia Journal of Law and Technology*, 5, 1522–1687.

Sundar, S.S., Edwards, H.H., Hu Y. and Stavrositu, C. (2007). Blogging for better health: Putting the 'public' back in public health. In M. Treymane (ed.) *Blogging, Citizenship, and the Future of Media* (pp. 83–102). London: Routledge.

Utz, S. (2005). Types of deception and underlying, motivation: What people think. *Social Science Computer Review*, 23, 49–56.

Viégas, F.B. (2005). Bloggers' expectations of privacy and accountability: An initial survey. *Journal of Computer-Mediated Communication*, 10 (3), 12. Retrieved from: http://jcmc.indiana.edu/vol10/issue3/viegas.html.

Wellman, B. and Gulia, M. (1999). Net surfers don't ride alone. In B. Wellman (ed.) *Networks in the Global Village* (pp. 331–366). Boulder, CO: Westview Press.

Whitty, M.T. and Carr, A.N. (2006). *Cyberspace Romance: The psychology of online relationships*. Basingstoke: Palgrave Macmillan.

Whitty, M.T. and Joinson, A.N. (2008) *Truth, Lies and Trust on the Internet*. London: Routledge.

3

THE MOTIVATIONS AND PERSONALITY TRAITS THAT INFLUENCE FACEBOOK USAGE

Graham Gilbert and Hannah Barton

Chapter summary

This chapter investigates the motivations and personality traits that influence people's Facebook usage. An online survey found that 'keeping in contact with existing friends' was the most commonly cited motive for using Facebook. However, boredom was not rated significantly differently from this social connectivity motive. It was found that different demographic groups use Facebook for different purposes: social connectivity (females) and boredom (males) both motivated the younger users more than the older ones. In an investigation of personality traits, those with high levels of conscientiousness trait were found to have a lower number of friends on their Facebook profiles; but overall, personality factors were not found to be as influential on Facebook usage as previous literature has suggested.

Introduction

'The Internet has changed the nature of human social interaction in such a way as to allow us to connect with many individuals' (Guadagno *et al.*, 2007, p. 1994). Boyd and Ellison (2007) explain that since their introduction, social networking sites (or SNSs) have attracted millions of users who have 'integrated these sites into their daily practices'. Wilson *et al.* (2009) claim that SNSs have come to play such an important role in facilitating communication and relationships for so many people – especially young people – that it would therefore seem imperative that the various factors that influence their usage be investigated.

There is a growing body of evidence indicating that individual differences on the Big Five factors of personality are associated with different types of Internet usage in general (Amichai-Hamburger and Ben-Artiz, 2003). However, despite the growth in Facebook usage and the high levels of media attention that Facebook receives, there have been very few formal investigations of the role played by personality traits on Facebook usage. For example, Wilson *et al.* (2009) state that research investigating the intrapersonal characteristics of people who access SNSs is limited. The research outlined in this chapter addresses this imbalance, thus increasing the pool of knowledge in relation to the ways social behaviours and interactions are adapting to SNS usage.

Social networking sites

Social networking sites are web-based services that allow individuals to construct a public or semi-public profile within a bounded system, articulate a list of other users with whom they share a connection and view and traverse this list of connections and those made by others within the system (boyd and Ellison, 2007). These researchers argue that the majority of SNS users are not necessarily 'networking' or looking to meet new people; they are seeking to communicate with people who are already in their extended social network. This is supported by Lampe *et al.* (2006), who concluded that people used SNSs primarily for 'social-searching' – finding out more about people whom they have met offline – rather than for 'social-browsing' – meeting people via their SNS with the intention of then meeting them offline. In addition, Lampe *et al.* contend that SNSs may also serve a surveillance type function; they enable users to monitor the actions, beliefs and interests of those they are friends with.

Specifically examining Facebook use, Joinson (2008, p. 1030) found that the most common cited functional uses were keeping awareness of contacts, sharing photos, organising groups and participating in applications. Joinson also found that 38.8 per cent of his participants visited Facebook daily, with a further 27.5 per cent visiting it more than once a day, and 22.5 per cent visiting it several times per week.

Personality traits and the Internet

Personality traits, according to Pervin *et al.* (2005, p. 223) refer to 'consistent patterns in the way individuals behave, feel and think', and can be used to summarise, predict and explain a person's conduct. The five personality traits of extraversion, neuroticism, agreeableness, conscientiousness and openness to experience are commonly studied and have been referred to as the 'Big Five' (Goldberg, cited in Pervin *et al.*, 2005, p. 254). McCrae and Costa (1996) contend that everyone possesses a certain level of each of the five factors, while John and Srivastava (2002, p. 7) explain that 'these five dimensions represent personality at the broadest level of abstraction, and each dimension summarises a large number of distinct, more specific personality characteristics'. Goby (2006) claims that personality may be the key to why some Internet users have more deep and satisfying online relationships than others. By reviewing the research into personality factors determining general Internet usage on a trait-by-trait basis, several observations have been made, and are outlined below.

Extraversion

According to Ross *et al.* (2009), extraversion denotes a tendency to be both sociable and able to experience positive emotions. In addition to liking people and being sociable, Costa and McCrae (1992) argue that extraverts are assertive, talkative, active and cheerful in disposition. At the other end of the continuum, Costa and McCrae (1992) contend that introversion should be considered as the absence of extraversion, rather than the opposite of it. They describe introverts as being reserved, independent and preferring to be alone; they are not unhappy or pessimistic. Extraversion has been found to be negatively related to higher levels of Internet usage among undergraduate students (Landers and Lounsbury, 2004). This finding suggests that in comparison to extraverts, introverts either have more spare time or are more attracted to the Internet's online appeal. Furthermore, extraverted people, according to Amiel and Sargent (2004), tend to use the Internet for instrumental purposes, such as researching, voicing their own opinions and sharing music with others, while tending to reject the use of the Internet for social purposes because they prefer social contact in more traditional contexts. In relation to SNSs, Anderson *et al.* (2001) found extraverts to have larger networks and show higher contact frequencies. Wehrli (2008) claims extraverts approach others more easily and engage in more social interaction; they are more outgoing and assertive.

Wilson *et al.* (2009) report that participants scoring high on extraversion in their study spent more time using a SNS, a finding inconsistent with that of Landers and Lounsbury's (2004) general Internet usage study. Wilson *et al.* speculate that the numerous functional abilities and unlimited contact with friends offered by SNSs may be specifically attractive to extraverts, who tend to require a high level of stimulation and a large social network.

Looking at research specifically investigating Facebook usage, although extraverts in Ross *et al.*'s (2009) study were found to belong to significantly more Facebook groups, a high level of extraversion was not found to be associated with the number of Facebook contacts or the communicative functions of Facebook. Ross *et al.* (2009) suggest this finding is consistent with Amiel and Sargent's (2004) findings, and they further suggest that 'although those high on the trait of extraversion may utilise Facebook as a social tool, they do not use Facebook as an alternative to social activities' (p. 582). However, in contradiction to these findings, Wehrli (2008) found that in relation to SNSs, extraversion had the largest influence on friendship, and that for a standard deviation increase in extraversion 'a student's expected mean number of friends increases by 29 per cent' (p. 11).

According to Amichai-Hamburger and Ben-Artzi (2003), both introverted and highly neurotic females were the most frequent users of the social services available on the Internet. They contend that these findings suggest that introverted and neurotic females may feel more protected and safer when using the Internet to socially interact, essentially because it is an anonymous, virtual environment that lacks the need to reveal physical appearance.

Neuroticism

Ross *et al.* (2009) explain that neuroticism reflects a person's tendency to experience psychological distress, with high scorers tending to display heightened sensitivity to perceived threats. In addition, high scorers can, according to Costa and McCrae (1992), be prone to having irrational ideas: 'to be less able to control their impulses and to cope more poorly than others with stress' (p. 14). In contrast, they consider individuals who score low on neuroticism to be emotionally stable: 'they are usually calm, even-tempered, and relaxed, and they are able to face stressful situations without becoming upset or rattled' (Costa and McCrae, 1992, p. 15). In addition, Amichai-Hamburger *et al.* (2002) and Amiel and Sargent (2004) found that neurotic people reported being comfortable and feeling a sense of belonging when interacting with others via the Internet. Amichai-Hamburger *et al.* (2002) state that introverted and neurotic people 'locate their "real me" on the Internet, while extraverts and non-neurotic people locate their "real me" through traditional social interaction' (p. 127). Wilson *et al.* (2009) found that neuroticism was not associated with increased levels of SNS usage. They contend that because of the insecure and anxious nature of neurotic people, posting photos and information on SNSs may not be an attractive proposition, and, like disagreeable people, they may prefer to use the Internet for other functions.

Agreeableness

Agreeableness is described by Ross *et al.* (2009) as a personality trait that reflects a tendency to be trusting, sympathetic and cooperative. According to Costa and McCrae (1992), the agreeable person is fundamentally altruistic; they are eager to help others, and believe others will be equally helpful in return. They claim that the disagreeable person is egocentric, sceptical of other people's intentions, and are competitive rather than cooperative. Agreeableness was found by Landers and Lounsbury (2004) to be negatively related to higher levels of Internet usage, suggesting that those who do not get along with others spend their time on the Internet, perhaps because there are fewer demands for agreeable behaviour. McCarty and Green (cited by Wehrli, 2008, p. 5) report agreeableness to have a favourable influence on social interactions, while Wehrli (2008) contends that agreeable individuals will not reject an offer of friendship. Agreeableness did not predict SNS usage in Wilson *et al.*'s (2009) study, with those researchers suggesting that although disagreeable people may use the Internet more, they are not necessarily engaging with other people socially on it; instead they are using it for more functional purposes.

Conscientiousness

Conscientiousness reflects dependability traits such as being careful, thorough, responsible, organised and planful (Hogan and John, both cited in Barrick and Mount, 1991, p.4). Others include these dependability traits but also include volitional variables such as hard working, achievement-oriented and persevering. Conscientiousness, according to Costa and McCrae (1992), has been linked to an individual's tendency to be competent, ordered, dutiful, achievement orientated, self-disciplined and strong-willed; and it contrasts with being lackadaisical and sloppy. High scoring is associated with academic and occupational achievement, but may lead to 'annoying fastidiousness, compulsive neatness, or workaholic behaviours' (Costa and McCrae, 1992, p. 16). Pervin *et al.* (2005) claim that low scorers on this dimension are aimless, less exacting in applying themselves, lazy, careless, lax, negligent, weak-willed and hedonistic. Lower scores on conscientiousness were also found by these researchers to be associated with high Internet use, and they suggest that this is due to the Internet's limited rules and unstructured policies. Conscientious people are dependable and careful, and have a high will to achieve. SNSs, according to Wehrli (2008), do not promise fast and obvious returns to conscientious people. As a consequence, therefore, high conscientiousness scorers may have lower numbers of contacts and networks in order to avoid distractions. In his study of 1560 student SNS users, Wehrli (2008) found that conscientiousness significantly reduced the number of friends a user had acquired on their SNS. Wilson *et al.* (2009) also found that those lower in conscientiousness spent more time using SNSs. They speculate that unconscientious people may occupy their time on SNSs while procrastinating about completing other tasks.

Openness to experience

Barrick and Mount (1991) claim that traits commonly associated with openness to experience include 'being imaginative, cultured, curious, original, broad-minded, intelligent, and artistically sensitive' (p. 5). Ross *et al.* (2009) contend that individuals who score high on this personality trait show a willingness to consider alternative approaches, are intellectually curious and enjoy artistic pursuits. According to Costa and McCrae (1992), they can also be unconventional, willing to question authority and prepared to entertain new ethical, social and political ideas. Also, according to these researchers, low scorers on openness to experience tend to be conventional in behaviour and conservative in outlook, preferring the familiar to the novel. Although agreeing with Landers and Lounsbury (2004) that introversion may predict general Internet usage, McElroy *et al.* (cited by Wilson *et al.*, 2009), found that neuroticism and openness to experience predicted higher levels of time spent online.

In relation to SNSs, Wehrli (2008) suggests that individuals with high scores on openness to experience would be more likely to try, to use, and to keep up with new social networking technologies. Regarding Facebook usage, in addition to their findings that high scorers on openness to experience have a tendency to seek sociable interactions on Facebook, Ross *et al.* (2009) found that high scorers tended to have lower levels of Computer-Mediated-Communication (CMC) skills. They suggest that this finding may be a result of high openness to experience, scorers being more interested in trying new things than they are in trying to figure out how things work.

Motivations for using SNSs

Pelling and White (2009) claim that young adults are more likely than any other age group to have an SNS profile and engage in higher levels of use: 1.46 hours per day and logging in 4.19 times per day, according to Raacke and Bonds-Raacke (2008, p. 171). However, despite the increasing popularity of SNSs, there is relatively little known about the motivations that predict people's level of use.

Lampe *et al.* (2006) reported that for their sample the main motivation for using Facebook was: 'to keep in touch with an old friend or someone I knew from high school'. In a longitudinal study looking at how use of Facebook has changed over a three-year period of time, Lampe *et al.* (2008) found that usage motives remained fairly constant and that their users were typically using the site to maintain light-weight contact with relationships they had developed offline. Only a few of their users reported that they used Facebook to make connections with people they did not know already. In agreement, Ross *et al.* (2009) found that a motivation to communicate was influential in terms of Facebook use.

In addition, the need to belong was found to correlate positively with the willingness to join a social network site by Gangadharbatla (cited by Christofides *et al.*, 2009, p. 342). Christofides *et al.* explain that for young adults, the need to be a part of their social group and their need for popularity are key elements in their lives. The need for popularity was therefore found to be a significant predictor of disclosure on Facebook and a motivation for using the site (Christofides *et al.*, 2009).

Research aims

A core objective of this study is to ascertain the individual personality characteristics that have a significant relationship with high levels of usage of the Facebook SNS. It is also an objective to investigate the individual personality characteristics that influence a specific online social networking behaviour – the number of contacts maintained. A further objective is to ascertain the most commonly cited motives for using the Facebook social network site.

Methodology

To achieve the above stated objectives, this study examined personality traits from a sample population of Facebook users via the Big Five Index (BFI) personality scale (John and Srivastava, 2002). The study examined the motivations for using Facebook via a demographic and Facebook usage questionnaire.

Participants

A convenience sample of 155 Facebook users, of mixed gender (males = 78; females = 77), formed the sample. A further criterion for inclusion to the sample population was that each participant had to be 24 years of age or over (Pervin *et al.*, 2005, contend that personality dimensions become more stable the further into adulthood a person is).

Materials

In order to obtain some of the demographic details of each of the participants, a demographic questionnaire was administered, which asked about gender, culture and age. A Facebook usage questionnaire was developed, which predominantly used a Likert-type five-point scale. The Big Five Index (John and Srivastava, 2002) is a 44-item measurement scale with high validity and reliability scores. It is a self-report inventory, comprising a five-point Likert scale with responses ranging from 'Disagree strongly' to 'Agree strongly' and provides overall measures of Extroversion; Openness; Agreeableness; Neuroticism and Conscientiousness

Results

The mean value for the length of time the participants in this study ($N = 155$) reported spending on each visit to Facebook was 27.58 minutes ($SD = 31.63$). Younger participants (aged 24–34 years) had a mean value of 32.66 minutes per visit ($SD = 4.30$), while those over 24 years had a mean value of 22.30 minutes per Facebook visit ($SD = 2.51$). The majority of participants (47.1 per cent) reported using Facebook at least once a day, with a further 43.6 per cent using Facebook at least once a week. Daily Facebook usage was higher among younger participants, with 57 per cent of 24–34 year olds compared to 36.8 per cent of over 34 year olds using their Facebook at least once a day

Motivations for using Facebook

Table 3.1 describes the scores given by participants to various potential motivations for using Facebook. Consistent with expectations, the highest score was given to the answer 'To keep in contact with existing friends'. Other high scoring motivations included 'To pass the time when I am bored' and 'To keep in contact with family and relations', while the lowest scores were given to items such as 'To possibly make romantic contacts' and 'For employment purposes'.

Gender differences in motivations for usage

Considering the two highest-scoring motivations – keeping in contact with existing friends and boredom – the results were further analysed for gender differences. Females were noted to give higher scores than males for keeping in contact with existing friends, while males gave slightly higher scores than females for the alleviation of boredom. These findings are outlined in Table 3.2.

TABLE 3.1 Motivations for using Facebook

Rank	Name	Answer statement	Mean	Standard deviation
1	Q1	To keep in contact with existing friends	3.68	.97
2	Q12	To pass the time when I am bored	3.54	1.05
3	Q2	To keep in contact with family and relations	3.10	1.12
4	Q10	To share photographs	3.10	1.15
5	Q8	To share information with others	3.02	1.18
6	Q6	To keep in contact with acquaintances I have previously met	2.98	1.03
7	Q5	To state what I am doing	2.22	1.16
8	Q13	To play games	2.18	1.32
9	Q14	To take quizzes	2.18	1.03
10	Q4	To express how I am feeling	1.98	1.04
11	Q7	To make contact with new people	1.75	.96
12	Q3	To keep in contact with persons I am already romantically involved with	1.69	1.08
13	Q11	For employment purposes	1.26	.70
14	Q9	To possibly make romantic contacts	1.14	.46

TABLE 3.2 Motivations for using Facebook by gender

Motive		Mean	Standard deviation
Q1: Keeping in contact with existing friends	Males	3.55	.91
	Females	3.82	1.01
Q12: Boredom	Males	3.56	.93
	Females	3.51	1.15

Comparison by age

For the purposes of analysing the differences in motivations for usage of Facebook based on the age of the participants, two distinct age groupings were compared: those aged 24–34 years ($n = 79$), and those over 34 years ($n = 76$). Participants aged 24–34 had a higher mean value for the motive of 'keeping in contact with existing friends' ($M = 4.01$, $SD = .09$) than those aged over 34 ($M = 3.34$, $SD = .97$). However, both age groups ranked this reason as their most common motivation for using Facebook. Participants aged 24–34 had a higher mean value for the motive of 'passing the time when bored' ($M = 3.81$, $SD = .93$) than participants over 34 years ($M = 3.25$, $SD = 1.08$). Both age groupings ranked this motive as their second most common motivation for using Facebook.

Personality traits and Facebook usage

Participants who reported having fewer than thirty friends generally scored higher on conscientiousness ($M = 36.03$, $SD = 4.23$) than those with more than 80 friends ($M = 32.53$, $SD = 6.26$). These results are depicted in Figure 3.1 and were found to be statistically significant ($U = 761.500$, $N_1 = 27$, $N_2 = 82$, $p = .015$, two-tailed).

To better understand the influences on conscientiousness scores, a stepwise regression was performed with the 'number of friends' and the 'length of time' per Facebook visit as predictors. Using the enter method, a significant model emerged: $F (2,152) = 7.484$, $p < .05$. However, the model only explained 7.8 per cent of the variance. Both number of friends and length of time were significant predictors of conscientiousness scores. A possible contributing factor could be usage levels. An investigation into the influence of usage levels on conscientiousness indicated that higher scoring tended to belong to the lower level of usage grouping. Participants in the usage grouping of 'fewer than three times a week' had a higher mean value for conscientiousness scores ($M = 34.72$) than participants in the 'three or more times a week' grouping ($M = 34.00$) and participants in the 'at least once a day' grouping ($M = 32.77$).

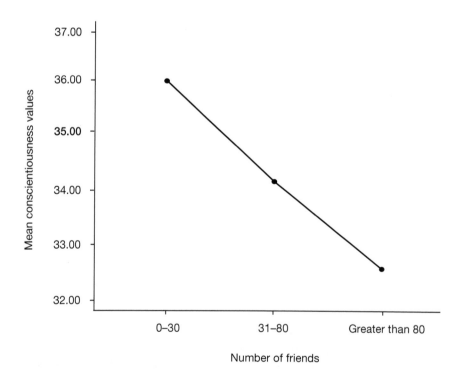

FIGURE 3.1 Conscientiousness scores by number of friends

No significant differences were found between the groups for other personality factors such as extraversion, agreeableness and openness to experience.

Overview of the main findings

The purpose of the present study was to examine the motivations and personality traits that influence Facebook usage. The results indicated that 'keeping in contact with existing friends' was the most commonly reported motive for using Facebook. However, the second most commonly cited motive – 'to pass the time when I am bored' – was not rated significantly differently. Younger adults more commonly reported both the 'keeping in contact with existing friends' and 'boredom' as their primary motivations than those aged over 34 years. Facebook users with low numbers of friends were found to score higher on the personality trait of conscientiousness than those participants reporting the highest number of friends, although scores on extraversion, agreeableness and openness to experience were not found to be significantly different.

In the present study, 47.1 per cent of the sample reported using Facebook at least once a day. However, this figure is not quite as high as Joinson's (2008) 66.3 per cent usage per day figure. This study also noted that older adults do not use Facebook as frequently as younger adults.

Motivations of Facebook users

Keeping in contact with friends was the highest scoring motivation mentioned in the study, with alleviating boredom achieving the second highest score. This is in keeping with the findings of Lampe *et al.* (2006), who concluded that 'keeping in touch with an old friend' was the main motivation for using Facebook, with this 'social capital' function being an important motive – users turned to Facebook seeking emotional support from their friends. However, none of the previous research drew conclusions that people were motivated to use Facebook because they were bored.

Personality

Facebook users with low numbers of friends differed significantly in conscientiousness scores than users with high numbers of friends. These findings replicate Wehrli's (2008) findings and support the contention that conscientiousness is associated with fewer friends maintained on a Facebook profile. As an explanation Wehrli (2008) surmised that SNSs do not promise fast and obvious returns to conscientious people. This study is also in agreement with Wilson *et al.*'s (2009) finding that low conscientiousness scorers spend a higher level of time using SNSs.

Extraversion was not found to have any impact on the number of friends on Facebook. The result also implies support for Ross *et al.*'s (2009) contention that although extraverts may use Facebook as a social tool, 'they do not use Facebook as an alternative to social activities' (p. 582).

Similarly, agreeableness scores were not found to impact on Facebook usage. This finding is consistent with the findings of the Ross *et al.* (2009) study. The findings suggest support for Wilson et *al.*'s (2009) conclusion that although the disagreeable people cited in the Landers and Lounsbury (2004) study may be using the Internet more than their agreeable counterparts, they are not using it for social networking reasons.

Openness to experience was not found to be associated with increased levels of Facebook usage. The findings are, however, consistent with the finding of the Wilson *et al.* (2009) study that openness to experience did not have any impact on SNS use. It should be remembered that Facebook has been popular for some time, and newer social networking technologies may have attracted those higher in openness to experience. It is possible that Facebook may no longer be considered a new innovation.

Conclusion

The results from the present study suggest that 'boredom' alongside 'keeping in touch' are major motivating factors for using Facebook, and that gender and age variables influence the level of these motivations. Paraphrasing Joinson (2008, p. 1035), it would seem likely that 'keeping in touch' is a polite way of saying 'checking up on regularly'. Furthermore, the findings imply that the time spent per visit is dependent on the uses being employed; it varies with age and gender.

If people are using Facebook because they are bored, it would seem imperative to design suitable content applications that address these needs alongside the applications that help build and maintain social connections. There is equally a need to recognise that not all users of Facebook have the same motivations for using it; different demographic groups use it for different purposes.

References

Amichai-Hamburger, Y. and Ben-Artiz, E. (2003). Loneliness and Internet use. *Computers in Human Behaviour*, 19, 71–80.

Amichai-Hamburger, Y., Galit-Wainapel, G. and Fox, S. (2002). 'On the Internet no one knows I'm an introvert': Extroversion, neuroticism, and Internet interaction. *CyberPsychology and Behaviour*, 5 (2), 125–128.

Amiel, T. and Sargent, S. (2004). Individual difference in Internet usage motives. *Computers in Human Behaviour*, 20, 711–726.

Anderson, C., John, O., Keltner, D. and Kring, A. (2001). Who attains social status? Effects of personality and physical attractiveness in three social groups. *Journal of Personality and Social Psychology*, 81, 116–132.

Barrick, M. and Mount, M. (1991). The Big-Five personality dimensions and job performance: A meta-analysis. *Personnel Psychology*, 44, 1–26.

boyd, D. and Ellison, N. (2007). Social network sites: Definition, history, and scholarship. *Journal of Computer-Mediated Communication*, 13 (1), article 11. Retrieved from: http://jcmc.indiana.edu/vol13/issue1/boyd.ellison.html.

Christofides, E., Muise, A. and Desmarais, S. (2009). Information disclosure and control on Facebook: Are they two sides of the same coin or two different processes? *CyberPsychology and Behaviour*, 12 (3), 341–345.

Costa, P. and McCrae, R. (1992). *NEO PI-R: Professional manual.* Boston, MA: Psychological Assessment Resources.

Goby, V. (2006). Personality and online/offline choices: MBTI profiles and favoured communication modes in a Singapore study. *Cyberpsychology and Behaviour*, 9 (1), 5–13.

Guadagno, R., Okdie, B. and Eno, C. (2007). Who blogs? Personality predictors of blogging. *Computers in Human Behaviour*, 24, 1993–2004.

John, O. and Srivastava, S. (2002). The Big-Five Trait taxonomy: History, measurement and theoretical perspectives. In L. Pervin and O. John (eds) *Handbook of Personality: Theory and research* (2nd edn). New York: Guilford Press.

Joinson, A. (2008). *'Looking at', 'looking up' or 'keeping up with' people? Motives and uses of Facebook.* Conference on Human Factors in Computing Systems (CHI). Florence: ACM Press, 1027–1036.

Lampe, C., Ellison, N. and Steinfield, C. (2006). A face(book) in the crowd: Social Searching vs. social browsing. Proceedings of the 2006 20th anniversary conference on computer supported cooperative work, 4–8 November, Banff, Alberta, Canada.

Lampe, C., Ellison, N. and Steinfield, C. (2008). Changes in use and perception of Facebook. *CSCW '08.* Proceedings of the ACM 2008 conference on Computer supported cooperative work, 721–730. Retrieved from: www.msu.edu/~nellison/LampeEllisonSteinfield2008.pdf.

Landers, R. and Lounsbury, J. (2004). An investigation of Big Five and narrow personality traits in relation to Internet usage. *Computers in Human Behaviour*, 22 (2), 283–293.

McCrae, R. and Costa, P. (1996). Toward a new generation of personality theories: Theoretical contexts for the five factor model. In J. Wiggins (ed.) *The Five-Factor Model of Personality: Theoretical perspectives* (pp. 51–87). New York: Guilford.

Pelling, E. and White, K. (2009). The theory of planned behaviour applied to young people's use of social networking web sites. *CyberPsychology and Behaviour*, 12, 755–759.

Pervin, L., Cervone, D. and John, O. (2005). *Personality: Theory and research* (9th edn). Hoboken, NJ: Wiley & Sons.

Raacke, J. and Bonds-Raacke, J. (2008). MySpace and Facebook: Applying the uses and gratifications theory to exploring friend-networking sites. *CyberPsychology and Behaviour*, 11 (2), 169–174.

Ross, C., Orr, E., Sisic, M., Arseneault, J., Simmering, M. and Orr, R. (2009). Personality and motivations associated with Facebook use. *Computers in Human Behaviour*, 25 (2), 578–586.

Wehrli, S. (2008). *Personality on Social Network Sites: An application of the Five Factor Model,* ETH Zurich Sociology Working Papers 7, ETH Zurich: Chair of Sociology.

Wilson, K., Fornasier, S. and White, K. (2009). Psychological predictors of young adults' use of social networking sites. *CyberPsychology and Behaviour*, 13 (2), 173–177.

4

MOBILE PHONE SEPARATION AND ANXIETY

Mark Siggins and Cliona Flood

Chapter summary

This research sought to investigate people's dependence on their mobile phones, their willingness to be separated from their mobile phones and the perceived anxiety associated with this separation. A group of mobile phone users aged 18–40 years old were recruited; their mobile phone dependence was measured using the Cellular Technologies Addiction Scale (CTAS) and anxiety scores calculated using the State Trait Anxiety Inventory (STAI). Participants were separated from their mobile phones for a twelve-hour period during which their anxiety levels were recorded and compared to a control group. No significant differences in anxiety levels were observed during the experiment. The study also provides insight into why a high proportion of individuals approached were unwilling to be separated from their mobile phones.

Introduction

The introduction of the mobile phone has had an enormous impact on the way people worldwide communicate and interact. Through the use of mobile phones people are no longer tied to landlines and are free to make phone calls almost anywhere, anytime. Mobile phones have evolved from expensive business-oriented tools into affordable and enormously popular devices. Today, mobile technology includes instant messaging, email, communication-orientated Internet sites such as blogs, dissemination of news, social networking and applications. Zichkur and Smith (2012) report that 46 per cent of Americans use smartphones, with reasons for using them including convenience, constant access to email, Internet, gaming, camera, texting and making phone calls. Subrahmanyam and Greenfield (2008) found that adolescents' usage of mobile technologies was mainly to reinforce existing relationships, with integration of these tools into their 'offline' worlds being a common feature.

Changes in behaviour due to mobile phone use

Once an individual begins to use their mobile phone, behavioural changes can often be observed. These include a compulsive checking of the phone for messages, using it as a crutch in awkward social situations and declining to memorise information when it can be stored in the mobile phone just as easily.

The use of mobile phones as a mass medium through which to disseminate news is indicative of another way our behaviour has been altered. In the wake of the Boxing Day tsunami in 2004, the majority of Finnish people learned of the tragedy from friends via their mobile phones or amateur websites. Kivikuru (2009) theorises that the pre-existing trust between sender and receiver and the need to disseminate news of such a magnitude in a sincere way lent itself towards mobile phone communication.

Some behaviour appears to be consistently influenced and encouraged by mobile phone use across many cultures. Among those that seem to transcend cultures is the behaviour that Norwegian researchers have termed hyper-coordination. Also known as a softening of time, it has led to the removal of taboos surrounding being late for appointments. The mobile phone allows people to organise and re-organise meetings with an abandon that many pre-mobile phone people would have found abhorrent (Ling and Haddon, 2003). Garcia-Montes (2006) has taken the idea of hyper-coordination and predicted that mobile phone usage will lead to people distancing themselves from immediate situations and even to a loss of ability to cope with situations as they arise.

Psychological traits associated with mobile phone use

Several researchers have examined the psychological traits that may be associated with mobile phone use. Bianchi and Phillips (2005) found higher levels of extraversion and lower self-esteem could be used to predict problem levels of mobile phone use. Neuroticism was investigated but not found to have any significant impact on problem use. Age was only a factor when it came to looking at the comparative number of text messages sent – with younger people sending more text messages than older people. Hall and Baym (2011) suggest that increased mobile phone usage does not necessarily result in improved relationships. In their study mobile phone usage increased expectations of relationship maintenance and positively predicted dependence, which increased satisfaction but positively predicted over-dependence, which in turn decreased satisfaction.

Reid and Reid (2007) investigated communication methods and compared voice calls and SMS messages within the constructs of social anxiety and loneliness. SMS messages were rated as less intimate but preferred by socially anxious people. Voice calls were preferred by those who scored highly on loneliness scales. The study theorises that voice calls allow for expression of the true self while SMS messages allow the user to construct their intended message more carefully. Similarly, Ha *et al.* (2008) found that excessive mobile phone use can be correlated with higher anxiety and lower self-esteem.

A study on a young female cohort found a correlation between urgency and impulsivity on the perceived dependence on their mobile phones. An expected link between trait anxiety and perceived dependence was not found (Billieux *et al.*, 2007). In contrast, research by Merlo and Stone (2007a) supports the claim that anxiety symptoms are associated with increased problematic mobile phone use. According to their data, anxious people seem more likely to be highly attached to their mobile phones.

Anxiety is a state often cited as an indicator of, or at least co-existing with, problematic mobile phone use. It is commonly measured across two scales – general/trait anxiety and state anxiety. General or trait anxiety will vary from person to person and is the default anxiety level experienced by a person. State anxiety is anxiety felt by a person at a particular moment, often in response to a particular threat. Such anxiety is very often short lived and seldom fails to diminish once the source of tension or fear is removed (Marks, 1978; Merlo and Stone, 2007b).

Mobile phone dependence and separation

The American Psychological Association's *Diagnostic and Statistical Manual, Fourth Edition (DSM-IV TR)* states that the 'abuse' part of addiction is identified through uncontrolled negative impacts on the sufferer's day-to-day life (APA, 2000). In proposals for the forthcoming *DSM-5*, there has been reference to the symptom of 'continued excessive Internet use despite knowledge of negative psychosocial problems' (APA, 2012) – this could be applied to problematic mobile phone usage.

Walsh *et al.* (2007) make the distinction between problem use and addiction, indicating that it is possible to excessively use the mobile phone without being addicted to it. They identify withdrawal symptoms when mobile phones are not available and cite the feeling of being 'lost without it' as the most cited symptom of withdrawal. In their study to determine why Australians use their mobile phones, they found that mobile phone use served to gratify three functions: self, social and security. It was those who derive self-gratification from their mobile phones who were most likely to demonstrate addictive symptoms. A common thread running through much of the literature is the sense of not being able to do without a mobile phone (Kamibeppu and Sugiura, 2005).

Katz (2006) conducted a 48-hour mobile phone separation. Of the 102 students invited to take part only 82 actually participated in the experiment. The number of participants who had not switched on their mobile phones was captured at regular intervals. Over 50 per cent were able to go 24 hours without their mobile phones, but only 6 per cent managed to go the full 48 hours without switching on their phones. The reasons cited for non-completion were that it was too hard and that situations arose in which they felt they needed to use their phones. Of those who completed the separation 70 per cent felt their lives were worse for the 48 hours without their phones. However, some students indicated that they enjoyed the experience.

Similarly, LaPorta (2006) indicate that as many as 30 per cent of Americans who own mobile phones claim they would not be able to live without it. Sánchez-Martínez and Otero (2008) found that 20 per cent of mobile phone users were unwilling to be separated from their mobile phones, and that 47 per cent did not turn their phones off in situations where they were instructed to do so. Extending these studies, the current research examines whether, when faced with the real possibility of separation, participants will willingly agree to be separated from their mobile phones. It also examines whether anxiety levels will increase if a person has no access to their mobile phone and whether such increases will vary over a period of separation. Two hypotheses were formulated: first, that separating a person from their mobile phone will result in increased situational anxiety levels for the duration of the separation when compared to a control group; second, that any increased anxiety levels experienced while a person is separated from their mobile phone will reach peak levels at the beginning of the separation period, reducing as the period of separation increases.

Method

Participants

Participants were owners and regular users of mobile phones and aged between 18 and 40 years of age. Convenience sampling was used. Forty-two individuals agreed to attempt the mobile phone separation (22 male, 20 female) and 63 declined to be separated from their phones and, as such, were included in a control sample. This gives a 'willingness to attempt mobile phone separation' figure of 40 per cent.

Materials

The CTAS was adapted for use in this study. The CTAS questionnaire quantifies an individual's addiction to their mobile device, and was previously used by Merlo and Stone (2007a). Two CTAS sub-scales measure dependency and mobile phone abuse.

The Spielberger STAI has been used extensively in research and clinical practice (Brook, 1976; Miller, 1979; Stauder and Kovacs, 2003). It comprises separate self-report scales for measuring state and trait anxiety. The S-Anxiety scale (State Anxiety – STAI Form Y-1) consists of twenty statements that evaluate how respondents feel 'right now, at this moment'.

A mobile phone use questionnaire was developed by the authors for this study and consisted of three parts: demographic information about the participants; information on their perceived mobile phone use; and willingness to go without their mobile phones for twelve hours.

The control and experimental groups were given printed booklets containing instructions on what they were required to do. These consisted of an introduction and instruction page, a checklist, five copies of the STAI Y-1 forms and a mobile phone usage form. Both booklets were identical except that the experimental group were asked to power off their phones for the twelve hours while the control group were not. Books were posted to participants, along with a small mobile phone sized elastic tag, which acted as a reminder to the control group participants to record their actual usage throughout the twelve hours. The elastic tag also served to remind the experimental group to record their compulsive or desired use throughout the separation period.

Procedure

Participants were directed to a secure web page where informed consent was obtained. They were invited to fill out the online survey, which consisted of the CTAS, STAI (form Y-2) and the mobile phone use questionnaire, by giving the most appropriate response to each item. Logic built into the questionnaire ensured that participants who agreed to try the twelve-hour separation were asked for a contact address, while those that refused were asked to provide the main reasons for not wanting to try the twelve-hour separation.

Anxiety scores were recorded ten minutes before the twelve hours began, ten minutes after the twelve-hour start, six hours into the twelve hours, ten minutes before the end of the twelve hours and, finally, ten minutes after the end of the twelve hours. Mobile phone usage was recorded throughout. Eligible participants who had agreed to try the separation were randomly assigned into two gender-balanced groups. These groups were randomly designated as the control and experimental groups. Both groups were given two weeks to complete the booklet. Participants who had provided an email address and not returned the forms were sent a reminder email at one and two weeks. This procedure is outlined in Figure 4.1.

Results

A total of 176 responses to the online questionnaire were recorded, of which there were 105 useable questionnaires (58 females and 47 males).

Of the 42 people who agreed to try separation, five had anxiety scores higher than the safe cut-off point and were excluded. Ages ranged from 19 to 40 years with a mean age of 29.1 years ($SD = 5.7$ years). The response rate to the instruction booklets that were sent out was found to be 67 per cent: 37 booklets were sent out, and 25 were returned. One of the experimental group reported switching on her mobile phone during the experiment, citing pressure to send out text messages for a group event she was organising. This returned booklet was not counted as a response.

Of all the participants 57 per cent said they used their phones mainly for social calls and texts only, 41 per cent used their mobile phones for business and social purposes equally, and 1.9 per cent used their mobiles for business reasons exclusively. Almost a third (30.5 per cent) of participants reported using their mobile

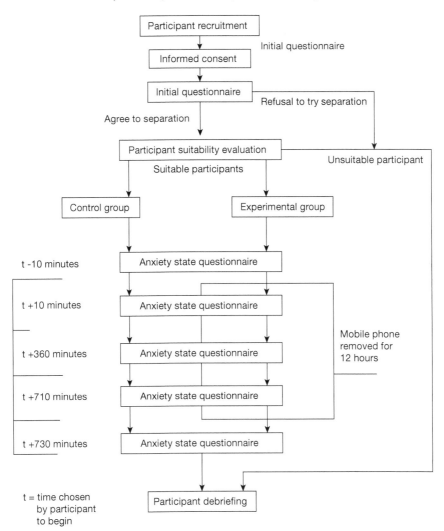

FIGURE 4.1 The procedure followed by participants

phones mainly for voice calls, 56.2 per cent used theirs primarily for text messages, while 13.3 per cent used theirs mainly for mobile Internet.

Addiction, dependence and anxiety

Higher average rates of mobile phone dependence were recorded for the group who declined to participate in the separation experiment (65.73) when compared to the group who agreed to try the separation experiment (62.83). The mean difference between conditions was 2.89, and the 95 per cent confidence interval for the estimated population mean difference is between −9.66 and 3.86. An independent t-test showed that the difference between conditions was not significant ($t = -.849$, $df = 103$, $p = .199$, one tailed).

Mobile phone separation experiment

The most common reason cited for initially not wanting to participate in the separation experiment was a need to be contactable all the time (26 per cent). Other common reasons cited were: 'No time to participate' (19 per cent), 'Unable go twelve hours without my phone' (14 per cent) and 'Prefer not to participate' (14 per cent).

A Mann-Whitney test to examine trait anxiety scores for the experimental group indicated that the participants who completed the separation (median = 41.0, range = 28.0) had higher scores than those who did not return forms (median = 28.0, range = 15.0). The difference was significant ($U = 16$, $N_1 = 14$, $N_2 = 5$, $p = .0435$, one-tailed). Trait anxiety levels for the group who returned their forms (median = 40.0, range = 26.0) were also higher than those who did not return their forms (median = 39.5, range = 25.0). This was not shown to be significant ($U = 28.5$, $N_1 = 11$, $N_2 = 6$, $p = .33$, one-tailed).

The raw anxiety scores for each recorded time were split by group and compared using the Mann-Whitney test. A line diagram showing the mean and standard deviation for each group for the duration of the experiment can be seen in Figure 4.2.

There was no significant difference between anxiety scores for each group at any of the recorded times (see Table 4.1).

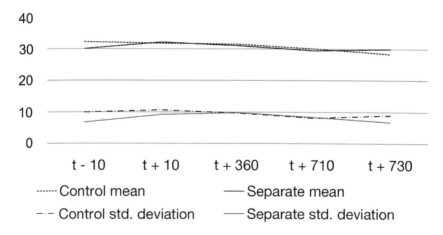

FIGURE 4.2 Mobile phone separation anxiety over time

TABLE 4.1 Anxiety scores between groups

Anxiety at $t - 10$ minutes	($U = 70.5$, $N_1 = 11$, $N_2 = 14$, $p = .363$, one-tailed)
Anxiety at $t + 10$ minutes	($U = 74.0$, $N_1 = 11$, $N_2 = 14$, $p = .446$, one-tailed)
Anxiety at $t + 360$ minutes	($U = 70.5$, $N_1 = 11$, $N_2 = 14$, $p = .363$, one-tailed)
Anxiety at $t + 710$ minutes	($U = 69.5$, $N_1 = 11$, $N_2 = 14$, $p = .343$, one-tailed)
Anxiety at $t + 730$ minutes	($U = 72.5$, $N_1 = 11$, $N_2 = 14$, $p = .404$, one-tailed)

TABLE 4.2 Anxiety scores between time intervals

Anxiety difference ($t - 10$ to $t + 10$)	($U = 63$, $N_1 = 11$, $N_2 = 14$, $p = .233$, one-tailed)
Anxiety difference ($t + 10$ to $t + 360$)	($U = 70$, $N_1 = 11$, $N_2 = 14$, $p = .363$, one-tailed)
Anxiety difference ($t + 360$ to $t + 710$)	($U = 70$, $N_1 = 11$, $N_2 = 14$, $p = .363$, one-tailed)
Anxiety difference ($t + 710$ to $t + 730$)	($U = 70.5$, $N_1 = 11$, $N_2 = 14$, $p = .363$, one-tailed)

Differences in anxiety score changes between recording times were also analysed, with the results depicted in Table 4.2. A greater increase was recorded for the first change in anxiety for the separation group, but no statistically significant differences in the rate of change in anxiety over time, between groups, was shown.

Discussion

While the primary hypothesis of the study was not supported, this research provides valuable insights into mobile phone separation anxiety.

Mobile phone separation and anxiety

The analysis of the anxiety questionnaires from the experimental and control groups indicated that the average scores for the experimental group were lower than those in the control group at every measurement point except one. No significant difference between the control group and the experimental group was found at any point during the twelve-hour separation. During the twelve-hour period the average anxiety levels actually fell steadily for both groups. This fall in anxiety levels and the high completion rate for the experimental group were unexpected, compared with the findings of Katz (2006) who found that many of his participants were unable to do without their mobile phones for even four hours.

Only one participant was unable to complete the twelve hours once it had begun. The reason given was to send out text messages to organise a meeting. Ling and Haddon (2003) have previously argued that the hyper-coordination mobile phones facilitate will lead to a diminished capacity to function without it. This may be a real world example of this and demonstrates that for some people the mobile phone is their preferred way of organising gatherings.

On average the separation experiment group displayed almost five times the level of increase in anxiety during the switching off period than the control group; however, once again the statistical significance of this change was not great enough to support the apparent pattern. Similarly, the separation experiment group displayed a greater reduction in anxiety after switching on their mobile phones although to a much lesser extent than the initial increase difference. The difference in reduction was not statistically significant.

When comparing the general anxiety levels for the separation group who had returned their forms with the separation group who had been sent forms but did not return them, a difference emerged. Those who had not returned their forms had an average general anxiety score that was less than the average for the group who had returned their forms. This difference was statistically significant. No such difference was present for the control group.

Willingness to try mobile phone separation

The results of this study indicate that 60 per cent of participants were unwilling to place themselves in a position where they could be required to go without their mobile phone for twelve hours. This figure is higher than the 18.2 per cent reported by Sánchez-Martínez and Otero (2008). The figure is also higher than that cited by LaPorta (2006) who claimed that 30 per cent of Americans were unwilling to go without their mobile phones. It seems likely that the difference between these studies is that the possibility of participants having to support the answers with actions was more overtly stated in the questionnaire employed in this study when compared to the others cited above.

A similar separation study to the experiment reported here was conducted by Katz (2006) where 12 per cent of participants were unwilling even to try separation when the threat of actual separation was real. The 60 per cent unwillingness found in the current study indicates a rise in unwillingness to be separated from mobile phones. If we apply the standard substance dependence model (APA, 2000), this would appear to indicate that we have moved from the craving stage of addiction into the tolerance stage where sufferers are more unlikely to voluntarily go without their dependent substance.

Reasons why people were unwilling to attempt the mobile phone separation are difficult to establish. The most frequent responses were that participants needed to be contactable all the time, that they had no time to participate and that they needed to have their phone on constantly for work reasons. For some, these reasons were certainly true; however, the 60 per cent unwillingness to attempt separation figure is so much higher than anticipated that other factors need to be examined. For ethical reasons, anxiety was specifically mentioned in the introduction, and this may have turned an already undesirable situation into one that outweighs any curiosity participants may have had about their chances of success. As one participant put it, there was a 'Dubious return for a difficult task'.

It must be remembered that it is not possible to verify that the participants in the current study actually switched off their mobile phones when requested to do so. In order to maintain ecological validity, data gathering was done in the participant's regular environment and not under the control of the researcher. This may mean that there were other factors at play that may have impacted on participants' anxiety levels during the twelve hours. Both groups were requested to complete the experiments during a time when they could not foresee a reason to use their mobile phones, and as such this should have helped to normalise the results. Participants were also free to utilise any other forms of electronic communication during the separation period. Another possible reason for the lack of increase in reported anxiety levels for this group may be that the separation period was of their own choosing and they had time to plan and organise for the lack of a mobile phone.

Conclusions

It appears that people are largely unwilling to be separated from their mobile phones. This research showed the difficulty in getting participants to complete a questionnaire about their attitudes to mobile phones when mention of potential separation is made. The findings indicate that a person who has been separated from their mobile phone in a planned manner will not be any more anxious than a person who is firmly connected.

References

American Psychological Association (2000). *Diagnostic and Statistical Manual of Mental Disorders: Text revision* (4th edn). Washington, DC: APA.

American Psychological Association (2012). *DSM-5 Development*. Retrieved from: www.dsm5.org/ProposedRevision/Pages/proposedrevision.aspx?rid=573.

Bianchi, A. and Phillips, J.G. (2005). Psychological predictors of problem mobile phone use. *CyberPsychology & Behaviour*, 8 (1), 39–52.

Billieux, J., Van Der Linden, M., D'Acremont, M., Ceschi, G. and Zermatten, A. (2007). Does impulsivity relate to perceived dependence on and actual use of the mobile phone? *Applied Cognitive Psychology*, 21, 527–537. doi: 10.1002/acp.1289.

Brook, R.M. (1976). Psychological evaluation stress on adolescents. *Journal of Clinical Psychology*, 32, 565–567.

Garcia-Montes, J.M. (2006). Changes in the self resulting from the use of mobile phones. *Media, Culture and Society*, 28(1), 67–82. doi: 10.1177/0163443706059287.

Ha, J.H., Chin, B., Park, D., Ryu, S. and Yu, J. (2008). Characteristics of excessive cellular phone use in Korean adolescents. *CyberPsychology & Behaviour*, 11 (6), 783–784. doi: 10.1089/cpb.2008.0096.

Hall, J.A. and Baym, N.K. (2011). Calling and texting (too much): Mobile maintenance expectations, (over)dependence, entrapment, and friendship satisfaction. *New Media & Society*, 14 (2), 316–331.

Kamibeppu, K. and Sugiura, H. (2005). Impact of the mobile phone on junior high-school students' friendships in the Tokyo Metropolitan Area. *CyberPsychology & Behaviour*, 8 (2), 121–131.

Katz, J. E. (2006). Mobile phones in educational settings. In J.E. Katz, *Magic in the Air: Mobile communication and the transformation of social life* (pp. 91–103). New Brunswick, NJ: Transaction.

Kivikuru, U. (2009). Tsunami communication in Finland revealing tensions in the sender–receiver relationship. *European Journal of Communication*, 21, 499. doi: 10.1177/0267323 106070013.

LaPorta, L.D. (2006). Cellular telephones: A new addiction? *Psychiatric Times*, 23 (11), 11–14.

Ling, R. and Haddon, L. (2003). Mobile telephony, mobility and the co-ordination of everyday life. In J. Katz (ed.) *Machines that Become Us: The social context of personal communication technology* (pp. 245–66). New Brunswick, NJ: Transaction.

Marks, I.M. (1978). *Living with Fear: Understanding and coping with anxiety*. London: McGraw-Hill.

Merlo, L.J. and Stone, A.M. (2007a). *Anxiety Linked With Increased Cell-Phone Dependence, Abuse Anxiety*. Gainsville, FL: Anxiety Disorders Association of America 28th Annual Meeting: Poster 55. 6–9 March.

Merlo, L.J. and Stone, A.M. (2007b). *Comorbidity of Anxiety Symptoms and Cellular Phone Addiction*. Poster presented at The Anxiety Disorders Association of America 28th Annual Meeting, Savannah, GA. 5–6 March.

Miller, S.M. (1979). Coping with impending stress: Psychophysiological and cognitive correlates of choice. *Psychophysiology*, 16, 572–581.

Reid, D.J. and Reid, F.J. (2007). Text or talk? Social anxiety, loneliness, and divergent preferences for cell phone use. *CyberPsychology & Behaviour*, 10 (3), 424–435. doi: 10.1089/cpb.2006.9936.

Sánchez-Martínez, M. and Otero, A. (2008). Factors associated with cell phone use in adolescents in the community of Madrid (Spain). *CyberPsychology & Behaviour*, 12 (1), 1–7. doi: 10.1089/cpb.2008.0164.

Stauder, A. and Kovacs, M. (2003). Anxiety symptoms in allergic patients: Identification and risk factors. *Psychosomatic Medicine*, 65, 816–823.

Subrahmanyam, K. and Greenfield, P. (2008). Online communication and adolescent relationships. *The Future of Children*, 18 (1), 119–146.

Walsh, S., White, K. and Young, R.M. (2007). Young and connected: Psychological influences of mobile phone use amongst Australian youth. In G. Goggin and L. Hjorth (eds) *Proceedings Mobile Media 2007* (pp. 125–134). Sydney: University of Sydney.

Zichkur, K. and Smith, A. (2012). Digital differences. Retrieved from: http://alexa. pewinternet.com/~/media/Files/Reports/2012/PIP_Digital_differences_041312.pdf.

5

A CROSS-CULTURAL COMPARISON OF DECEPTION IN ONLINE DATING PROFILES USING LANGUAGE ANALYSIS

Nicola Fox Hamilton and Gráinne Kirwan

Chapter summary

Previous research has found that in the free text 'About Me' element in online dating profiles, liars unconsciously produced different word patterns to those being truthful. In this research, language variables indicating deception were investigated through the programme Linguistic Inquiry and Word Count (LIWC). Additionally, emergent coding was used to examine how profile authors write about themselves, specifically in relation to describing themselves as honest and trustworthy. The free text 'About Me' element of 150 Irish and 150 American Caucasian, male, online daters' profiles was analysed, and the differences were compared across the two cultures. The results found that the Irish profiles used more language variables indicating deceptive language than American profiles, and yet the Irish males were more likely to describe themselves as trustworthy or honest. This dichotomy is an interesting one, and is worthy of further study. Applications of this research include online dating profile analysis, and social network and other profile analysis.

Introduction

In many cultures across the world, it has become increasingly acceptable for individuals to find love online (Rosen *et al.*, 2008). As more people utilise these services, important questions pertaining to successful communication strategies can be raised. For example, does the manner in which people present themselves on dating sites affect how others will perceive them?

Past research has shown that the free text component of a dating profile is the second most important element – after the profile photograph – in determining attractiveness and trustworthiness (Fiore *et al.*, 2008; Toma, 2010). Online daters are therefore likely to make judgements about compatibility on the basis of what others write, as well as how they look. A potential problem with meeting online, however, lies in the propensity for individuals to stretch the truth. Indeed, it has been suggested that people will alter the manner in which they present themselves online to be more in line with the values that the prospective date expects from them (Rowatt et al., 1998). As self-presentation is a key element to a dater's success in finding a partner, the manner in which they choose to write about themselves is likely to be a careful consideration.

This research seeks to further study into the free text element of online dating profiles through the use of language analysis. The text element of online dating profiles from two cultures, Ireland and America, will be analysed for variables indicating deceptive language, and those variables will be compared across the two cultures.

Self-presentation in online dating

There has been a lack of research examining the free text element of online dating profiles or of other online self-descriptions. Rosen et al. (2008) found that in online dating the amount of emotionality and self-disclosure in initial emails affected perception of a potential partner. There was a slight tendency for online daters to prefer low self-disclosing emails, supporting social information processing theory (SIP theory; Walther and Parks, 2002). SIP theory proposes that people adapt to the medium and imbue textual communication with information about character-istics, attitudes and emotions. Information is also extrapolated from interpreting contextual and stylistic cues. This allows for a normal or enhanced relational communication to occur. Ellison et al. (2006) found support for SIP theory in a naturalistic setting in studying online dating profiles. In initial interactions on a dating site, stylistic elements of the communication such as message length, timing and grammar appear to be as important as the message content itself, indicating that when non-verbal cues are reduced, remaining cues become more salient.

Ellison et al. (2006) and Whitty (2008) found that most online dating participants' self-presentation strategy revolved around their profile and that participants strove to present a positive but accurate representation of themselves. They balanced their desire to self-market with accurate self-presentation, prompted by their desired outcome of a face-to-face meeting (Ellison et al., 2006). Many participants described their ideal self rather than their actual self in their profiles – this encouraged some to change their behaviour before meeting face to face, for example, by losing weight in order to match their profile description (Ellison et al., 2006). However Norton et al. (2007) found that daters who encountered profiles that appeared 'too good' – whose profiles more closely resembled their ideal self than real self – were liked less.

Whitty (2008) found that 51 per cent of participants had misrepresented themselves in some way in their profiles, with men more likely to lie about their relationship status or having children. Toma et al. (2008) found that while deception was rife in dating profiles, the amounts by which people lied were very small. They found that men were more likely to intentionally lie about their height and women about their weight. Gibbs *et al.* (2006) found that those who anticipated greater face-to-face interaction were motivated to present themselves authentically, and as such were more likely to disclose both the positive and negative aspects of themselves to potential dates, with the majority claiming to be truthful in their profiles. Fiore and Donath (2005) found that when daters had a perception that others on the dating site were being deceptive about information such as age, they felt that they also had to be deceptive or they would be at a disadvantage. However, the amount by which they changed their age was small and was designed to get around constraints of the site rather than to intentionally misrepresent themselves, and they tended to inform partners with whom they entered into conversation early in the exchange (Ellison *et al.*, 2006).

Cultural, personality and language differences between Ireland and America

In 2004, Hofstede and McCrae suggested that 'the idea that a population or part thereof possesses collective mental characteristics is probably as old as populations themselves' (p. 53). Hofstede and McCrae (2004) contend that personality traits and culture interact in a manner that shapes the behaviour of both individuals and social groups. At an individual level this means that the set of characteristic adaptations that a person develops is reflective of both individual and culturally contextual contributions (McCrae and Costa, 1999). Hofstede and McCrae (2004) found that mean personality scores of cultures correlated strongly and significantly with dimensions of culture and proposed that environmental and temperamental variations may provide an explanation for these variances. Their research found a number of correlations between cultural context and traits, including strong correlations between individualism and extraversion, uncertainty avoidance and neuroticism.

A study by Lester (2000) analysed the rates of cultural variables such as murder, crime, divorce, smoking, suicide and cirrhosis mortality that had been clearly and consistently identified from past research as being correlated with either extraversion or neuroticism. This study found differences in the levels of extraversion between Ireland and America, and found similar levels of neuroticism, showing that Ireland had an overall score as 'stable introvert' and America as 'stable extravert'. Lester's (2000) study therefore also demonstrates that cultural variables and personality traits are interlinked.

Van Hemert *et al.* (2002) measured personality traits across different countries using the Eysenck Personality Questionnaire (EPQ; Eysenck and Eysenck, 1975). Irish participants were found to have a higher score on psychoticism ($n = 2804$, $M = 4.65$) than American participants ($n = 4153$, $M = 3.67$). Ireland also demonstrated a lower level of extraversion ($M = 18.85$) than America ($M = 20.83$), and Ireland had a lower level on the lie scale ($M = 9.72$) than America ($M = 11.54$). The mean across all twenty-six countries for psychoticism was 4.96, meaning that Ireland's score was lower than average and America considerably lower than average. The mean for extraversion over all countries was 18.63, placing Ireland close to average and America above average. The mean for the Lie Scale across all twenty-six participating countries was 13.23, with Ireland below the average and America below but closer to the average. The mean age across all populations was 27.46 ($SD = 9.30$; Van Hemert et al., 2002).

It has been suggested that language differences partly arise from cultural transmission, alongside biological evolution and individual learning. Furthermore, interactions between the three adaptive systems, learning, culture and evolution combine to create language (Kirby et al., 2007). Christiansen et al. (2009) also argue that the processes of cultural evolution are the principal factors affecting the evolution of linguistic structure.

Language analysis

There is a long history of a lexical approach to examining personality traits and other factors in individuals, with the idea that patterns of words used may reveal dimensions of the self. Recent research has found relationships between textual self-descriptions in online dating profiles and personality traits such as neuroticism (Fiore et al., 2010). Relationships have been found between language and personality traits from both the NEO-PI Five-Factor Personality inventory (Costa and McCrae, 1992) and EPQ (Eysenck and Eysenck, 1975) scales. Relationships have also been found between language and deception (Newman et al., 2003; Toma and Hancock, 2010).

Toma and Hancock (2010) and Toma et al. (2008) found that in the free text 'About Me' element in online dating profiles, liars unconsciously produced different word patterns to those being truthful. The act of lying is more cognitively difficult than truth telling and results in the use of more concrete and simple language. Liars also psychologically distance themselves from their writing by using fewer references to themselves and more negations. They also write fewer words than truth-tellers, possibly in order to avoid contradicting themselves. The linguistic variables identified by Toma et al. (2008) accounted for 23 per cent of the variance in the deception index that they had devised, and had a large effect size. It was possible to accurately identify 63 per cent of profiles using these variables. Analysis of other text samples has shown that deceptive language contains fewer third-person references and fewer exclusions (Newman et al., 2003), and contains more motion words than truthful language (Newman et al., 2003; Toma and Hancock, 2010).

Research question and hypotheses

This study attempts to determine whether there is a cultural difference in the language used by Irish and Americans in their online dating profiles, particularly in variables indicating deception. Research has shown the Irish score higher in psychoticism than Americans (Lester, 2000; Van Hemert et al., 2002). As psychoticism has been found to correlate negatively with conscientiousness (Avia et al., 1995; Draycott and Kline, 1995; Saggino, 2000), and integrity has a significant positive correlation with conscientiousness (Korchin, 1987; Murphy and Lee, 1994), it would be expected that the Irish would score lower in conscientiousness, and therefore lower in integrity, than Americans.

The study hypothesises that analysing the free text component 'About Me' of online dating profiles for language signifiers of deception will find that Irish online dating profiles have greater use of language variables indicating deception than American profiles.

Method

Design

This research was undertaken to determine if there is a cultural difference in the language used in self-presentation by Irish and American people in their online dating profiles, particularly relating to signifiers of deception. A mixed method quantitative and qualitative content analysis of the data in the online dating profiles was completed.

Participants

This research was a between-participants design in which a stratified, random sample of 300 profiles was selected from two online dating websites in Ireland and America. The two websites chosen both had openly accessible profiles with their data in the public domain. The dating profiles from each site were constructed in a similar manner with sections for photographs, fixed-category questions such as religion, marital status and body characteristics, and free text spaces to describe both themselves and a positive date scenario. The main difference between the two sites was that the Irish site contained a free text element where the dater could describe their ideal partner, whereas the American site did not.

A total of 150 profiles from Ireland and 150 from America were chosen, taking a spread from across urban and rural areas of the two countries. In America four zip codes were chosen from major urban areas – Austin, Los Angeles, Brooklyn and Billings – and daters were chosen from within a 200-mile radius of those zip codes. This allowed for a mix of urban and rural daters to be chosen to represent different areas of the country. In Ireland the search for profiles included all counties in the Republic, and profiles were chosen to reflect a spread across the country. Caucasian, heterosexual, male adults over the age of 18, born in America or Ireland, who gave no indication that they were born or had lived for a large proportion of their lives outside America – for American daters – or Ireland – for Irish daters – were chosen for the study to ensure that ethnicity, sexual orientation and gender did not provide confounding variables. The Irish profile authors ranged in age from 23 to 71 with a mean age of 40.1 (SD = 10.208), and the American authors ranged in age from 19 to 74 with a mean age of 37.99 (SD = 12.461). The age of the two groups was compared using an independent samples t-test and no significant difference was found (t = 1.541, df = 298, p = .124).

Materials

The data collected from each profile consisted of the free text component 'About me' describing the dater and the age of each profile author. This was analysed using the LIWC software (Pennebaker *et al.*, 2001), which contains a dictionary consisting of approximately 80 output variables including standard linguistic dimensions, word categories that mine psychological constructs and personal concern categories. There are two types of words: function words, which are used in how something is said; and content words, which are the topic of what is said. There are 80 word categories consisting of over 4,500 words and word stems. Results are reported as a percentage of the total words in the sample. (Pennebaker *et al.*, 2001). LIWC has shown good reliability across topics and testing occasions (Pennebaker *et al.*, 2007). The free text content of the 'About Me' section of the dating profiles was analysed for language signifiers identified in the previous research indicating deception using the LIWC 2007 standard dictionary categories.

Procedure

The text content of the 'About Me' section of the profiles was prepared according to the directions in the LIWC user manual and included spell checks, removal of extra punctuation, removal of abbreviations or text speak and removal of numerals where a word was intended. All of the data were anonymised for the purposes of this study.

There was a significant difference in the average length of the Irish and American profiles, with Americans writing considerably more than Irish authors. This may have been partly due to the fact that the American dating site had only one text box labelled 'About Me' and no box in which to describe their ideal partner, while the Irish site had both 'About Me' and 'My Ideal Partner' text boxes. American authors sometimes used this 'About Me' section to describe aspects of their ideal partner. Thus in the process of cleaning up the profile text data, direct references in American profiles to their ideal partner were removed from the 'About Me' text box. After the references to the ideal partner were removed, Americans still had a considerably higher word count than Irish daters, with Americans writing on average 149.02 words ($SD = 104.328$) in their profiles and Irish daters writing only 41.99 on average ($SD = 40.857$). Use of an independent t-test showed that the difference between the nationalities' word count was significant ($t = -11.699$, $df = 298$, $p < .0005$) with a large effect size ($d = 1.4743$). All profile texts were placed into individual text documents, and LIWC was used to analyse them.

Content analysis – themes

In addition to the analysis of the data using LIWC, the profiles were analysed to identify and compare the language across the two cultures, and to identify any language that LIWC might have miscounted due to issues of context. Siedel (1998) proposed a three-stage process of noticing, collecting and thinking that is iterative, progressive, recursive and holographic in nature, and this process was followed to identify an emergent coding system.

Results

The results of the profile text analysis using LIWC word categories related to deception were compared using independent samples t-tests, and a number of significant findings were made. Differences were found between American and Irish dating profiles in the use of language associated with deception. In addition to the LIWC word count analysis, the profile texts were subject to content analysis to identify emergent themes.

Quantitative data from LIWC analysis of profiles

LIWC captured over 91 per cent of the words in daters' textual self-descriptions. The Irish and American results for each LIWC word category were compared using independent samples t-tests.

Examination of deception related word categories

The LIWC word categories associated with deception and the results of the independent t-test comparison between Ireland and America for these categories can be seen in Table 5.1. Highly significant results are detailed below.

TABLE 5.1 Findings for LIWC word categories with a relationship to deception

Categories with a positive relationship to deception							
Category	Mean IRE	SD	Mean USA	SD	t	df	sig two-tailed (p)
Motion	1.9328	3.1465	2.0698	1.4371	−.485	298	.628
Negations	1.3544	2.6078	1.6242	1.6970	−1.062	298	.289

Categories with a negative relationship to deception							
Category	Mean IRE	SD	Mean USA	SD	t	df	sig two-tailed (p)
Exclusions	2.411★	3.7470	3.5274	2.5869	−3.003	298	.003
First person singular	5.4087★	5.0770	9.7944	3.3334	−8.844	298	.000
Negative emotion	1.93	3.9325	.8970★	1.0257	3.119	298	.002
She/he	.0752★	.4482	.2156	.5554	−2.409	298	.017
They	.0799★	.3431	.2309	.5113	−3.004	298	.003
Word count	41.99★	40.8570	149.0200	104.3280	−11.699	298	.000

Note: ★ significant results.

The results show a significantly greater use of exclusions in Irish profiles with a moderate effect size ($d = .35$). In American profiles the use of the first person singular was significantly greater than in Irish profiles, with a large difference effect ($d = 1.0429$). There was a significant difference in the use of negative emotion words between the two nationalities, with Irish daters scoring higher than American daters, with a moderate effect size ($d = .4174$). Americans show significantly greater use of she/he words, with a small effect size ($d = .28$). Americans used the third person plural significantly more than the Irish, with a moderate effect size ($d = .3535$). The total word count of the profiles was significantly higher in American texts, also with a large effect size ($d = 1.4743$).

Qualitative content analysis

Additional content analysis of the American and Irish profile texts was undertaken to uncover themes that might have been missed by the LIWC software. During this analysis a new theme emerged that was not apparent in the LIWC analysis. Authors of profile texts sometimes referred to themselves as being honest or trustworthy.

The content theme was identified as a category, and the profiles were coded nominally. The coded data was analysed using a chi-square test and was found to have differences between nationalities at a significant level. Irish daters described themselves as honest or trustworthy significantly more frequently ($n = 35$; 23.3 per cent of Irish profiles) than American daters ($n = 20$; 13.3 per cent of American profiles). The relationship between being Irish and describing the self as honest was significant: χ^2 (1, $N = 300$) = 5.009, $p = .025$. The association was of small strength: $\phi = .129$ and thus being Irish accounted for 1.6641 per cent of the variance in honesty as a description.

Discussion

In summary, support was found for differences between the two cultures in deceptive language variables. Irish daters scored significantly higher than American daters on many of the markers of deception, supporting the hypothesis. In the LIWC categories Ireland was positive for five of the relevant categories, American daters for one, and only two categories were shared. This suggests that Irish daters may be more deceptive in their online profiles than American daters. Additionally, this data is supported by previous findings of higher psychoticism in the Irish, where psychoticism leads to lower measures of integrity.

The free text element of male dating profiles has been rated more attractive when the language used is rated higher for appearing genuine, trustworthy, extraverted and feminine (Fiore et al., 2008). Irish daters have higher results for deceptive language in this study, and yet the qualitative data found that they were significantly more likely to describe themselves as trustworthy or honest. This dichotomy between what they are expressing and their underlying process is an interesting one, and is worthy of further study to discover if they are attempting to cover their deception by stating their honesty or if, indeed, they are being consciously deceptive at all. It would also be interesting to discover whether stating these attributes actually contributes to the rating of attractiveness of the textual element, or whether the rating of attractiveness is attributed to more subtle language cues.

If honesty is a preferred trait or a cultural norm with Americans, there may be greater repercussions for Americans who are not honest in their profiles, and therefore it may be more advantageous to them in the context of online dating to present themselves honestly because of the desired outcome of a face-to-face meeting. Considering that being honest about both the positive and negative attributes of the self in a dating profile has been shown to be an unsuccessful strategy (Rosen *et al.*, 2008), Irish daters may be balancing the tension of conveying their honesty, and not being completely honest in their profiles in order to be more successful.

This research would benefit from greatly expanded study involving considerably more profiles across both genders, and across sexual orientation. The results of the study cannot be generalised outside online dating participants, as this cohort may constitute a unique sub-group of the population with different factors at play to the population in general.

Where different numbers of significant variables were found it was suggested that the nationality with the higher number of significant variables was higher in deceptive language. In general, the results of this research mirrored previous research into the mean levels of traits in the two cultures, suggesting that it may be a valid method of measuring personality across cultures. However, there is no validation in this study as to whether the profile authors were being honest or not. Further research with participants deliberately creating deceptive and honest profiles would be a useful extension of this study.

As many social networking and business networking profiles are composed of similar elements to online dating profiles, including self-descriptive text, language analysis could be used to determine deceptive characteristics from the textual elements of those profiles, and also in other areas such as curriculum vitae and application letters for employment. This could be useful for employers, team builders and educators working with student learning styles and creating adaptive learning, and in many other areas.

References

Avia, M.D., Sanz, J., Sánchez-Bernardos, M.L., Martínez-Arias, M.R., Silva, F. and Graña, J.L. (1995). The five-factor model-II: Relations of the NEO-PI with other personality variables. *Personality and Individual Differences*, 19, 81–97.

Christiansen, M.H., Chater, N. and Reali, F. (2009). The biological and cultural foundations of language. *Communicative and Integrative Biology*, 23, 221–222.

Costa, P.T., Jr and McCrae, R.R. (1992). *Revised NEO Personality Inventory (NEO-PI-R) and NEO Five-Factor Inventory (NEO-FFI) Manual*. Odessa, FL: Psychological Assessment Resources.

Draycott, S.G. and Kline, P. (1995). The big three or the big five – the EPQ-R vs. the NEO-PI: A research note, replication and elaboration. *Personality and Individual Differences*, 6, 801–804.

Ellison, N., Heino, R. and Gibbs, J. (2006). Managing impressions online: Self-presentation processes in the online dating environment. *Journal of Computer-Mediated Communication*, 11, 415–441.

Eysenck, H.J. and Eysenck, S.B.G. (1975). *Manual of the Eysenck Personality Questionnaire.* London: Hodder & Stoughton.

Fiore, A.T. and Donath, J.S. (2005). Homophily in online dating: When do you like someone like yourself? *Computer-Human Interaction 2005*, 1371–1374.

Fiore, A.T., Shaw T.L., Mendelsohn, G.A. and Hearst, M.A. (2008). Assessing attractiveness in online dating profiles. *Computer-Human Interaction 2008*, 797.

Fiore, A.T., Taylor, L.S., Zhong, X., Mendelsohn, G.A. and Cheshire, C. (2010). Who's right and who writes: People, profiles, contacts, and replies in online dating. *Proceedings of Hawaii International Conference on System Sciences*, 43, Persistent Conversation Minitrack.

Gibbs, J.L., Ellison, N.B. and Heino, R.D. (2006). Self-presentation in online personals: The role of anticipated future interaction, self-disclosure, and perceived success in Internet dating. *Communication Research*, 33 (2), 1–26.

Hofstede, G. and McCrae, R.R. (2004). Personality and culture revisited: Linking traits and dimensions of culture. *Cross-Cultural Research*, 38 (1), 52–88.

Kirby, S., Dowman, M. and Griffiths, T.L. (2007). Innateness and culture in the evolution of language. *Proceedings of the National Academy of Sciences of the United States of America*, 104 (12), 5241–5245.

Korchin, S. (1987). Personality correlates of a measure of honesty. *Journal of Business and Psychology*, 1, 236–247.

Lester, D. (2000). National differences in neuroticism and extraversion. *Personality and Individual Differences*, 28 (1), 35–39.

McCrae, R.R. and Costa, P.T., Jr (1999). A Five-Factor Theory of personality. In L.A. Pervin and O.P. John (eds) *Handbook of Personality: Theory and research*, 2nd edn (pp. 139–153). New York: Guilford.

Murphy, K. and Lee, S. (1994). Personality variables related to integrity test scores: The role of conscientiousness. *Journal of Business and Psychology*, 8, 413–424.

Newman, M.L., Pennebaker, J.W., Berry, D.S. and Richards, J.M. (2003). Lying words: Predicting deception from linguistic styles. *Personality and Social Psychology Bulletin*, 29(5), 665–675.

Norton, M., Frost, J. and Ariely, D. (2007). Less is more: The lure of ambiguity, or why familiarity breeds contempt. *Journal of Personality and Social Psychology*, 92, 97–105.

Pennebaker, J.W., Francis, M. E. and Booth, R.J. (2001). *Linguistic Inquiry and Word Count (LIWC): LIWC2001.* Mahwah, NJ: Erlbaum.

Pennebaker, J.W., Chung, C.K., Ireland, M., Gonzales, A. and Booth, R.J. (2007). *The Development and Psychometric Properties of LIWC2007.* Austin, TX and Auckland: University Texas at Austin and University of Auckland.

Rosen, L., Cheever, N., Cummings, C. and Felt, J. (2008). The impact of emotionality and self-disclosure on online dating versus traditional dating. *Computers in Human Behaviour*, 24(5), 2124–2157.

Rowatt, W.C., Cunningham, M.R. and Druen, P.B. (1998). Deception to get a date. *Personality and Social Psychology Bulletin*, 24 (11), 1228–1242.

Saggino, A. (2000). The big three or the big five? A replication study. *Personality and Individual Differences*, 28, 879–886.

Seidel, J.V. (1998). Qualitative data analysis. Qualis Research. Retrieved from: www.qualis research.com.

Toma, C.L. (2010). Perceptions of trustworthiness online: The role of visual and textual information. *Proceedings of the 2010 ACM Conference on Computer Supported Cooperative Work* (CSCW '10), 13–22.

Toma, C.L. and Hancock, J.T. (2010). Reading between the lines: Linguistic cues to deception in online dating profiles. *Proceedings of the 2010 ACM Conference on Computer Supported Cooperative Work* (CSCW '10), 5–8. Retrieved from: http://doi.acm.org/10.1145/1718918.1718921.

Toma, C., Hancock, J. and Ellison, N. (2008). Separating fact from fiction: An examination of deceptive self presentation in online dating profiles. *Personality and Social Psychology Bulletin*, 34, 1023–1036.

Van Hemert, D., van Devijver, F., Poortinga, Y. and Georgas, J. (2002). Structural and functional equivalence of the Eysenck Personality Questionnaire within and between countries. *Personality and Individual Differences*, 33 (8), 1229–1249.

Walther, J.B. and Parks, M.R. (2002). Cues filtered out, cues filtered in: Computer-mediated communication and relationships. In M. L. Knapp and J.A. Daly (eds) *Handbook of Interpersonal Communication*, 3rd edn (pp. 529–563). Thousand Oaks, CA: Sage.

Whitty, M.T. (2008). Revealing the 'real' me, searching for the 'actual' you: Presentations of self on an Internet dating site. *Computers in Human Behaviour*, 24, 1707–1723.

6

THE INFLUENCE OF GENDERED WEB DESIGN ON FEMALE SCIENCE CAREER MOTIVATION

Donna McCabe, Olivia Hurley and Cliona Flood

Chapter summary

The low number of women working in science, technology, engineering and mathematics (STEM) careers has become a global issue (Moss-Racusin *et al.*, 2012; Sanz Casado *et al.*, 2011; Tajmel, 2009). Reasons for this lack of female participation in science careers has been investigated (Baker, 2011; genSet, 2010; Miller, 2006; Pawley, 2004; Williams and Ceci, 2012), with the Internet highlighted as an effective means of promoting STEM careers among young people (Quinn *et al.*, 2009). However, little research exists on how the Internet could be used to specifically encourage female participation in STEM careers. The current research sought to investigate how the graphic design of STEM websites is perceived by female students, how these perceptions might influence their motivations to pursue careers in STEM, and whether designing science websites in a more female-orientated manner might encourage greater female participation in STEM careers. In summary, the female population investigated preferred non-gendered science websites. However, when motivation towards STEM careers was examined, students with lower motivation appeared to prefer more female-specific web design. Web design also appeared to play an important role in influencing student attitudes towards STEM, as well as having the power to evoke strong emotional reactions.

Introduction

Female motivation and STEM careers

Motivation is derived from a 'need', such as a need for achievement or a need for uniqueness. In the context of Maslow's Hierarchy of Needs, which identified a number of levels of motivation (Maslow, 1943), students may believe that particular career choices allow them to earn enough money to ensure the provision of basic needs such as food and shelter. However, at a higher level, a sense of belongingness, being accepted by others and feeling self-fulfilled may be greater 'drivers' of career motivation. It is likely that an expectancy to conform to group norms exists among such a population of female students (Turner *et al.*, 1987). Turner's (1985) theory of self-categorisation proposed that social group members who share group identities are more comfortable aligning their behaviours and beliefs to those of the group. This suggests that peer group approval of a career choice could be a strong motivator for females when choosing their career path. While being careful to avoid reinforcing stereotypes (Cheryan *et al.*, 2011), it is possible that young females may be more motivated to work in STEM careers if they see a strong online presence of successful female STEM role models.

Kerger *et al.* (2011) reported that female students were less interested in science than boys because they saw it as something inherently masculine that threatened their sense of femininity. Kerger *et al.* reported that girls' interest in scientific concepts was significantly higher when they were presented in the context of interesting topics relevant to females. They recommended using more feminine topics in science to increase personal interest among female students. However, using such feminised content had a negative impact on boys, who showed a significant decrease in interest in science when it was presented in a feminine context.

Using the Internet to promote STEM careers

O'Neill *et al.* (2011) reported that almost 75 per cent of Irish teens use the Internet daily, while 85 per cent of teens in Europe use it for school work (Haddon and Livingstone, 2012). This suggests that the Web is worth pursuing as a way to promote gender equality in science. The YOSCIWEB study (Quinn *et al.*, 2009) investigated the effectiveness of science websites in promoting STEM among young people. Negative and stereotypical perceptions of scientists were examined, as well as the influence of the media. However, the report did not focus on female evaluations of the websites in question.

The role of web design in promoting STEM careers

Benford *et al.* (2009) proposed that affect, pleasure, fun and aesthetics contribute to the overall experience of the web user. Assessing the user experience for female students visiting STEM promotion websites could help to determine guidelines for developing effective web design that positively motivate females to select science careers, thus helping to eradicate gender stereotyping in this area.

Schaupp and Bèlanger (2005) reported that satisfaction derived from the user experience is essential for continued engagement online. Szmanski and Hise (2000) also commented that perception of website design can greatly influence feelings of user satisfaction. According to Keller's 'Attention Relevance Confidence Satisfaction' (ARCS, 1987) model of motivational design, a key element in student learning motivation is content that captures their attention, is relevant to them, instils confidence and leads to an overall sense of satisfaction. Female-specific websites appear to promote a common identity group of users (Prentice *et al.*, 1994), where the content and design aims to appeal to females who are looking for positive reinforcement regarding the study of science as acceptable, and even praised.

'Gender neutral' in science language

The current literature acknowledges that there is much debate regarding the use of the term 'gender neutral' in the language used to describe science content on websites. Spertus (1991) investigated sexual biases present in language, particularly concentrating on the field of computer science and reported that 'gender neutral' language is often not truly neutral. Indeed, Miller and Swift (1977) reported that when people think of the generic term 'man' in reference to humankind, the word evokes images of a male. In the present study, the term 'gender neutral' was replaced with terms considered 'non-sexist' or 'non-traditional'. For example, it was recommend that non-gender specific terms such as 'analyst' or 'programmer' be used, thus avoiding reference to the scientist's gender. Whyte (1986) referred to 'girl-friendly science' after finding that workshops with school children produced illustrations of scientists who were predominately male. Chambers (1983) employed the Draw-a-Scientist Test (DAST) to measure children's stereotyping of scientists and also reported that children's drawings of scientists were predominately male.

While content obviously targeted at a female audience in its tone and imagery may be put forward as empowering for female students, there is little empirical evidence to support this to date. Clearly there is a lack of consensus for which language approach is most effective in science communications. Similarly, there is a lack of strong empirical data to show whether non-gendered web design, or female-specific web design, is more effective in promoting STEM careers online among female students. The proposed research sought to examine these questions and make use of the terms 'female-specific' or 'feminine-specific' to refer to web content that is aimed at a female audience with regard to the domain name, web design (colour and primary imagery) and language style. Where a website did not clearly target one gender over another, the term 'non-gender specific' rather than the term 'gender-neutral' was employed.

Research question

In summary, then, the literature has suggested that female career stereotypes have a detrimental effect on women pursuing careers in STEM. New methods for communicating positive images of female role models in these fields are required. Of particular interest to this research study was the relationship between motivation and the design and content of science websites. The Internet provides a means for communicating directly with female students, giving them access to science content depicting female scientists in a positive manner that is available twenty-four hours per day and that is not influenced by parents and teachers. Specifically, the research questions asked in the present study were: (i) Would feminising the design and content of websites promoting STEM careers make them more appealing to female students? (ii) Would this lead to an increase in their science-career motivation?

From these questions the following hypotheses were derived:

H1 Female-specific science websites would be more appealing to female students then non-gender specific science websites.
H2 Less motivated students would prefer female-specific science websites.

Method

Design

The study utilised a mixed methods, within groups design (Leech and Onwuegbuzie, 2007).

Participants

The sampling frame consisted of a cross-sectional, convenient sample of 94 female second-level science students aged sixteen years and over. Four female-only schools were selected from the same geographical urban area, and from a similar socio-economic background, in order to minimise possible confounding variables. The participating students were studying one of the main science subjects, physics, chemistry or biology, or a combination of the three. The study sought to investigate the motivation of these female students to study these science subjects, rather than female students not studying a science subject, as the question of motivation within this science-studying group was most relevant to the present study (see Table 6.1).

TABLE 6.1 Overview of participants by subject choice

Subject	Number of students
Physics	17
Chemistry	33
Biology	44
Total	94

Subject mixes	Number of students
Physics + Biology	5
Physics + Chemistry	2
Biology + Chemistry	24
Physics + Chemistry + Biology	1

Materials

The online questionnaire entitled 'Perceptions of Science and You' Questionnaire (PSUQ) was adapted from Glynn *et al.*'s (2008) thirty-item Likert-scale Science Motivation Questionnaire (SMQ). The PSUQ was designed and located on an online survey website. It was available to potential participants for four weeks.

The first part of the PSUQ, which was pilot tested before the main data collection took place, consisted of thirteen questions from the SMQ measuring intrinsic motivation for a science career. Participants indicated their responses on a five-point scale (with 1 = 'never'; 5 = 'always'). Images of homepages for two different science promotion websites were included in the online survey. Image A was taken from a female-orientated website. Image B was from a non-gender specific website. These two images were approved by two independent researchers for their appropriateness before being selected for the survey. The second part of the PSUQ consisted of seven questions asking participants to rate the images, and their associated terms. These questions were devised by the researcher and were also approved by two independent researchers for their appropriate inclusion in the PSUQ.

Procedure

Teachers were invited by email to carry out the data collection as part of a national science week with their students. As the participants were under 18 years, there were ethical issues to consider. Schools were provided with a full outline of the study plan, a copy of the PSUQ, consent forms and the debriefing document. They were advised that participation in the study was voluntary and anonymous. Teachers were given an opportunity to provide feedback on any changes or issues they had with the research materials before they were finalised. Potential participants were given consent forms to be signed by their parents or guardians prior to participating in the study. All participants' rights were assured (American Psychological Association, 2002).

Teachers either invited students to complete the online survey during class time or set it as a piece of homework. Students were given (i) the web address to log on to and (ii) clear instructions for how to complete the survey. Participants were given the name and contact details of the researcher and her supervisor. They were advised that all information provided would remain confidential and anonymous, and that the survey would take approximately fifteen minutes to complete. They were also advised that participation in the study was voluntary. Students were then asked to press the link to continue to the PSUQ, if they so wished. Upon completion of the PSUQ, participants were thanked for their participation in the study.

Results

Quantitative analysis

All statistical data was analysed using statistics software PASW 18 (PASW Statistics, 2009). Hypothesis 1 stated that female-specific science websites would be more

TABLE 6.2 Results showing expected and observed website preference of the total survey population

Website preference	Observed	Expected
Non-gendered (Image A)	49	31.3
Female-specific (Image B)	29	31.3
No preference	16	31.3
Total	94	

appealing to female students than non-gender specific science websites. A goodness-of-fit chi-square test was used to test this hypothesis. As seen in Table 6.2, the goodness-of-fit chi-square test actually indicated that there was a significant difference in the proportions of those who preferred the non-gendered website identified in the sample (49 per cent) compared to the expected 31.3 per cent, $\chi^2 (1, N = 94) = 1.6$, $p < .0005$. This was in direct contrast to the expected finding.

Motivation and preference

Hypothesis 2 stated that less motivated female students would prefer female-specific science websites over the non-gendered websites. An independent t-test was used to compare which website the participants preferred (the grouping variable) with how they had scored for motivation (the dependent variable). A significant difference in science motivation was found to exist between those who preferred the non-gendered website and those who preferred the female-specific website ($t = 2.87$, $df = 76$, $p = .0025$, one-tailed). Students with no preference were excluded from the analysis. Those who preferred the non-gendered website had higher mean motivation scores ($M = 41.59$, $SD = 7.57$) than those who preferred the female-specific website ($M = 36.03$, $SD = 9.32$). The magnitude of difference between the means was large (mean difference = 5.56, 95 per cent CI: 1.702–9.412; $d = .657$; see Table 6.3).

Qualitative analysis

Three questions in Part II of the PSUQ gave participants the opportunity to give free-text responses, where more detailed answers were provided. These were

TABLE 6.3 Mean motivation score and standard deviation for website preference

Website preference	N	Mean motivation score	Standard deviation	Standard error mean
Non-gendered	49	41.59	7.574	1.082
Female-specific	29	36.03	9.322	1.731

questions relating to: which website image they preferred; which of the websites would be more attractive to females in their opinion; and, finally, which website they felt was most relevant to them. Of the survey participants ($N = 94$), 80 students provided free text responses. Of these, 24 per cent indicated a preference for the female-specific website, 14 per cent had no preference, and 43 per cent preferred the non-gendered website. Keywords were identified across the responses, and these were then coded as either positive or negative. The frequency of positive or negative words used in response to both websites were counted and verified. An inter-rater reliability analysis using Kappa was conducted to determine consistency among the raters, $k = .50$ ($p < .003$), 95 per cent CI (.309, .501).

For a number of the participants, the free text responses produced strongly worded, emotional responses when discussing the female-specific website. For example, one participant said, 'Image B is condescending and looks like a cheap girly magazine. I find it offensive, graphic heavy and I, as a girl, object to the blatant stereotyping.' Participant 28 stated, 'I would consider image B to be very condescending, as I am a very practical person who doesn't consider gender to have any relevance in the portrayal and uptake of science', while participant 71 commented 'The second [website] seems to target a stereotype girl which isn't that present in today's society. I find it quite sexist that it is still assumed that the girl will like the pink website.'

For other participants, the reverse was found to be true, and positive comments were made in relation to the female-specific website. Participant 70 remarked, 'It stands out to me as it's eye-catching and relates to me as I am a girl', while participant 74 said, 'The colours are vibrant and immediately you see happy girls having fun and their fun and laughter draws you in.'

In another instance, Participant 39 chose the female website for being more relevant to her, as she remarked, 'It states that girls are struggling with maths and various sciences, and I find this very relevant.'

For some participants the non-gendered website was seen as being more credible, or authentic. For example, Participant 99 said, 'I would be more likely to browse the website in Image A as I would feel more assured that the information given would be accurate and objective, rather than skewed to appeal to female audiences.'

While a large number of comments referred to the female-specific website as being 'too-girly' or 'sugar-coated' (Participant 98), others felt that the non-gendered website lacked a 'feminine touch' (Participant 95). A small number of participants questioned the need to separate content or design for different genders. For example, Participant 40 remarked, 'You can learn about science in both of the websites so it doesn't really make a difference', while Participant 81 commented, 'Girls like to be equal, not have separate websites.'

Discussion

The current research investigated the influence of feminised or gendered web design on female science student attitudes and motivation towards a science career.

The research specifically considered the role that web design might play in helping to improve the engagement of female students with science subjects. The results showed that the female-specific science website was not more appealing to female students; thus Hypothesis 1, which stated that female-specific science websites would be more appealing to female students than non-gender specific science websites, was not supported. More females preferred the non-gendered website than was expected. However, when the sample was scored for motivation, it was possible to look more closely at which website design was preferred by the participants in the low motivation category. The results suggest that less motivated females preferred the female-specific website design; thus Hypothesis 2, which stated that less moti-vated students would prefer female-specific science websites, was supported.

It is felt that the sample size ($N = 94$) gave an adequate representation of the student population in question. Similarly, the age range and selection criteria of surveying only female students from all-female schools who were studying science subjects and came from the same geographical location and socio-economic bracket helped to minimise confounding factors. As the students were studying one or more science subjects it was felt they would have some opinion of, or interest in, working in this area. By measuring the motivation score of the sample, it was then possible to determine which students were low in motivation. This finding should be of particular interest to researchers and policy makers looking to encourage more female students to consider STEM careers. It should be noted, however, that the lack of women in STEM is predominantly in the areas of the 'physical sciences'; the majority of students surveyed in the present study were biology students.

Implications of findings of the present study

The implication of the findings for policy makers and web designers promoting STEM careers to young females using the Internet is that a careful balance must be struck between attractive, eye-catching and engaging content that is relevant to females, and design and content that is seen as mature, credible and professional. While many participants did not react positively to what they felt was the presence of gender stereotyping, less motivated female students appeared to consider this design approach to be more attractive. If policy makers are looking at specifically engaging this group, their websites should adopt a more female-friendly design and include a stronger presence of female role models to provide encouragement and reinforcement.

Strengths and limitations of the present study

The current research has gone beyond looking at the potential of the Internet to engage females in science careers by looking more closely at the role of gender within web design, to see how it can impact on attitudes and motivation. The research has added to the literature where a gap existed as it proposes solutions for using appropriate web design to help address the issue of low female participation in STEM careers. In confirming that web design has an influence on the attitudes and perceptions of female science students towards science websites, the research has shown that careful consideration must be given to how web design and content are presented to this audience, particularly in terms of gender and the presence of stereotypes. This study shows that this approach may be effective for students with low motivation towards a science career; however, it may not work for all students.

It is acknowledged that students carrying out the survey in class time may have been affected by the presence of the teacher, and that this is a potential limitation of the study. As the students also participated in the study during Science Week, a national awareness campaign promoting science, there may have been a response bias, where the participants felt obliged to give positive responses in this science-focused research study.

It is acknowledged that only students studying science subjects participated and that these were students who perhaps already saw themselves as *scientists*. This may, in part, explain why there was a strongly negative reaction by some participants to the female-specific website. If scientific material is seen as inherently masculine, and web users see themselves as 'scientific', they perhaps prefer to disassociate themselves from the female imagery.

It was apparent that many participants felt the female-specific website was 'too childish', and thus the image used to demonstrate the female-specific website did not appear to be as age appropriate to the survey sample as the image selected to demonstrate a non-gendered STEM website. This may have contributed to responses indicating that the non-gendered website was seen as more 'mature', while the female-specific website was seen as 'un-serious'. Future research should address this by ensuring that both images are equally age appropriate for the survey sample. The survey also failed to ask students if they were planning to pursue careers in STEM. This was considered a missed opportunity. However, it was felt that as the survey took approximately fifteen minutes to complete, keeping students engaged long enough to complete it was crucial, and not allowing the survey to become too long was important. Exploring participants' intention to pursue a career in STEM in the context of STEM websites and web design preference may be an area for further research. A final limitation worth noting is the danger of alienating male students. Kerger *et al.* (2011) reported that boys exhibited less interest in science when the content was presented in a feminine context. As the global STEM community struggles to produce enough STEM graduates of both genders, this is an important consideration. As suggested in the Kerner *et al.* study, a possible solution to address this issue would be to allow students to self-select the web content most preferable or relevant to them, and to use multimedia to produce such material in a manner they feel most appropriate to their own design tastes, regardless of gender.

Further research

Further studies would benefit from looking more closely at the relationship between STEM career motivation and science promotion website design, to investigate if the prolonged use of one design type, to the exclusion of another, could increase motivation towards a career in STEM. This would be particularly relevant for those students with lower motivation. Lanoven *et al.* (2008) noted that personal encouragement plays a strong role in influencing career motivation, so the role of teachers and the relevance of their experience, as well as the scheduling of school resources, merits further study also. A broader study using the wider female student population – that is, those who have not chosen to study science subjects – would also be of interest, to determine the reasons for the general lack of female participation in STEM subjects at post-primary school level.

Future research could also include testing sub-sections within the female student population, for example, investigating the design preferences of students who are generally more experienced at using the Web, and to explore social and cultural factors more deeply, such as the careers of their parents, what their peers' opinions are of female scientists, and asking them about their own career aspirations in more depth. A cross-cultural study of this nature could reveal how female science students in the same age range differ or compare across different cultures globally, as well as perhaps within different ethnic groups in Ireland itself.

Conclusion

It has been acknowledged that the issue of low female participation in STEM careers across the globe needs to be addressed. The underlying reasons appear to be strongly linked to how females perceive science as relevant, accessible, of personal interest and in line with their sense of femininity and social identity. These factors influence their attitudes and motivation towards STEM careers. The current research investigated how web design may be used to more effectively engage female students, and asked whether making the design of STEM websites more female-orientated could help to encourage more female interest towards STEM careers. The female population investigated preferred non-gendered science websites. However, students with lower motivation appeared to prefer more female-specific web design. Web design appeared to play an important role in influencing student attitudes towards STEM. It also had the power to evoke strong emotional reactions. The non-gendered website was seen as credible, professional, scientific, and associated with more success. However, the design was found to be 'boring'. In contrast, the female-specific website was seen as 'fun' and 'pleasurable', but 'unscientific, condescending, childish' and associated more with failure. The current research proposes that STEM websites should utilise a design that is 'eye-catching' and colourful, but not to the detriment of content. The design approach should ensure the content appears genuine and is seen as credible and scientific, while still attractive to females, thus encouraging them to feel that it is personally relevant to them. The findings of the study should be of interest to policy makers, educators and web designers tasked with promoting STEM careers to female students and aiming to increase the number of females participating in the STEM workforce.

References

American Psychological Association (2002). Ethical principles of psychologists and code of conduct. *American Psychologist*, 57, 1060–1073.

Baker, B. (2011). Having a life in science. *Bioscience*, 61 (6), 429–433.

Benford, S., Giannachi, G., Koleva, B. and Rodden, T. (2009). From interaction to trajectories: Designing coherent journeys through user experiences. In *CHI 2009: User experience*. Boston, MA: ACM.

Chambers, D.W. (1983). Stereotypic images of the scientist: The Draw-A-Scientist test. *Science Education*, 67, 255–256.

Cheryan, S., Siy, J.O., Vichayapai, M., Druary, B.J. and Kim, S. (2011). Do female and male role models who embody STEM stereotypes hinder women's anticipated success in STEM? *Social Psychological and Personality Science*, 2, 656–664.

genSET (2010). Consensus seminar report. Science in society programme of the european commission 7th framework. Retrieved from: www.genderinscience.org.

Glynn, S.M., Taasoobshirazi, G. and Brickman, P. (2008). Science motivation questionnaire: Construct validation with non-science majors. *Journal of Research in Science Teaching*, 46, 127–146. Retrieved from: www.coe.uga.edu/smq.

Haddon, L. and Livingstone, S. (2012). *EU Kids Online: National perspectives*. London: The London School of Economics and Political Sciences. Retrieved from: www.lse.ac.uk/media@lse/research/EUKidsOnline/Home.aspx.

Keller, J.M. (1987). Development and use of the ARCS model of motivational design. *Journal of Instructional Development*, 10 (3), 2–10.

Kerger, S., Martin, R. and Brunner, M. (2011). How can we enhance girls' interest in scientific topics? *British Journal of Educational Psychology*, 81, 606–628.

Lavonen, J., Gedrovics, J., Byman, R., Meisalo, V., Juuti, K. and Uitto, A. (2008). Motivational orientations and career choice in science and technology: A comparative investigation in Finland and Latvia. *Journal of Baltic Science Education*, 7 (2), 86–102.

Leech, N.L. and Onwuegbuzie, A.J. (2007). A typology of mixed methods research designs. *Quality and Quantity Journal*, 43 (2), 265–275.

Maslow, A. (1943). A theory of human motivation. *Psychological Review*, 50, 370–396.

Miller, C. and Swift, K. (1977). *Words and Women*. New York: Anchor Press.

Miller, P.H. (2006). Gender differences in high school students' views about science. *International Journal of Science Education*, 28, 363–381.

Moss-Racusin, C.A., Dovidio, J.F., Brescoli, V.L., Graham, M.J. and Handelsman, J. (2012). Science faculty's subtle gender biases favour male students. Proceedings from the National Academy of Sciences. Social Sciences. *Psychological and Cognitive Sciences*, 109 (41), 16474–16479.

O'Neill, B., Grehan, S. and Olafsson, K. (2011). Risks and safety for children on the Internet: The Ireland report. Initial findings from the EU Kids Online survey of 9–16 year olds and their parents. London School of Economics. Retrieved from www.webwise.ie.

PASW Statistics (2009). *Release Version 18.0.0*. Chicago: SPSS.

Pawley, A. (2004). The feminist engineering classroom: A vision for future educational innovations. Proceedings from the 2004 American Society for Engineering Education Annual Conference and Exposition. Retrieved from http://purdue.academia.edu/AlicePawley/Papers/191025/The_Feminist_Engineering_ Classroom_a_Vision_for_Future_Educational_Innovations.

Prentice, D.A., Miller, D.T. and Lightdale, J.R. (1994). Asymmetries in attachments to groups and to their members: Distinguishing between common-identity and common-bond groups. In T. Postmes, R. Spears, M. Lea and S. Reicher (eds) *SIDE effects centre stage: Recent developments in studies of de-individuation in groups* (pp. 63–78). Amsterdam: KNAW.

Quinn, A., McGee, A. and Schroeter, B. (2009). Young people and the images of science on websites (YOSCIWEB). Glasgow Caledonian University. Retrieved from: www. docstoc.com/docs/77338205/best-practices-and-recommendations-guide.

Sanz Casado, E., De Filippo, D. and Nieves Millán Reyes, A. (2011). *National assessments in Gender and STI European Report*. Madrid: University Carlos III.

Schaupp, C.L. and Bèlanger, F. (2005). A conjoint analysis of online consumer satisfaction. *Journal of Electronic Commerce Research*, 6 (2), 95–111.

Spertus, E. (1991). Why are there so few female computer scientists? MIT Artificial Intelligence Laboratory technical report 1315. Retrieved from: http://people.mills.edu/spertus/Gender/pap/pap.html.

Szmanski, D. and Hise, R. (2000). E-satisfaction: An initial examination. *Journal of Retailing*, 76 (3), 309–322.

Tajmel, T. (2009). *Science Education Unlimited: Approaches to equal opportunities in learning science*. Münster: Waxmann Verlag.

Turner, J.C. (1985). Social categorisation and the self-concept: A social cognitive theory of group behaviour. In E. Lawler (ed.) *Advances in group process: Theory and research*, (2). Oxford: JAI Press.

Turner, J.C., Hogg, M.A., Oakes, P.J., Reicher, S.D. and Wetherell, M.S. (1987). *Rediscovering the Social Group: A self-categorisation theory*. New York: Basil Blackwell.

Whyte, J. (1986). *Girls into Science and Technology: The story of a project*. London: Routledge.

Williams, W.M. and Ceci, S.J. (2012). When scientists choose motherhood. *American Scientist*, 100, 138–145.

PART III

Personality and Internet use

The previous section presented a number of studies that looked at how new media is changing how we communicate; this section considers our trust and personality in the use of new media. The changes in usage of the Internet over the past decade due to the greater social interaction allowed by Web 2.0 affects online behaviour – previously anonymity and identity experimentation was common, whereas contemporary online behaviour focuses more on identification of the self, with accurate, but positive, self-representation. Nevertheless, there are still some instances where misrepresentation occurs, more frequently in some contexts than others. For example, it is still expected that pseudonyms are used in some online settings, such as online gaming and boards, which can lead some users to misrepresent themselves. In contrast, the use of pseudonyms and inaccurate portrayals of the self in social networking sites is discouraged. Other types of online profiles (such as online dating profiles) fall somewhere in the middle. New media is being used by millions of people to provide social contacts and intimate interactions. This is an area of study attractive to both technologists and psychologists. If the area is examined solely from a technological viewpoint the importance of personality can be lost, whereas a purely psychological perspective can ignore important changes in new media technologies.

Chapter 7 examines the issue of trust through the growing use of virtual assistants in telecommunication customer support. The research examines the effectiveness of virtual assistants in online commercial roles and seeks to take the study beyond the familiar question-and-answer support and website navigation used to date. Chapter 8 looks at the phenomenon of gender-bending online, specifically in virtual worlds. Gender-bending occurs when someone consciously crosses or bends expected gender roles, and it has existed online since the creation of virtual environments and chat-rooms. The research described in this chapter examines the relationship between gender-bending online and 'Need for Achievement' in goal-orientated and non-goal-orientated environments. Chapter 9 explores the psychological factors that contribute to online recommendation sites, specifically how altruism and narcissism act as motivation for online informational giving. In Chapter 10 the issue of online identity theft is investigated, with a specific focus on the differences between victims and non-victims regarding anxiety, precautions and uses of the Internet. Looking at the differences between those who have been victims of online identity theft and those who have not, it examines anxiety levels online, and precautions and measures when shopping and banking online. Chapter 11 focuses on the issue of Facebook phishing. Phishing is a well-documented social phenomenon whereby an individual or group poses as a trustworthy source to lure an unsuspecting user to give up sensitive, personal details willingly; this data is deceitfully utilised in identity theft, cash transfer and fraudulent credit card transactions. The findings indicate individuals who score highly in cognitive instability, a sub-scale of impulsivity, log in more frequently and identify fewer phishing stimuli than those who score low in cognitive instability.

7

VIRTUAL ASSISTANTS

Trust and adoption in telecommunication customer support

Phelim May and Gráinne Kirwan

Chapter summary

Virtual assistants are used to deliver question-and-answer support and as website navigation aids, but there is little research on their effectiveness in these or other online commercial roles. This study addresses this gap by investigating the hypothesis that trust and likely adoption of a telecommunication network switching experience are significantly higher when mediated by a virtual assistant. The experiment replicated a traditional online network switching form and created an alternative version mediated by an interactive chat bot. It used mixed methods: a usability test followed by a within-group online experiment. The online experiment failed to support the hypotheses. Some interesting findings on usability, deployment strategy and future research were uncovered and are discussed.

Introduction

Customer service has become a critical success factor for modern telecom-munications companies (telcos). Service breadth and product complexity can increase the volume of customer enquiries that are not adequately serviced by telco websites and result in the customer calling directly for support (Dixon *et al.*, 2010). At the same time, price competition and the steady migration away from voice services, a core revenue stream for all telcos, has led to intense pressure for each telco to protect its customer base by reducing the drivers for customer defection (Chappuis *et al.*, 2011). Poor customer service is one such driver, but customer service is also one of the most expensive functions for a telco to deliver (Gustafsson *et al.*, 2005). Complex product sets and processes call for agents that have 'the ability to interact with a customer and . . . guide them to an answer to their question' (Beck, 2010, p. 32). It is prohibitively expensive to deliver this level of service solely through live agents and so an alternative approach must be found.

This study investigated whether a virtual assistant (VA) would be trusted, whether it would outperform a traditional network switching order form in a mock online exercise, and whether it would be adopted by telecommunication customers. The following sections introduce the concepts of artificial intelligence and chat bots, outlining how they can relate to the psychology of problem solving and trust to deliver enhanced online self-care capabilities.

Artificial intelligence and chat bots

Alan Turing suggested a test, called The Imitation Game, during which a participant has a conversation with either another unidentified human or a computer. If the participant cannot tell the difference between the two, the computer has passed what is now described as the 'Turing Test' (DeAngeli and Brahnam, 2008; Turing, 1950). It seems that humans are predisposed to interact in a natural manner with computers (Kerr and Bornfreund, 2005). Reeves and Nass (1996) found that people are inclined to treat computers with the same social norms as they apply to human interactions. Given these findings and previous research showing that consumers prefer to find answers to their questions over the Internet (Dixon et al., 2010), there is a significant opportunity to deliver customer service via virtual assistants or computer programs that display 'characteristics that we associate with human intelligence: learning, inference, adaptability, independence, creativity' (Lieberman, 1997, p. 1). This is not a new concept – many telcos have deployed virtual assistants (Chatbots.org, 2012), but there is limited academic research to support their effectiveness when deployed to deliver customer support.

The psychology of problem solving, information seeking and interaction

Cognitive psychology focuses on the relationships between perception, problem solving, memory and language and is closely linked to the development of artificial intelligence as a research discipline (Chi et al., 1982). Cognitive research has shown that expert individuals tend to have a superior memory capacity – this ability to relay relevant facts is exactly what a virtual assistant needs to mimic when used in customer support.

It is common for a telecommunication customer to search their provider's website for a solution to a problem they are experiencing (Dixon et al., 2010). In a typical search, the best matches are presented in a list to the customer. If this leads to information overload, which can exist at both a sensory and a cognitive level (Milord and Perry, 1977), the resulting behaviour is that the customer either disregards or spends less time on individual pieces of information leading to 'confused and dysfunctional' behaviour (Jacoby et al., 1974).

Virtual assistants can do a lot to prevent information overload; it has been shown that increasing the levels of interaction a user has with media reduces the associated 'cognitive load and improve[s] self-efficacy' (Zheng et al., 2009, p. 790).

Interactive multimedia also increase the level of control offered to the user, which has also been shown to promote self-efficacy and improve cognitive performance (Lurie, 2004).

The aim of the virtual assistant is to act as a repository of knowledge that is easily accessible for each user on the telco's website. Critical to the success of the VA is its ability to process and interpret queries received in natural language, to ask clarifying questions when necessary and to effectively engage and interact with the user. Natural Language Processing (NLP) is used to interpret text input and match it with a specific knowledge set in a database (Chowdhury, 2003). NLP does this by calculating statistical probability or by pattern matching, and it is an enabling tool for the VA. The challenge for the telco VA is not just to process natural language; it is to engage with the customer in a way that delivers a natural language interaction. Graesser *et al.* (2008) note that recent advances in 'discourse processing and computational linguistics' (p. 299) make practical humanoid animated agents possible.

The importance of avatar design

Avatars are defined as 'general graphic representations that are personified by means of computer technology' (Holzwarth *et al.*, 2006, p. 20). The novelty and presence of an avatar on a website can encourage information seeking and present an opportunity for the telco to interact in a more personal manner with its customers (Holzwarth *et al.*, 2006). The role of the avatar is not just to act a focal point for the interaction; it also has to make itself appealing to the maximum number of users. Avatar design is therefore critical to the success of a virtual assistant. Holzwarth *et al.* (2006) set about showing that the mere presence of an avatar would increase the effectiveness of a website. Their premise was that an avatar can have the same positive influence that a human sales agent has on attitudes and purchase intention. The interaction is moderated by the user's level of purchase involvement; attractive avatars were found to be more influential when the consumer had low involvement in the purchase, and expert avatars were found to be more influential when the consumer had high involvement. This highlighted the potential benefits of deploying multiple avatars in telecommunications sales and support.

Appearance

Nowak and Rauh (2008) suggest that the visual characteristics of the avatar have such a strong influence on the person interacting with it that it outweighs the influence of actual behaviour in the interaction. They also suggest that the more anthropomorphic a character is, the higher its perceived credibility. Reliance on visual characteristics for success should also be tempered by the Uncanny Valley phenomenon (Mori, 1970). The Uncanny Valley describes the process by which our perception of an inanimate representation of a human improves with the quality of that representation, but only to a point. At a certain level, approaching a lifelike appearance, the viewer reacts with an instinctive feeling of revulsion. The reaction is explained by Mori (1970) as a visual association with death; the closer the representation is to a human form the more difficult it is to make it appear lifelike. It would be prudent to set the design goal for the avatar to be anthropomorphic but not realistic, for example, using a cartoon representation. Although Mori (1970) did not substantiate his hypothesis, it has been supported by a number of subsequent studies (Misselhorn, 2009).

Virtual assistance: impact on trust and adoption

Rousseau *et al.* (1998) define trust as 'a psychological state comprising the intention to accept vulnerability based upon positive expectations of the intentions or behaviour of another' (p. 395). Trust is a prerequisite to adoption and frequent use; it is also a prerequisite for most economic exchanges. If a customer does not trust the VA to give them the correct answer, then they will not continue to use it.

Beldad *et al.* (2010) point out key differences between offline and online trust. Offline trust is directed at the individual and/or the organisation whereas online trust is focused on the technology and how it is deployed as well as the organisation itself. The broad influence of institutional reputation was also highlighted by Mayer *et al.* (1995). Trust is also subjective; individual attitudes, beliefs, experience and culture all mediate propensity to trust (Beldad *et al.*, 2010).

Keeling *et al.* (2010) highlight the importance of customer-salesperson interaction in the development of trust and in supporting positive purchase intention. In offline sales, trust is generated through face-to-face communication, high levels of interaction, personalisation and likeability. In a human–computer interaction, the avatar can mimic the role of a sales assistant by encouraging natural language interactivity. This was shown by Keeling *et al.* (2010) to have a positive effect on both trust and behavioural intent. They demonstrated that there are three key elements to the successful implementation of an avatar in an online sales experience: appearance, website positioning and interaction style. A shortcoming of Keeling *et al.* (2010) is that they developed a simplistic online purchase experience that merely showed the participant images of what an avatar-supported interaction might look like without exposing participants to an actual sales experience.

Walsh and Mitchell (2010) showed that there is a connection between conscious and unconscious confusion and trust. If the customer is confused, then there is an increased likelihood of postponing or making an irrational purchasing decision. Trust will also be negatively impacted if there is a significant volume of data or level of ambiguity in the information being presented to the customer. Walsh and Mitchell (2010) were primarily concerned with looking at inter-product choices and individual susceptibility to confusion. However, the relationships that are drawn between overload, confusion and trust are very relevant to the present study, as a key goal for the VA should be to reduce the cognitive load on the user.

Bart *et al.*'s (2005) empirical study supports the assertion that perceived ease of use and the capability to direct the user to their desired goal quickly leads to the formation of trust. In turn, this trust positively influences behavioural intent. Bart *et al.* (2005) argue that the existence of a virtual assistant may increase user trust as it both supports decision-making and enhances credibility.

Research question

This study comprised two parts: a usability test (Study 1) and an online experiment (Study 2). The aim of Study 1 was to test the usability of the interface by tracking eye movement during the experience and capturing qualitative data in a post-experience interview. Study 2 investigated whether measures of trust and likely adoption of a telecommunication network switching experience were significantly higher when the experience was mediated by a virtual assistant (Bart *et al.*, 2005; Keeling *et al.*, 2009). The primary hypothesis stated that respondents would have higher trust for a switching experience that uses a virtual assistant to guide them through a complex online request when compared with a traditional linear online form. It was also predicted that behavioural intent would be higher for a switching experience that uses a virtual assistant when compared with a traditional linear online form.

Study 1: usability

A traditional online network switching process was replicated in two ways: a direct copy and a version mediated by a VA. This type of online transaction was chosen for two reasons. First, in its traditional form, an online network switching process is lengthy and complex, with a high user abandonment rate. Second, the focus on one specific aspect of customer service limited the lexicon required for the conversational agent, making the build process more feasible.

Three customer journeys were developed to aid participant progress through the switching scenario; each was designed to support a different problem solving style (Zheng *et al.*, 2009). At the outset of the assisted switching experience the participant was asked how they would like to be helped to select a service package. Participants with a low need for cognition could choose the 'budget' route, which began with setting an end goal, then progressed by asking an allocation question before automatically choosing the most suitable package. At the other end of the spectrum, participants with a high need for cognition could choose 'usage' or 'help' and be stepped through each element of the service package.

A female cartoon-style avatar was designed to evoke the maximum potential appeal (Baylor, 2009). The bias that the avatar design could have on the participants' perceptions of the experience needed to be kept to a minimum as this study tested the influence only of its presence and the interactivity produced by a natural language interface. The design of the VA interface consisted of a speech bubble in a primary position on the top of the screen, an input bar under that and a supplementary window at the bottom of the screen. Figure 7.1 shows a sample screen of the completed design.

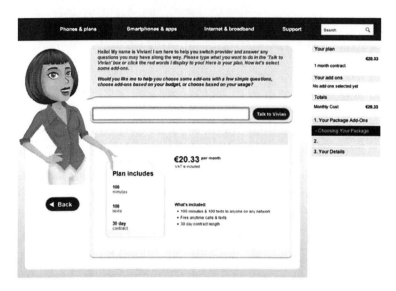

FIGURE 7.1 Virtual assistant user interface

Method

Study 1 was a laboratory usability study designed to monitor a small number of participants completing the experience under observation by the researcher. It was undertaken to evaluate ease of use and expose any significant design flaws. On completion of the study the participants were interviewed by the researcher to gain further insight into their views and opinions.

Participants

A demographic and Internet experience cross-section of six consumers was recruited using quota sampling. Nielsen and Landauer (1993) found that the law of diminishing returns becomes valid after approximately five or six usability test iterations. They proposed that the maximum cost-benefit ratio was achieved by the first four tests, with additional benefits becoming negligible after approximately twelve tests.

Materials

The HTML from an existing switching experience was captured and reproduced on a web-accessible server. In order to create a context for the experiment and to simplify the process, a basic mobile communication package was selected, and the user-testing centred around supporting the selection of additional package elements, described as 'add-ons'. A second version of the same sales flow, mediated by a virtual assistant, was created.

The order the switching experiences were presented in was randomised using a browser session identifier and a time stamp. This was to negate any order-effect bias. Following each experience the participant was asked to complete a short self-reported questionnaire that used a validated scale of trust and adoption from Bart *et al.* (2006). The questionnaire measured trust, behavioural intent (likely adoption) and efficacy.

The laboratory used a dual screen computer equipped with an eye tracker system and an Internet browser. The participant used the primary monitor; the secondary monitor was offset so that it would not distract the participant and was used by the researcher to monitor the progress of the participant and the performance of the eye tracking software.

Procedure

The usability evaluation study used a mixed-methods, within-groups design. The independent variable was the method used to mediate the online switching experience and the dependent variable was the resulting self-reported measures of trust, efficacy and likely adoption.

Once the experiment was over, the real-time screen capture and eye-tracking position was replayed to the participant, each of whom was prompted to recall their experience. Retrospective Think Aloud (RTA) was used to stimulate accurate recall of the process (Guan *et al.*, 2006) and to help gather more detailed qualitative feedback.

Results

Four out of six of the participants preferred the traditional experience. Each participant took approximately forty-five minutes to complete the experience and post-experience interview. Order bias was observed to be strong; there was a certain amount of confusion when each of the participants started the experience, especially when the VA was first presented. The learning effect was observed to have a positive impact on the second experience. Three out of the four participants who preferred the traditional experience received the VA first.

Participants 4 and 6 chose a decision route that took them to the end of the package selection process very quickly. In both cases this increased their level of uncertainty about the validity of their choice. As a result, Participant 4 restarted the process and Participant 6, whose observed computer self-efficacy was low, felt that this impacted negatively on his level of trust.

The eye tracking results for the usability test found that there was more eye movement in the traditional form. The heat maps confirm that the traditional switching flow displays a conventional 'F' shaped visual path and a much more scattered page scan. Figures 7.2 and 7.3 show the eye track heat map for a typical page on both experiences.

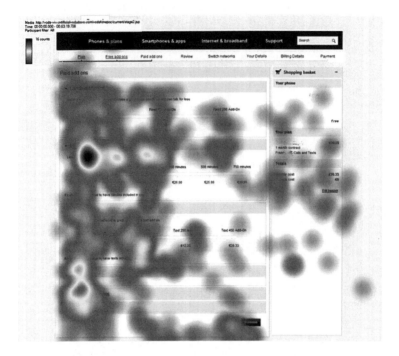

FIGURE 7.2 Eye tracking heat map of the traditional experience

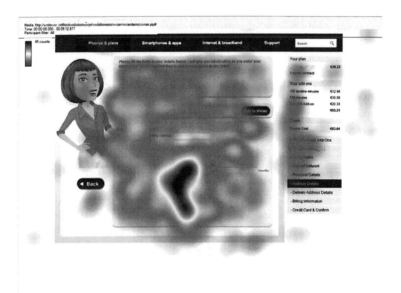

FIGURE 7.3 Eye tracking heat map of the VA experience

Participant 1 did not like the VA, indicating that it did not seem real to her. She commented that 'it felt like spam', which may have been a response to the VA suggesting packages or doing too much for the participant. Participant 1 also suggested using a headline for each section; she possibly felt a bit lost and needed this for a navigational bearing. She was also frustrated by the lack of an ability to review a prior submission, commenting that 'it wouldn't let me go back'. This participant was observed to have a lower computer self-efficacy, driving the requirement to revisit and check her selection and the comment that she 'would not be comfortable buying from the VA'.

Participant 2 became stuck after typing the first response to the VA – she needed to be told how to interact with the VA: 'Once I was told to press "Ask Vivian", it was a lot more clear to complete the task.' Participant 2 was very meticulous in her approach to the task. Eye tracking did not work as the participant had to move closer to the screen. It was confirmed later that the VA screen text size was too small for this participant.

Participant 3 opted for the 'budget' flow; she appeared to understand it and completed the process very quickly. She had significant Internet experience and had used click-to-chat services in the past. When asked for some free association comments about the VA, Participant 3 remarked that it was 'more personal, more fun and trusted'. Trust was observed to be more strongly correlated with brand and practical Web browser experience rather than with the experience itself.

Participant 5 did not like the way the VA presented information in a piecemeal fashion, commenting that he would prefer to have all the options presented at the same time. Even though this participant preferred the traditional process, he commented that he thought that the VA 'looked good' and also mentioned that it was a 'more enjoyable experience dealing with it'. This participant was in the process of considering switching his account at the time of the test so he made more specific and realistic selections.

Discussion

The usability test showed that a VA interface was not immediately intuitive and that some of the terminology used was not clearly understood. The results of the usability test indicate that trust and likely adoption are lower for the VA experience when compared to the traditional experience. Yet four participants also indicated that they liked the virtual assistant, which points to other usability or design issues. The context may have been too complex, which possibly had an impact on the resulting measures of trust and adoption.

The eye tracking results show that there was significantly less scanning activity required to complete the VA experience. It is posited that as the virtual assistant presents information in a more piecemeal fashion, and contains this information in a speech bubble, the user has to expend less cognitive resource in a VA flow.

Participant expectations of a natural language interface were higher once they realised what that interface could do. There was an immediate expectation that the virtual assistant should be able to answer any question. This resulted in a high degree of frustration when this was not the case. Context, content and interaction design is key. The VA required more context for the user before the experience started; it needed to tell the user where they were in the process and what they needed to do next. The VA interaction also required training at the beginning of the experience as it was not immediately intuitive, but it became natural very quickly.

Study 2: online experiment

Study 2 was designed to discover if measures of trust and likely adoption of a telecommunication network switching experience were significantly higher when mediated by a virtual assistant.

Method

Participants

Convenience sampling was used. The target population for the experiment was drawn from a list of company employees who had volunteered to take part in service testing and new product introductions. The group was newly formed, so the group members had not yet been asked to take part in a test event. The researcher was given access to 150 names and email addresses. A total of 103 responses were received. Three responses were discarded as they had insufficient data. Of the 100 usable responses, 71 per cent were male and 29 per cent were female.

Materials

The materials and design used were similar to Study 1. The issues identified in the usability test were addressed with the addition of a welcome page before the VA experience started, a transitional explanation after the welcome screen and an amended preamble introducing the second half of the experiment.

The text was made larger and the first response line was highlighted using black text and a font that was one size bigger than the surrounding text. Additionally, the input bar was moved inside the speech bubble to make it feel like a unified area for question input and response delivery.

The validated scale used by Bart *et al.* (2005) has been replicated in this experiment. Each question is detailed in Table 7.1. Each item was scored on a five-point Likert scale.

Procedure

An email invitation was sent to all potential participants with a statement of purpose, a link to the experiment and a request to complete the process within forty-eight

TABLE 7.1 Validated scale used to measure trust and adoption

Trust items	
T1	This site seems to be more trustworthy than other sites I have visited
T2	The site represents a company or organisation that will deliver on promises made
T3	My overall trust in this site is
T4	My overall believability of the information on this site is
T5	My overall confidence in the recommendations on this site is

Adoption (behavioural intent) items	
A1	I would purchase an item at this site
A2	I would recommend this site to a friend
A3	I am comfortable providing financial and personal information on this site
A4	I would bookmark this site
A5	I would register at this site

Source: Bart *et al.*, 2005.

hours. The mix of VA and traditional presentation order was monitored to ensure an equal distribution (51 per cent of respondents received the VA experience first).

Results

The virtual assistant took an average of just under six minutes to complete whereas the traditional experience took an average of five minutes to complete. The majority of participants completed the VA experience within the range 75–600 seconds, and the traditional experience was completed within the range 60–400 seconds. The standard deviation from the mean is similar for both experiences at three and a half minutes for the VA experience and just under four for the traditional experience. The overall experiment took an average of 13 minutes and 52 seconds to complete.

Trust

The mean trust for the VA experience was 2.152 (SD = .7231) compared to a mean of 2.150 (SD = .6352) for the traditional experience. The difference between the two conditions was not significant (t = .022, df = 99, p = .491, one-tailed).

Adoption

The mean behavioural intent for the VA experience was 2.252 (SD = .8402) compared with a mean of 2.238 (SD = .7503) for the traditional experience. The difference between the two conditions was not significant (t = .141, df = 99, p = .444, one-tailed).

Efficacy

A measure of efficacy was included in the questionnaire. It asked respondents to rate whether 'the process was easy to complete' and whether they were 'satisfied that [they] completed the process correctly'. The mean efficacy score for the VA condition was 3.91 (SD = 1.9233) and the score for the traditional condition was 3.68 (SD = 1.2861), There was no significant difference between both experiences (t = .962, df = 99, p = .169, one-tailed).

Preference

A question was included to gauge the self-reported preference between the two conditions. Ninety-eight participants answered the preference question, with 59.2 per cent preferring the VA experience. The test showed that the virtual assistant was preferred over the traditional experience to a level that approaches significance χ^2 (1, N = 98) = 3.306, p = .069. There was no relationship between experience preference and gender: χ^2 (2, N = 94) = .245, p = .621. There was also no relationship found between experience preference and the order in which each was completed by the participant: χ^2 (2, N = 98) = .028, p = .867.

Discussion

While the virtual assistant experience was preferred by the majority of participants, this preference is not supported by the self-reported measures of both trust and likely adoption. The hypotheses of the study were therefore rejected.

Efficacy was also measured, and it showed that both experiences scored poorly. These results indicate that there may have been usability issues with both the experiment and the experience chosen as the context for the experiment. One participant commented that he found 'the chat bot thing a bit confusing. I didn't know what I was supposed to do sometimes'.

Neither age nor gender had an impact on experience preference. The presentation order bias that was observed in Study 1 was not supported in the results of Study 2; this could be attributed to using a sample population that was more familiar with the language, concepts and processes used in the experiment scenario. The experience would need to be tested with a sample more representative of the general population to confirm whether this is the case.

There are indications that a virtual assistant can improve decision making, trust, adoption and recall when used as pedagogical agents (Bart et al., 2005; Graesser et al., 2005; Graesser et al., 2008; Patrick, 2002). The findings of Study 2 do not support earlier research, but as this approach is novel it should be viewed as the first step toward the development of a method of testing the effectiveness of virtual assistants when deployed as supportive agents on commercial websites. From the qualitative feedback it is clear that there was a positive reaction to using a VA, with only two participants articulating an irrevocable objection to the concept.

Overall discussion

For the majority of participants there was a positive association with using a virtual assistant, but usability issues negatively impacted the experience. Once a website design progresses from delivering simple text and input forms to delivering natural language interaction, the expectations of the user increase substantially. The complexity of the scenario used in this online experiment and the lack of interactivity of the virtual assistant have negatively influenced the measures of trust and adoption. The comments received from the online study did not significantly reveal more issues than were collated during the usability test reinforcing Nielsen and Landauer's (1993) claim that most issues will have surfaced after approximately six test iterations.

Implications of the study

There are two significant implications of the findings of both studies. First, more testing is required before being able to ascertain if a virtual assistant can have an impact on trust and behavioural intent. Second, user expectations of usability and interactivity are higher when presented with an interactive agent, which poses a significant design challenge; 'a prettier experience, however the assistant is very one dimesional [sic] . . . I expected more interactivity and more flexibility . . .' (Study 2, Participant 42). A commercial rollout of a virtual assistant would need to be mindful of the above feedback by limiting the scope of a first iteration to focus more effort on populating the lexicon and ensuring that any usability issues are resolved.

It cannot be assumed that a natural language interface is intuitive for the user. As was evident from the usability test many participants were initially confused when presented with a speech bubble, an input box and an invitation to 'talk to Vivian'. Indeed, one user from Study 2 interpreted that invitation to 'talk' literally and expected that the virtual assistant would both speak and listen to their reply. A simple training demonstration that could be played when the VA starts would be sufficient to show the user how to interact with the chat bot.

The design of the chat interface also requires careful planning and testing. Complex offerings that require verbose explanations are not supported easily by a chat interface. This experiment used two active areas: a speech response bubble and an additional information window underneath the input bar. Some participants in the usability test commented that they did not know where to look to get the information that they required. The challenge to mimic complex face-to-face communication processes with a chat bot should not be underestimated and should be met with considered interaction design. It is recommended that a virtual assistant should be introduced first as an agent that can answer frequently asked questions and support navigation on the telco's website by co-browsing with the user, moving them to a specific page to aid the completion of an established task. There are many positive comments that indicate that there is significant goodwill towards a virtual assistant: 'I like Viv, it's more user friendly and personal, the web form is too serious and texty' (Study 2, Participant 81).

From the free text comments in Study 2 the avatar design appears to have received a mixed review: on the positive side, 'Virtual assistant seems a little more personal' (Study 2, Participant 73); and on the negative side, 'looks unprofessional' (Study 2, Participant 17) and 'Found this . . . a bit cartoonish and therefore would have been less inclined to complete a purchase for real using this site' (Study 2, Participant 79). The negative comments support Nowak and Rauh's (2008) finding that the more anthropomorphic a character is the higher its perceived credibility. But, contrary to the findings of Holzwarth et al. (2006), this study did not show that the mere presence of an avatar would increase the effectiveness of a website.

The usability study revealed a strong relationship between the institutional reputation of the organisation/website and trust. On enquiring if the usability participants felt that they trusted the VA experience, participants mentioned that they trusted the company or brand, and this appeared to have the highest influence on trust for the website, supporting Mayer et al. (1995).

Avatars have been shown to have a positive impact on trust (Keeling et al., 2010), and the relationship between trust and behavioural intent has also been established (Bart et al., 2005) but there was no research found on the impact that a virtual assistant can have on a commercial website. The fact that no such link has been supported by this novel experiment may be partially due to the usability issues with the experiment. The complexity of the scenario used, combined with the problems highlighted in this section, impacted the resulting measures of trust, adoption and efficacy. A quotation from one of the participants adequately summarises the situation: 'I prefer the Vivian option but it is confusing at the moment. The process is not as simple and easy to follow as the normal web form' (Study 2, Participant 4).

Limitations and future research

While the design of the experiment was adequate, the most significant limitation was the complexity of the scenario that the participant was asked to undertake. A sales flow was chosen to limit the required size of the lexicon and to provide a commercial background to the activity. From the efficacy measure of both the traditional and the VA experiences it is clear that this type of sales flow is overly complex.

The avatar was not animated, and a single image was used throughout the process. To improve the sense of interactivity a number of expressions could have been developed and deployed according to type of response from the virtual assistant. Another significant issue with the virtual assistant was that its conversational capability was underdeveloped. Of the participants that entered a comment 18 per cent mentioned that the VA was not able to answer their question.

The sample population used in this research was a segment of telecommunication employees. Their product knowledge and website experience resulted in an experiment population that had specific knowledge and experience, which possibly reduced the impact the virtual assistant had in simplifying the switching experience.

Reeves and Naas (1996) indicated that we are predisposed to interact with digital media in a humanlike manner, but that does not mean that a virtual assistant can be deployed without consideration for both usability and user training. Both will have to be carefully considered in subsequent research. It would also be advisable to include a baseline measure of computer self-efficacy, which could be used to cross-tabulate capability with measures of trust and adoption.

Conclusion

The aim of this study was to add to the body of knowledge in the area of virtual assistance and to measure its effectiveness when deployed to deliver customer support. The study found no support for the hypotheses that respondents would have greater trust or behavioural intent for a network switching experience that used a virtual assistant compared to an online form. Further research is required to build on the preference result from this study, which showed that 60 per cent of participants would prefer to interact with a virtual assistant over a traditional web form.

References

Bart, Y., Shankar, V., Sultan, F. and Urban, G.L. (2005). Are the drivers and role of online trust the same for all web sites and consumers? A large-scale exploratory empirical study. *The Journal of Marketing*, 69 (4), 133–152.

Baylor, A.L. (2009). Promoting motivation with virtual agents and avatars: role of visual presence and appearance. *Philosophical Transactions of the Royal Society B: Biological Sciences*, 364 (1535), 3559–3565.

Beck, K. (2010). Anybody's bot. *CRM Magazine*, 14 (10), 32–36.

Beldad, A., de Jong, M. and Steehouder, M. (2010). How shall I trust the faceless and the intangible? A literature review on the antecedents of online trust. *Computers in Human Behaviour*, 26 (5), 857–869.

Chappuis, B., Gaffey, B. and Parvizi, P. (2011). Are your customers becoming digital junkies? *McKinsey Quarterly*, 3, 20–23.

Chatbots.org (2012). Telecoms and utilities – virtual assistants, virtual agents, chat bots, conversational agents, chatterbots, chatbots: examples, companies, news, directory. Retrieved from: www.chatbots.org/industry/telecoms_utilities/

Chi, M.T.H., Glaser, R. and Rees, E. (1982). Expertise in problem solving. In R.J. Sternberg (ed.) *Advances in the Psychology of Human Intelligence* (p. 7–75). Hillsdale, NJ: Erlbaum.

Chowdhury, G.G. (2003). Natural language processing. *Annual Review of Information Science and Technology*, 37 (1), 51–89.

DeAngeli, A. and Brahnam, S. (2008). I hate you! Disinhibition with virtual partners. *Interacting with Computers*, 20 (3), 302–310.

Dixon, M., Freeman, K. and Toman, N. (2010). STOP trying to delight your customers. *Harvard Business Review*, 88 (7/8), 116–122.

Graesser, A.C., McNamara, D.S. and VanLehn, K. (2005). Scaffolding deep comprehension strategies through point and query, AutoTutor, and iSTART. *Educational Psychologist*, 40 (4), 225–234.

Graesser, A.C., Jeon, M. and Dufty, D. (2008). Agent technologies designed to facilitate interactive knowledge construction. *Discourse Processes*, 45 (4/5), 298–322.

Guan, Z., Lee, S., Cuddihy, E. and Ramey, J. (2006). The validity of the stimulated retrospective think-aloud method as measured by eye tracking. *Proceedings of the SIGCHI conference on Human Factors in Computing Systems*, CHI 2006 (pp. 1253–1262). New York: ACM.

Gustafsson, A., Johnson, M.D. and Roos, I. (2005). The effects of customer satisfaction, relationship commitment dimensions, and triggers on customer retention. *Journal of Marketing*, 69 (4), 210–218.

Holzwarth, M., Janiszewski, C. and Neumann, M.M. (2006). The influence of avatars on online consumer shopping behaviour. *Journal of Marketing*, 70 (4), 19–36.

Jacoby, J., Speller, D.E. and Kohn, C.A. (1974). Brand choice behaviour as a function of information load. *Journal of Marketing Research*, 11 (1), 63–69.

Keeling, K., McGoldrick, P. and Beatty, S. (2010). Avatars as salespeople: communication style, trust, and intentions. *Journal of Business Research*, 63 (8), 793–800.

Kerr, I.R. and Bornfreund, M. (2005). Buddy bots: how Turing's fast friends are undermining consumer privacy. *Presence, Teleoperators and Virtual Environments*, 14 (6), 647–655.

Lieberman, H. (1997). Autonomous interface agents. Retrieved from http://web.media. mit.edu/~lieber/Lieberary/Letizia/AIA/AIA.html.

Lurie, N.H. (2004). Decision making in information-rich environments: the role of information structure. *Journal of Consumer Research*, 30 (4), 473–486.

Mayer, R.C., Davis, J.H. and Schoorman, F.D. (1995). An integrative model of organizational trust. *The Academy of Management Review*, 20 (3), 709–734.

Milord, J.T. and Perry, R.P. (1977). A methodological study of overload. *Journal of General Psychology*, 97 (1), 131–137.

Misselhorn, C. (2009). Empathy with inanimate objects and the uncanny valley. *Minds and Machines*, 19 (3), 345–359.

Mori, M. (1970). The uncanny valley. *Energy*, 7 (4), 33–35.

Nielsen, J. and Landauer, T.K. (1993). A mathematical model of the finding of usability problems. *Proceedings of the INTERACT '93 and CHI '93 conference on Human Factors in Computing Systems*, CHI 1993 (pp. 206–213). New York: ACM.

Nowak, K.L. and Rauh, C. (2008). Choose your 'buddy icon' carefully: the influence of avatar androgyny, anthropomorphism and credibility in online interactions. *Computers in Human Behaviour*, 24 (4), 1473–1493.

Patrick, A. (2002). Building trustworthy software agents. *IEEE Internet Computing*, 6 (6), 46–53.

Reeves, B. and Nass, C. (1996). The media equation: how people treat computers, television, and new media like real people and places. Stanford, CA: CSLI Publications.

Rousseau, D.M., Sitkin, S.B., Burt, R.S. and Camerer, C. (1998). Not so different after all: a cross-discipline view of trust. *Academy of Management Review*, 23 (3), 393–404.

Turing, A.M. (1950). Computing machinery and intelligence. *Mind*, 59 (236), 433–460.

Walsh, G. and Mitchell, V.W. (2010). The effect of consumer confusion proneness on word of mouth, trust, and customer satisfaction. *European Journal of Marketing*, 44 (6), 838–859.

Zheng, R., McAlack, M., Wilmes, B., Kohler-Evans, P. and Williamson, J. (2009). Effects of multimedia on cognitive load, self-efficacy, and multiple rule-based problem solving. *British Journal of Educational Technology*, 40 (5), 790–803.

8

GENDER-BENDING IN VIRTUAL WORLDS

Investigating 'Need for Achievement' between goal-orientated and non-goal-orientated environments

Eily Coghlan and Gráinne Kirwan

Chapter summary

Gender-bending has existed online since the creation of virtual environments and chat-rooms. This research examines the relationship between gender-bending online and 'Need for Achievement' in goal-orientated and non-goal-orientated environments. Participants responded to an online questionnaire to find out their motivations for gender-bending and their level of Need for Achievement. Findings showed women in a goal-orientated virtual environment with high Need for Achievement were more likely to gender-bend than women with lower Need for Achievement. Findings also showed that men who gender-bend have lower Need for Achievement than men who do not gender-bend in a goal-orientated environment. There was no difference in Need for Achievement scores between individuals who do and those who do not gender-bend in a non-goal-orientated environment.

Introduction

The online social world of the Internet has provided people with extensive ability to explore their identities. Individuals are provided with an environment where identity can be explored anonymously, reducing fears of persecution or judgement (Parks, 1998). This freedom has led to many interesting facets of human behaviour being displayed openly online. One of these is gender-bending – where an individual can present a gender that is different from their biological sex (Roberts and Parks, 1999). There is research to show that most people who gender-bend generally return to their actual gender (Kafai *et al.*, 2008); nonetheless, there are still those who continue to stay the gender opposite that of their biological sex (Francino and Guiller, 2011).

In order to engage in a conversation with another individual online, there are certain factors that need to be identified before any kind of trust is developed (Nowak and Rauh, 2005). During text-based chat rooms, the most commonly requested identifying factor is an individual's gender – in the format of 'a/s/l', standing for age/sex/location (Lim and Larose, 2003). This displays how gender is considered one of the most important identifying factors when interacting online.

Suler's initial research (2004) found that men swap gender more often than females. Suler's hypothesis was that society forces men not to display any kind of feminine characteristics, and therefore they move to online environments where they can explore their curiosities in privacy and security. Suler (2004) also discovered that one of the reasons men play as a female avatar in an online gaming environment was to progress faster in the game. Female avatars attract more attention from male players and, as a result, they receive gifts and help throughout the game that enable them to progress quicker. Research by Wadell (2012) also shows that users with more attractive avatars receive more help in a game by receiving more gifts and aids to help with the gaming process. This trend makes the goals of the game easier to achieve.

Research by Hussain and Griffiths (2008) showed that women gender-bend because as a male character they believe that they are taken more seriously and they do not receive unwanted help and attention. They can compete in a Massively Multiplayer Online Role Playing Game (MMORPG) – experiencing the game without any help.

This study examines two online environments – World of Warcraft and Second Life. World of Warcraft (WoW) is a MMORPG that was created by Blizzard Entertainment in 2004. WoW is an online real-time strategy game in which users create their own avatar, and they use their character to interact with the environment and other avatars in the 3D virtual world. Game play involves users interacting in the game environment and completing missions, tasks and goals in-game as well as either teaming-up with other players or going into combat against them. Users create their own avatar, choosing everything from their outward appearance and dress to their gender. WoW can be described as a goal-orientated, achievement-focused environment with goals defined by the in-game story and the in-game levelling process.

Second Life differs significantly from World of Warcraft: Second Life is a virtual social world. It is an Internet-based virtual world launched in 2003 and developed by Linden Research, Inc. It is a virtual world that changes much faster than the real world. It was created to represent the real world, but without physical limits. The Second Life game play involves creating an avatar – choosing clothing, appearance and gender – and then moving this avatar around various virtual worlds and interacting with other avatars. There is no end-goal achievement to Second Life – it is simply a virtual world where people can interact.

Achievement motivation is described as 'an individual's tendency to desire and work toward accomplishing challenging personal and professional goals' (Byrne *et al.*, 2004, p. 204), and to excel to impress others (Meijer and Van Den Wittenboer, 2004). The main goal operating in achievement motivation is the desire to demonstrate high ability in order to feel and appear competent to others. Need for Achievement (nAch) refers to an individual's desire for accomplishment, mastering of skills, control or high standards (McClelland, 1965). It is related to the difficulty of tasks people choose to undertake. Those with low nAch may choose very easy tasks in order to minimise risk of failure, or highly difficult tasks, such that a failure would not be embarrassing. Those with high nAch tend to choose moderately difficult tasks, feeling that they are within reach but challenging enough to feel as if they have achieved something significant.

Another characteristic of achievement-motivated people is that they seem to be more concerned with personal achievement than with the rewards of success (McClelland, 1965) – the rewards are not as essential as the accomplishment itself. They get more satisfaction out of winning or solving a difficult problem than they get from any money or praise they receive. High nAch scorers tend to set achievable goals for themselves, master tasks and achieve high satisfaction from successfully completing tasks; they constantly strive for improvement and have a strong sense of initiative (Hodson, 2001).

These same nAch characteristics can apply to aspects of online gaming. Wan and Chiou (2006) used Need for Achievement to investigate which factors cause adolescents to become addicted to online gaming. They found that adolescents who reported high Need for Achievement also displayed behaviours consistent with online gaming addiction (Wan and Chiou, 2006). As MMORPGs can be very reward-based and goal-orientated, the adolescent's Need for Achievement in these environments is high. Wan and Chiou (2006) suggest that this may not be the case for these adolescents in a real world environment. They suggest that the adolescents may actually display very low levels of nAch in a real world environment.

While Need for Achievement has been studied as a connection to online gaming and addiction, it has not been investigated in relation to game play motivations. As Suler's (2004) research showed, one of the reasons males are motivated to gender-bend is that female avatars receive more help, gifts and aid during the game play. This help and aid results in a more social game, as well as a less challenging game. McClelland's research (1965) shows that individuals who set easily achievable goals score low in the Need for Achievement questionnaire. It is therefore suggested that males who gender-bend in a goal-orientated game will have a low Need for Achievement score.

Women who gender-bend as males experience a more difficult game, as Suler's research (2004) shows that male avatars have a more solitary game, and receive less help and gifts from other players. It is proposed that women who play as males will therefore score higher in the Need for Achievement scales, as McClelland's research (1965) finds that people who set difficult, but achievable goals for themselves have a high Need for Achievement score. This study therefore hypothesises that women who gender-bend in World of Warcraft have higher Need for Achievement than women who do not gender-bend in World of Warcraft, while men who gender-bend in World of Warcraft have lower Need for Achievement than men who do not gender-bend in World of Warcraft. It is expected that there will be no difference in Need for Achievement scores between gender benders and non-gender benders in Second Life.

Methodology

This study employed a survey design with a sample of 258 participants. These were recruited by requesting participation on forums, and frequenting popular areas in the games, requesting willing participants to take part in the study. Participants completed a short demographic and gaming habits questionnaire, and they specified whether they played Second Life or World of Warcraft. They then answered questions about the length of time they had played their chosen game, how many years they had been playing it, how many avatars they actively played, and whether or not they were gender-benders online.

Participants also completed the Ray-Lynn Achievement Orientation Scale (Ray, 1979), which was used as a measure of achievement motivation. The scale was developed and validated in Australia and the United Kingdom and has better criterion validity than most other objective measures with correlations ranging from .17 to .58 on different criteria directly related to the achievement motive, and .36 on criteria combining a variety of indicators. Cronbach's alpha for this scale is .85, reliability is .81. The scale consists of twenty-eight items with a three-point scale – potential responses being 'Yes', 'No' or 'Don't Know'. The scoring of the instrument consisted of a simple summation, with several of the items being reversed to account for the reverse polarity of the particular item.

Because of the nature of the study, the demographic question regarding gender also provided options for transgender. Approximately equal numbers of males and females took part – 126 females (48.8 per cent) and 125 males (48.4 per cent). Two individuals identified as female to male transgender (.8 per cent), while five individuals identified as male to female transgender (1.9 per cent). The overall mean age of participants was 31.46 years ($SD = 13.095$). Further information on the mean age for each of the genders is shown in Table 8.1.

TABLE 8.1 Age and gender of participants

	Frequency	Per cent (%)	Mean age	Standard deviation
Male	125	48.4	31.88	14.473
Female	126	48.8	30.62	10.712
F-M Transgender	2	.8	32.50	2.121
M-F Transgender	5	1.9	42.00	27.928
Total	258	100	31.46	13.095

Note: The individual percentages do not add up to 100% because of rounding.

A majority (77.5 per cent) of respondents identified as Heterosexual (n = 200), 13.2 per cent of respondents identified as Bi-Sexual (n = 34), 6.2 per cent identified as Homosexual (n = 16) and 8 per cent gave no response (n = 8).

Results

After adjusting for gender, the ANCOVA showed that there was a significant effect of gender-bending on Need for Achievement ($F(1,251)$ = 424.02, p = .01).

In World of Warcraft, the mean nAch of women who gender-bend was higher (65.80, SD = 6.985) than the women who did not gender-bend (54.52, SD = 8.504) (see Table 8.2). The mean difference between nAch scores was 11.28, and the 95 per cent confidence level for the estimated population mean difference was 7.29 and 15.28. An independent t-test showed that the difference between the nAch scores was significant (t = 5.653, df = 59, p < .0005, one-tailed).

The mean nAch of men who gender-bend in World of Warcraft was lower (55.38, SD = 6.985) than the men who did not gender-bend (64.35, SD = 8.504). The mean difference between nAch scores was 8.97, and the 95 per cent confidence level for the estimated population mean difference is −12.483 and −5.462. These results are outlined in Table 8.3. An independent t-test showed that the difference between the nAch scores was significant (t = −5.107, df = 63, p < .0005, one-tailed).

The mean nAch of individuals who gender-bend in Second Life was 59.92 (SD = 9.716), and for individuals who did not gender-bend it was 61.23 (SD = 1.064). The mean difference between nAch scores was −1.32. The 95 per cent confidence level for the estimated population mean difference is −4.475 and 1.847. An independent t-test showed that the difference between the nAch scores was not significant (t = −.822, df = 128, p = .412, one-tailed).

TABLE 8.2 Women, gender-bending, mean and standard deviation

Engage in gender-bending?	Frequency	nAch mean	Standard deviation
Yes	30	65.80	6.985
No	31	54.52	8.504
Total	61	60.07	9.597

TABLE 8.3 Men, gender-bending, mean and standard deviation

Engage in gender-bending?	Frequency	nAch mean	Standard deviation
Yes	34	55.38	6.729
No	31	64.35	7.437
Total	65	59.66	8.347

Gender and hours played in World of Warcraft

An ANOVA was conducted to see if there was any significant relationship between the level of nAch and the number of hours played daily by male and female World of Warcraft players. Table 8.4 shows the means and standard deviations. The results showed that there was a significant difference ($F(34,93) = 3.909$, $p < .0005$ partial $\eta2 = .58$).

Qualitative analysis

Participants were also given the option to elaborate on their gender-bending responses. Participants in World of Warcraft expressed the view that players in a gaming environment did not like males playing as female avatars and vice versa: 'those players usually do not react well to the fact that a male player would play a female character'.

Participants who did not gender-bend also expressed their upset and disapproval of people who do gender-bend: 'it would feel weird to be playing a guy'; 'it feels deceiving'; 'I don't see the point in misrepresenting myself'; 'I feel less connection with my male alt then I do with my female characters'.

World of Warcraft players appeared to have more strategic and visual reasons for gender-bending than in Second Life: 'What looks best I go with'; 'a tough looking deathknight'; '[male avatars] I play less due to their lower levels'; 'I choose male cos[sic] it looks cooler'; 'males are harder to level . . . there's so much support for female avatars'.

Second Life responses were fewer, and indicated reasons unrelated to achievement. Fewer comments were made regarding treatment in-game of gender-bending participants: 'I have tried a few times to use my boyfriend's male avatar but it made me feel very uncomfortable'.

Responses from Second Life characters indicated that they would not be able to depict a gender online that was the opposite of their biological gender: 'Totally unable to act/feel like a guy'; 'I role play my characters'.

TABLE 8.4 World of Warcraft, number of hours played and nAch

Hours Played	Mean nAch	Standard deviation	Frequency
Less than 1 hour	48.33	5.680	6
1 hour	54.75	9.362	8
2 hours	58.09	6.934	23
3 hours	57.47	8.207	34
4 hours	57.12	5.932	16
5 hours	62.42	6.585	12
6 hours	67.00	8.155	13
More than 6 hours	69.50	5.955	16
Total	59.88	8.878	128

These results indicate that gender-bending reasons are varied across environment types, and can often depend on the end-goal of the game or environment they are interacting with. Second Life has non-specific goals, and this freedom inspires varied gender-bending reasons. Reasons for gender bending in World of Warcraft tend to be more specific because it is a goal-orientated environment – the overall reason for gender-bending appears to be goal related.

Discussion

This study demonstrated that women who gender-bend in goal-orientated environments have higher nAch than women who do not. Men who gender-bend have lower nAch than men who do not. A non-goal-orientated virtual environment shows no difference between nAch scores across gender. These findings support the original three hypotheses.

World of Warcraft female players

In World of Warcraft, a goal-orientated virtual environment, female players who chose to play male avatars scored a higher level of Need for Achievement than those who played with a female avatar. These results supported the hypothesis and supported the previous research into Need for Achievement, which found that people with high nAch scores tend to set goals for themselves that are achievable but are challenging. Individuals who set low, easily achievable goals for themselves felt less rewarded for achieving those targets than if they had set higher, harder goals to reach (McClelland, 1965).

Playing as a male character in a goal-orientated virtual environment did not make the goal of the game unachievable, but it made the game more challenging, and this resulted in female gender-bending players deriving more satisfaction upon completing challenges and tasks within the game. It has been documented that female avatars receive more gifts and help in game (Donath, 1998; Suler, 2004; Wadell, 2012), which make the goals of the game easier to achieve and, as a result, less satisfying for individuals with high nAch scores.

These findings suggest that women who gender-bend perhaps do so to experience a challenging, but achievable, game. Playing as a male character can lead to a less social, more challenging game than playing as a female character. Essentially, they are experiencing a more difficult game (Suler, 2004).

World of Warcraft male players

For male World of Warcraft players who gender-bend during game play, lower levels of nAch were scored than male players who did not gender-bend. These results supported the second hypothesis, and are consistent with the research that shows individuals who set easier-to-reach goals for themselves tend to display lower levels of nAch then those who set more challenging, but achievable, goals

(McClelland, 1965). This is also consistent with Suler (2004), whose research showed that males who play as females in goal-achieving environments experience an easier game because female characters receive more gifts and help in game.

Second Life and Need for Achievement

The hypothesis that there would be no difference in Need for Achievement scores between participants who do and do not gender-bend was supported in this study. As Second Life is a non-goal achieving environment, where the residents do not level-up and do not take part in cooperative combat, there is no obvious motivation for users to gender-bend.

Time spent in World of Warcraft

Results showed that the amount of time spent involved in World of Warcraft correlated with the players' level of nAch. This research also supports that of Wan and Chiou (2006), who found that individuals who played online for lengthy periods reported higher levels of nAch. As World of Warcraft is a goal-orientated environment, these results show that as the game constantly requires a user to improve, win and succeed, these factors are associated with high levels of nAch, and the user feels personally rewarded as a result.

Implications and evaluation

These findings support the previous research that online virtual worlds are strongly adhering to gender norms that exist in the real world (Shaw and Ardener, 2005). These results do not support the early expectations that the Internet would become a genderless environment (Haraway, 1991; Plant, 1993); gender roles still feature strongly even in online virtual worlds. In World of Warcraft there is no programmed in-game advantage of having a female avatar as opposed to a male avatar; the advantages and disadvantages are created by the society and culture where the avatars exist and interact.

There was difficulty trying to recruit individuals who would be willing speak about gender-bending, and this occurred at various stages throughout the research. The problem was most evident in Second Life. When requests for participation were made in a public arena, many individuals responded publicly, expressing their disgust and/or making derogatory comments. This could have discouraged any individual who may have been willing to take part. Commonly, individuals who did respond were only curious about the research and expressed interest in what the researcher was doing; however, they were not of the demographic that the researcher requested and, as a result, could not contribute to the research.

Future research could examine other aspects of the psychology of why people gender-bend online, beyond Need for Achievement. It could also examine genderless games – where avatars are androgynous, or avatars are similar to robots, with no visual aspects that identify an avatar's gender. Further research could also examine the use of 'alts' in online gaming in relation to gender-bending. 'Alts' are additional avatars that are alternate to the user's primary avatar.

Conclusion

Massively multiplayer online environments have often been discussed as a promising environment in which to conduct psychological research (Bainbridge, 2007; Castronova, 2006). Our understanding of how humans are changing and adapting in this medium is still developing (Williams, 2010). While there is a wealth of existing research, many of the studies to date cover a relatively small number of the social intricacies that are occurring every day, and much research is still required. Need for Achievement clearly appears to be one motivator for gender-bending in a goal-orientated environment, where users may win or lose depending on how they play and interact in the game. Realistically there are probably many more factors that encourage this behaviour, and these need to be examined.

References

Bainbridge, W.S. (2007). The scientific research potential of virtual worlds. *Science*, 317, 472–476. Retrieved from: www.sciencemag.org/cgi/content/abstract/sci;317/5837/472.

Byrne, Z.S., Mueller-Hanson, R.A., Cardador, J.M., Thornton, G.C., Schuler, H., Frintrup, A. and Fox, S. (2004). Measuring achievement motivation: Test of equivalency for English, German, and Israeli versions of the achievement motivation inventory. *Personality and Individual Differences*, 37, 203–217.

Castronova, E. (2006). On the research value of large games: Natural experiments in Norrath and Camelot. *Games and Culture*, 1 (2), 163–186.

Donath, J. (1998). Identity and deception in the virtual community. In P. Kollock and M. Smith (eds) *Communities in Cyberspace* (pp. 29–59). London: Routledge.

Francino, F. and Guiller, J. (2011). Is that your boyfriend? An experiential and theoretical approach to understanding gender-bending in virtual worlds. In A. Peachey and M. Childs (eds) *Reinventing Ourselves: Contemporary concepts of identity in virtual worlds* (pp. 153–175). London: Springer.

Haraway, D. (1991). *Simians Cyborgs and Women: The reinvention of nature*. New York: Routledge.

Hodson, C. (2001). *Psychology and Work*. London: Routledge.

Hussain, Z. and Griffiths, M.D. (2008) Gender swapping and socializing in cyberspace: An exploratory study. *Cyberpsychology and Behaviour*, 11 (1), 47–53.

Kafai, Y., Heeter, C., Denner, J. and Sun, J. (2008). Pink, purple, casual, or mainstream games: Moving beyond the gender divide. In Y. Kafai, C. Heeter, J. Denner and J. Sun (eds) *Beyond Barbie and Mortal Kombat: New perspectives on gender and gaming* (pp. 11–25). Cambridge, MA: Massachusetts Institute of Technology (MIT) Press.

Lim, L. and Larose, R. (2003) *Interpersonal Attraction Online: Do trust and gender differences play a part in determining attraction due to attitudinal similarity?* San Diego, CA: International Communication Association. Retrieved from www.allacademic.com/meta/p111493_index.html.

McClelland, D.C. (1965) Toward a theory of motive acquisition. *The American Psychologist*, 20, 321–333.

Meijer, A.M. and Van Den Wittenboer, G.L.H. (2004). The joint contribution of sleep, intelligence and motivation to school performance. *Personality and Individual Differences*, 37, 95–106.

Nowak, K.L. and Rauh, C. (2005). The influence of the avatar on online perceptions of anthropomorphism, androgyny, credibility, homophily, and attraction. *Journal of Computer-Mediated Communication*, 11 (1), article 8. Retrieved from: http://jcmc.indiana.edu/vol11/issue1/nowak.html.

Parks, M.R. (1998). Love and relationships on the Internet. Workshop presented at the Conference on Successful Relating. University of Arizona, Tucson, AZ.

Plant, S. (1993). Beyond the screens: Film, cyberpunk, and cyberfeminism. *Variant*, 14, 12–17. Retrieved from: http://archive.fact.co.uk/tools/archive_download.php?id=47.

Ray, J.J. (1979). A quick measure of achievement motivation: validated in Australia and reliable in Britain and South Africa. *Australian Psychologist*, 14, 337–344.

Roberts, L.D. and Parks, M.R. (1999). The social geography of gender-switching in virtual environments on the Internet. *Information, Communication and Society*, 2 (4), 521–540.

Shaw, A. and Ardener, S. (2005). *Changing Sex and Bending Gender*. New York: Berghahn Books.

Suler, J.R. (2004). Do boys (and girls) just wanna have fun? In A. Kunkel (ed.) *Gender Communication* (pp. 149–153). Dubuque, IA: Kendall/Hunt Publishing.

Wadell, F.T (2012). It's not easy trying to be one of the guys: The effect of avatar attractiveness, avatar gender, and purported user gender on the success of help-seeking requests in an online game. Unpublished master's thesis, Virginia Polytechnic Institute and State University, Virginia, United States. Retrieved from: http://scholar.lib.vt.edu/theses/available/etd-05142012-184457/unrestricted/Waddell_Thomas_F_D_2012.pdf.

Wan, C.S. and Chiou, W.B. (2006). Why are adolescents addicted to online gaming? *CyberPsychology and Behaviour*, 9, 762–766.

Williams, D. (2010). The mapping principle, and a research framework for virtual worlds. *Communication Theory*, 20, 451–470

9

EXPLORING PSYCHOLOGICAL FACTORS FOR CONTRIBUTING TO ONLINE RECOMMENDATION SITES

Mary O'Brien, John Greaney and Hannah Barton

Chapter summary

This study explores altruism and narcissism as motivation for online informational giving. There is a dilemma about whether helping generally is motivated by altruism or egoism (Bierhoff, 2002). Recent research has also shown a propensity for narcissists to move online to places where they can gain more exposure and access a larger number of shallow relationships (Baldwin and Stroman, 2007). For this study, forty-four participants from an online travel recommendation website took the Narcissistic Personality Inventory (NPI), which measures sub-clinical narcissism (Raskin and Hall, 1979), the Interpersonal Reactivity Index (IRI), which measures altruism (Davis, 1983), and an open-ended question about motivation. No significant results were found, though reciprocation was given as the most common reason for reviewing, thus raising questions about the direction of future research in the area.

Introduction

Online word-of-mouth communication (e-WOM) is any 'positive or negative statement made by potential, actual, or former customers about a product or company, which is made available to a multitude of people and institutions via the Internet' (Hennig-Thurau *et al.*, 2004, p. 39). They can have a powerful influence on potential consumers, with even the order that positive and negative recommendations are presented having an impact on brand evaluation (Coker, 2012). Although many studies have been carried out in the area of e-WOM communication generally, few studies have been published on the motivation behind online WOM activities or the reason for individuals' engagement in them (Sun *et al.*, 2006). This chapter explores the possible motivations for contributing, with a particular focus on exploring the personality factors of altruism and narcissism. Data was collected from people who contribute to a popular travel recommendation website.

Alruism online

Klisanin (2011) has argued that the Internet is giving rise to new forms of altruism. These include initiatives that rely upon user-generated content and sharing of expertise created for the public good, such as Linux and Project Gutenberg, as well as activities designed to help other people, animals or the environment, using a click-to-donate format or as an integrated aspect of social networking, searching, shopping or gaming.

The type of goods exchanged in online review systems and other online consumer communities are referred to by economists as public goods (Kollock, 1999). Online information exchange has the characteristics of a public good because everyone in the community may benefit regardless of whether they helped to create it or contributed to it in any way. It further has the characteristic that it is indivisible, as one person's usage does not diminish the overall good, and it is non-excludable because it is usually impossible to exclude anyone from benefiting, whether or not they contributed. Information exchange in online travel recommendation systems satisfies these criteria.

The literature has widely recognised an inherent danger in systems where public goods are exchanged. There is the temptation to 'free-ride' (Kollock, 1999, p. 4) or to 'leech' (Giesler, 2006, p. 287), where some individuals only take (i.e. they do not contribute). This may threaten the ongoing viability of the entire system. Curien et al. (2005) refer to this as the 'tragedy of the digital commons' (p. 2), where there is the danger of overexploitation of a common (digital) shared resource. Ekeh (1974) refers to the dangers of a system of 'generalized exchange' (p. 48), in which the gift given is not reciprocated by the recipient but by someone else in the group. Though this system appears generous, there is the risk that many people will benefit without taking the trouble to contribute. The potential social dilemma proposed here is that individually reasonable behaviour will lead to collective disaster. This study therefore aims to explore the motivation behind online informational gift-giving in order to shed more light on how these systems survive, despite these threats, in the hope of ensuring long-term sustainability.

What motivates people to contribute online reviews?

There are many possible motivations for contributing to WOMs. Researchers have argued that the decision to post a review may be influenced by a number of factors. For example, it has been postulated that users mainly contribute when their product expectations are not met (Anderson, 1998) and that positive WOM is motivated differently to negative WOM (Sundaram et al., 1998). Similarly, 'brag-and-moan' theory states that moderate reviews do not get posted (Hu et al., 2006, p. 15) and that only very positive or negative experiences are written about.

Personality factors of the individual may also play a part; in other words, some people may be more disposed to write about a particular experience than others. The particular focus of this chapter is to contrast personal motivations that are more self-centred (narcissistic) with those that might be more other-centred (demonstrating a more empathetic or altruistic pro-social personality).

Altruism as a motivation for contributing online reviews

Altruism was one of a range of possible motives for contributing online that were identified by Sundaram *et al.* (1998), who built on previous research by Dichter (1966) and Engel *et al.* (1993). The motives identified were: altruism, product involvement, self-enhancement, helping the company, anxiety reduction, and retaliation against the company for a negative experience (Hennig-Thurau *et al.*, 2004).

Altruism is a concern for the welfare of others; specifically, it is a type of helping where the benefactor provides aid to another without any anticipation of external rewards for providing that aid (Macaulay and Berkowitz, 1970). It is difficult to interpret a person's motivation for any good deed in absolute terms, and behaviour may be motivated by a mixture of ego-centric and other-regarding aspects. For example, the good feelings experienced from helping others may relieve bad feelings, so the helping gives the reward of improving the helper's mood. In particular, from the negative state relief model, we see that if people feel distressed, sad or tense, they are egoistically motivated to improve their own welfare by helping others (Cialdini *et al.*, 1987). Batson (1991) argued that as long as the receiver gets some benefit from the act and the giver's primary motivation is the benefit of the other – in particular where they feel empathy for the other – then even if the giver gets some egoistic benefit, the act is still altruistic.

Empathy and altruism

There is now a convergence of findings indicating that there is a prosocial personality (Bierhoff, 2002) and the most consistently found personality trait across studies using different research methods is *dispositional empathy*. Dispositional empathy is a consistent tendency to empathise with the emotional experiences of others, to see their viewpoint, and as a result to offer help. Empathic concern is associated with prosocial behaviours such as helping, and has been considered a chief enabling process to altruism by Batson (1991). It is widely believed that empathy encourages prosocial or altruistic behaviour, and numerous studies appear to support this view (e.g. Batson *et al.*, 1987).

Measuring altruism through the Interpersonal Reactivity Index

The Interpersonal Reactivity Index (Davis, 1980, 1983) is a multi-dimensional measure of dispositional empathy. This twenty-eight-item Likert scale contains four seven-item sub-scales. The perspective taking (PT) scale measures the reported tendency to spontaneously adopt the psychological point of view of others in everyday life. The empathic concern (EC) scale assesses the tendency to experience feelings of sympathy and concern for unfortunate others. The personal distress (PD) scale taps self-oriented feelings of distress and anxiety in response to tense interpersonal situations. The fantasy (FS) scale measures the tendency to imaginatively transpose oneself into the feelings of fictional characters in plays, books or movies.

When might contributing online be self-interested?

In what ways might motivation to contribute online be self-interested rather than altruistic? Ego rewards and areas of self-interest that have been the subject of some research to date include *status seeking* as motivation for disproportionate gift giving in offline communities (Harbaugh, 1998), *prestige and reputation* in online communities (Kollock, 1999) and *self-efficacy* (Bandura, 1995) where in an online environment the contributor can have a great effect on society from a relatively small effort. Another self-interest motivation that has been identified is the pleasure derived from discussing or talking about a loved product or experience (Solomon *et al.*, 2006).

Status-seeking, celebrity and exhibitionism

There are many different ways to interact online, such as: social news sites (e.g. Digg, Reddit) where participants interact by voting for articles and commenting on them; social networking sites (e.g. Facebook, Last.FM); and social photo and video sharing sites (e.g. YouTube, Flickr). Online review sites present an opportunity for a type of fame, for celebrity reviewers (Lampel and Bhalla, 2007), for individuals' own mini-celebrity – a means for putting oneself 'out there', for exhibitionism. Lasch (1979) says:

> The media give substance to and thus intensify narcissistic dreams of fame and glory, encourage the common man to identify himself with the stars and to hate the 'herd', and make it more and more difficult for him to accept the banality of everyday existence.
>
> (pp. 55–56)

Though the balance of power is shifting from a mass media information system to the more democratised Internet, this brings with it the shadow of 'de-massified individual media that incubate a new electronic narcissism' (Shane, 2001, p. xiii). 'The Internet has many democratizing possibilities, but its use as a vehicle to grab attention and its potential for fuelling narcissism in millions of Americans deserves special comment' (Derber, 2000, p. xvii).

Lampel and Bhalla (2007) have argued that status-seeking is a strong driver of online contributions. Online status can be more difficult to achieve than offline status – the connection between social, economic and professional status being much clearer in the latter (Lampel and Bhalla, 2007). Kollock (1999) suggests that reputation is an important input to status and prestige, stating that 'impressive technical details . . . and elegant writing can all work to increase one's prestige in the community' (p. 228).

Offline, reputation is one of a number of resources available to improve people's standing in the community; in an online environment, by contrast, reputation is often the main resource that can be used for this purpose. This is especially true of a system where reviewers are complimented and rated as helpful by other reviewers, and can also earn tokens indicating expertise from the system administrators. Lampel and Bhalla (2007) found two status-seeking strategies online: one where contributors are focused on a specific area of expertise; and a second where contributors demonstrate knowledge of multiple areas – what is referred to as 'a diverse display of authority' (p. 12). They indicate how posters draw on diverse sets of experience and how they demonstrate their own 'discerning tastes' (p. 13) in topics such as music and fashion, while others hint at their not insubstantial financial resources. This body of research strongly suggests the presence of exhibitionism in online recommendation communities.

Multiple reviewing as its own reward

As seen earlier, multiple reviewing is reinforced by e-WOMs. The value of contributions in travel recommendation websites can be rated with destination expert badges, which is marked by the display of a 'tangible ego-incentive' (Lampel and Bhalla, 2007, p. 17) in the form of a digital logo displaying expertise status (p. 15). Lampel and Bhalla (2007) conclude that the gift in e-WOMs comes with a message about the gift-giver; it contains information about the identity and status of the individual contributor.

Narcissism as motivation

Despite what is known already about non-altruistic motivation, little light has been shone on the part played by personality traits such as those exhibited in narcissism and any impact this may have on online informational gift giving. Narcissism refers to a set of character traits concerned with self-centredness, specifically 'A pervasive pattern of grandiosity (in fantasy or behaviour), need for admiration, and lack of empathy' (American Psychiatric Association, 1994). Males show higher levels of narcissism than females; narcissism levels decline with age, and people from more individualistic societies report more narcissism (Foster et al., 2003).

According to the social-psychological view of narcissism, the person has an unconscious dependency on others for self-esteem and self-concept. Narcissists therefore usually initiate many relationships, are popular initially and seek opportunities and forums for self-enhancement, bragging and public glory (Buffardi and Campbell, 2008).

Several recent studies have focused on the issue of narcissists in social networking sites (SNSs). Two key features of SNSs that are seen to attract narcissists are: first, the context of *many shallow relationships* (friends) commonly formed in these communities, featuring short sound-byte type interactions; and, second, the ability to control their web page and therefore their *self-presentation* (Marcus et al., 2006; Vazire and Gosling, 2004). However, the number of studies that have looked at narcissistic traits in online communities is few to date; this study therefore proposes to add to this body of knowledge by exploring narcissism in travel e-WOMs.

A travel review study carried about by Gretzel et al. (2007) found that along with altruistic and reciprocative motives for contributing, there was also strong evidence of motivation out of 'a need for extraversion and positive self-enhancement' (p. 5). This study set out to investigate whether exhibitionism (one of the components of narcissism) as defined by Raskin and Hall (1979) is significant for frequent online contributors to these systems.

Individuals may be clinically diagnosed as pathologically narcissistic and suffering from narcissistic personality disorder or they may be studied at the sub-clinical level and classified as *normal narcissists*. Among other things, normal narcissism is characterised by self-centredness, self-aggrandisement and a manipulative inter-personal orientation (Emmons, 1987; Paulhus, 1998). This study is designed to address whether higher levels of narcissism do indeed exist among prolific reviewers, as the anecdotal evidence suggests. This research has been conducted at the sub-clinical level and was not designed to detect narcissistic personality disorder. Hereafter, the term narcissism refers to normal narcissism.

Method

The study employed two online survey questionnaires delivered through an online travel recommendation website. Participants completed the measures of narcissism and altruism outlined above followed by an open-ended question about motivation for contributing to online travel reviews generally.

Participants

Forty-two English-speaking adults participated in the study. Participants were divided into 'frequent contributors' (defined as ten or more contributions in the past year) and 'infrequent contributors' (having less than or equal to five contributions, but greater than one contribution in the last year). Gender breakdown was twenty-two males and twenty females. Age ranged from 20 to 65 with a mean of 41.36.

Participants were recruited by choosing a selection of towns and cities from around the world, in all continents, browsing from the most recent contribution date and moving backwards. Those reviewers who did not fall into the 'frequent' or 'infrequent' categories were excluded, as were foreign language contributors, due to the complexity of translating. Contributors who had been a member of the online community for less than one year or who had been inactive for a year or more were also excluded.

Measuring narcissism

The NPI (Raskin and Hall, 1979) was used to measure narcissism and exhibitionism in the present study. This is a self-report measure where each of forty questions consists of two statements representing pairs of attitudes, to which the participants are asked to select one. This study uses the forty-item seven-factor version that produces a full-scale narcissism score and seven-factor-based sub-scale scores, specifically authority, self-sufficiency, superiority, exhibitionism, exploitiveness, vanity and entitlement. Each component sub-scale is composed of between three and eight non-overlapping items.

Content analysis

Content analysis was used to describe, analyse and interpret themes from the open-ended question. Responses were coded and grouped with the assistance of a co-researcher for purposes of validation.

The literature was used as a foundation for seeking expected themes: Kollock (1999) identified reciprocity, reputation and efficacy as motives, while Lampel and Bhalla (2007), expanding on this, found that motivation to contribute online informational gifts is shaped mainly by altruism, norms of reciprocity, positive self-image, status-seeking status and product promotion. This study used a two-stage analysis of the content. In stage one the themes identified from the literature were combined and used for a preliminary scan of the text data. These themes were then ruled in or out, depending on whether or not they reflected what occurred in the study data, and further themes were added as new concepts emerged from content.

Data from the open-ended question were analysed so that one or more phrases from each participant response were matched to the following labels: (1) Recipro-cation; (2) Efficacy; (3) Altruism; (4) Product promotion; (5) 'brag-and-moan' (Hu *et al.*, 2006, p. 15); (6) Sustainability; and (7) Objective source of information.

Results

By far the most common reason given for contributing reviews was *reciprocation* at 39 per cent, with *objective source of information* (17 per cent) the next largest category, followed by *sustainability*, *altruism* and *efficacy* all at 13 per cent each and smaller numbers for both *brag-and-moan* and *product promotion*.

Is frequent reviewing related to measures of narcissism and empathy?

The results did not support the hypothesis that there is a positive relationship between frequent reviewing and either narcissism or exhibitionism. The results partially supported the hypothesis that there is a negative relationship between infrequent reviewing and altruism. This study found that higher number of reviews tended to coincide somewhat with lower levels of empathy, although this was not a significant (reliable) difference. In technical terms, there was a weak negative correlation between IRI (measuring dispositional empathy) and number of reviews, which implies a small correlation in the direction predicted between altruism and lower levels of reviewing but which is not considered significant.

Most of the participants (78 per cent) were in the age range 20–50. The mean NPI score for the oldest age group (51–65 years) was the lowest at 10.33, and highest in the 31–40 age group at 14.91; this being a 4.58 difference in means. Age may be a confounding variable as generational difference over twenty-five years has been found to be twice as large as the current sex difference in narcissism, making generation a better predictor of narcissism scores than gender (Foster et al., 2003). Results differed also along demographic patterns for altruism, but not as much as for narcissism. As altruism generally increases with age, the bias in this sample towards the under-fifties may have skewed the results.

Interpreting the results

NPI results for this study (mean score = 12.48) show the mean to be less than the average score in the general population, which Foster et al. (2003) identified as 15.2. Although there is no specific cut-off score for which a person is considered a clinical narcissist (Foster and Campbell, 2007), a score of more than 16 or 17 is considered more narcissistic. However, it is worth noting that though the results did not achieve statistical significance, seventeen participants from the sample of 42 did, in fact, score 17 or higher, with five of those scoring 20 or higher on the NPI scale. Those five participants represent participants who answered half or more of the items in a narcissistic direction.

One possible reason for non-significant results is the susceptibility to both social desirability bias and inaccurate introspection on self-reports such as the NPI (Nisbett and DeCamp Wilson, 1977). Attitudes on the NPI include questions such as 'I like to show off my body' and 'If I ruled the world, it would be a better place', so it is possible that someone given narcissistic and non-narcissistic attitudes from which to select might elect to make themselves more socially desirable by selecting non-narcissistic options.

Discussion

Reciprocation was given more often (39 per cent) than any other single reason as the motivation for contributions. Kollock (1999) notes that group reciprocity can sometimes be seen as a type of 'system of generalized exchange' (p. 8). This means that a form of credit is permitted where users can take now and pay later. They can make use of others' contributions without feeling the need to reciprocate immediately. Such systems usually have a sense of approximate balance over time, where good citizenship is encouraged and people see that the group is better off if they reciprocate.

Curian *et al.* (2005) make the point that by generating reciprocity more contributions will be created and the 'tragedy of the commons' avoided (p. 2). Kollock (1999) notes that this is particularly true in communities where contributions can be seen by the whole group and where they are publicly praised and valued (e.g. by expert badges and compliments). A feature of e-WOMs that encourages reciprocation is 'a well defined and defended group boundary' (Kollock, 1999, p. 8), where participants do not feel that there is a strong likelihood of people taking advantage of group resources before leaving. If reciprocation is indeed confirmed as a key motivator of e-WOMs, these communities could look to their membership and boundary definition to help ensure future sustainability.

Online communities are increasingly playing a role in shaping the choices of millions of people. The motivations for participating in such communities may vary – from the self-serving to the genuinely altruistic. Future research has the potential to help unravel the various factors at play in the decision to participate in these communities. This in turn will help to ensure the long-term viability and credibility of this modern means of relying on word-of-mouth testimony.

References

American Psychiatric Association (1994). *Diagnostic and Statistical Manual of Mental Disorders* (4th edn., text revision). Washington, DC: APA.

Anderson, E.W. (1998). Customer satisfaction and word-of-mouth. *Journal of Service Research*, 1 (1), 5–17.

Baldwin, T. and Stroman, A. (2007). How self-esteem classes are breeding a selfish generation. *The Times*, 1 March.

Bandura, A. (1995). *Self-Efficacy in Changing Societies.* New York: Cambridge University Press.

Batson, C.D. (1991). *The Altruism Question: Toward a social-psychological answer.* Hillsdale, NJ: Erlbaum.

Batson, C.D., Fultz, J. and Schoenrade, P.A. (1987). Adults' emotional reactions to the distress of others. In N. Eisenberg and J. Strayer (eds) *Empathy and its Development* (pp. 163–184). New York: Cambridge University Press.

Bierhoff, H.W. (2002). *Prosocial Behaviour.* Hove: Psychology Press.

Buffardi, L.E. and Campbell, W.K. (2008). Narcissism and social networking web sites. *Personality and Social Personality Bulletin*, 34(10), 1303–1314.

Cialdini, R.B., Schaller, M., Houlihan, D., Arps, K., Fultz, J. and Beamen, A.L. (1987). Empathy-based helping: Is it selflessly or selfishly motivated? *Journal of Personality and Social Psychology*, 52 (4), 749–758.

Coker, B.L.S. (2012). Seeking the opinions of others online: Evidence of evaluation overshoot. *Journal of Economic Psychology*, 33, 1033–1042.

Curien, N., Fauchart, E., Laffond, G. and Moreau, F. (2005). Online consumer communities: Escaping the tragedy of the digital commons. Retrieved from: www.cnam-econometrie.com/upload/OLC-CUP(2).pdf.

Davis, M.H. (1980). A multidimensional approach to individual differences in empathy. *JSAS Catalog of Selected Documents in Psychology*, 10, 85.

Davis, M.H. (1983). Measuring individual differences in empathy: Evidence for a multidimensional approach. *Journal of Personality and Social Psychology*, 44 (1), 113–126.

Derber, C. (2000). *The Pursuit of Attention: Power and ego in everyday life.* New York: Oxford University Press.

Dichter, E. (1966). How word-of-mouth advertising works. *Harvard Business Review*, 44 (Nov.–Dec.), 147–166.

Ekeh, P.P. (1974). *Social Exchange Theory: The two traditions*. Cambridge, MA: Harvard University Press.

Emmons, R.A. (1987). Narcissism: Theory and measurement. *Journal of Personality and Social Psychology*, 52, 11–17.

Engel J.F., Blackwell R. D. and Miniard P. W. (1993), *Consumer Behaviour*. New York: Dryden Press.

Foster, J.D. and Campbell, W.K. (2007). Are there such things as 'narcissists' in social psychology? A taxometric analysis of the Narcissistic Personality Inventory. *Personality and Individual Differences*, 43 (6), 1321–1332.

Foster, J.D., Campbell, W.K. and Twenge, J.M. (2003). Individual differences in narcissism: Inflated self-views across the lifespan and around the world. *Journal of Research on Personality*, 37, 469–486.

Giesler, M. (2006), Consumer gift systems. *Journal of Consumer Research*, 33, 283–290.

Gretzel, U., Yoo, K. H. and Purifoy, M. (2007). *Tripadvisor Online Travel Review Study: Role and impact of online travel reviews*. Retrieved from: www.Tripadvisor.com/pdfs/Online TravelReviewReport.pdf.

Harbaugh, W.T. (1998). The prestige motive for making charitable transfers. *American Economic Review*, 88 (2), 277–282.

Hennig-Thurau, T., Gwinner, K.P., Walsh, G. and Gremler, D.D. (2004). Electronic word-of-mouth via consumer-opinion platforms: What motivates consumers to articulate themselves on the Internet? *Journal of Interactive Marketing*, 18 (1), 38–52.

Hu, N., Pavlou, P.A. and Zhang, J. (2006). Can online word-of-mouth communication reveal true product quality? Experimental insights, econometric results, and analytical modeling. A submission to Information Systems Research. Retrieved from: http://sloan. ucr.edu/blog/uploads/papers/ISR_HU_PAVLOU_ZHANG_SUBMITTED.pdf.

Klisanin, D. (2011). Is the Internet giving rise to new forms of altruism? *Media Psychology Review* [Online], 3, 1.

Kollock, P. (1999). The economics of online cooperation: Gifts and public goods in cyberspace. In M.A. Smith and P. Kollock (eds) *Communities in Cyberspace* (pp. 220–239). London: Routledge.

Lampel, J. and Bhalla, A. (2007). The role of status seeking in online communities: Giving the gift of experience. *Journal of Computer-Mediated Communication*, 12 (2), article 5.

Lasch, C. (1979). *The Culture of Narcissism: American life in an age of diminishing expectations*. New York: Norton.

Macaulay, J. and Berkowitz, L. (1970). *Altruism and Helping Behaviour*. New York: Academic Press.

Marcus, B., Machilek, F. and Schutz, A. (2006). Personality in cyberspace: Personal websites as media for personality expressions and impressions. *Journal of Personality and Social Psychology*, 90, 1014–1031.

Nisbett, R.E. and DeCamp Wilson, T. (1977). Telling more than we can know: Verbal reports on mental processes. *Psychological Review*, 84 (3), 231–259.

Paulhus, D.L. (1998). Interpersonal and intrapsychic adaptiveness of trait self-enhancement: A mixed blessing? *Journal of Personality and Social Psychology*, 74 (5), 1197–1208.

Raskin, R. and Hall, C.S. (1979). A narcissistic personality inventory. *Psychological Reports*, 45, 590.

Shane, E. (2001). *Disconnected America: The consequences of mass media in a narcissistic world*. New York: M.E. Sharpe.

Solomon, M., Bamossy, G., Askegaard, S. and Hogg, M.K. (2006). *Consumer Behaviour: A European perspective*, 3rd edn. London: Prentice Hall–Financial Times.

Sun, T., Youn, S., Wu, G. and Kuntaraporn, M. (2006). Online word-of-mouth (or mouse): An exploration of its antecedents and consequences. *Journal of Computer-Mediated Communication*, 11 (4), article 11.

Sundaram, D.S., Mitra, K. and Webster, C. (1998). Word-of-mouth communications: A motivational analysis. *Advances in Consumer Research*, 25, 527–531.

Vazire, S. and Gosling, S.D. (2004). e-perceptions: Personality impressions based on personal websites. *Journal of Personality and Social Psychology*, 87, 123–132.

10

ONLINE IDENTITY THEFT

An investigation of the differences between victims and non-victims with regard to anxiety, precautions and uses of the Internet

Karen Reilly and Gráinne Kirwan

Chapter summary

This research examined the possible differences between those who had been victims of online identity theft and those who had not. In particular, it examined anxiety levels online, precautions and measures when shopping and banking online, and the amount of information that participants provided online. The research was divided into two studies: a content analysis of Facebook profiles and a survey of online security behaviours and anxiety levels. Results revealed a difference in anxiety levels of victims and non-victims, with victims experiencing higher levels of anxiety. The results showed that victims of online identity theft are less likely to use personal information as passwords than non-victims. However, there was little difference between the precautions and measures undertaken by victims and non-victims online. This study highlights the after-effects of being a victim of online identity theft.

Introduction

The present study examines the difference in precautions taken by victims of online identity theft and non-victims. The research also identifies whether victims of online identity theft experience higher levels of anxiety online. This literature review will briefly discuss identity, identity theft, victims of online identity theft, and availability of identity information and precautions. The present study and hypotheses will then be discussed.

What is identity?

Finch (2007) describes identity as 'a multi-faceted concept that is best understood by a division into three categories: personal, social and legal' (p.29). Personal identity is characterised by a sense of continuity, an ability to know that we are different now than we were then and that life progresses (Locke, 1690). Social identity is the identity viewed by others in society (Burr, 2003), or how others see us. Social and personal identity can evolve and change over time. Legal identity relates to the way that pieces of information can distinguish one person from another – it answers the questions 'Who is this person?' and 'Is this the same person?' (Torpey, 2000). Legal identity cannot be changed, but more facts and information can be added to it (such as changes in marital status and educational achievements). Legal identity allows individuals to prove who they are at any point in time, and it also has a cumulative element in that it provides a historical continuity of an individual's past. Legal identity becomes more comprehensive as an individual ages (Torpey, 2000). With regard to identity theft, the legal aspect is the most important factor of an individual's identity. The purpose of legal identity is to create an unbreakable association between a collection of factual information and the individual to whom it relates.

What is identity theft?

Identity theft is the misuse of an individual's personal information (mainly legal identity such as date of birth, name, address) to commit fraud (Gonzales and Majoras, 2007). Identity theft is rarely just one crime, and it can be linked to a variety of crimes that are well known to most people. Identity theft is commonly associated with crimes such as: cheque and card fraud; various financial crimes; telemarketing and Internet scams; theft aided by fraudulent documentation; counterfeiting and forgery; and many more (Maxfield and Clarke, 2004; Newman and Clarke, 2003).

Smith (2010) indicates that while identity theft is not a new criminal activity, it is facilitated by information technology. New technologies make it easier to access personal information and to fabricate important identity documents. The Internet has played a major role in distributing information about identity theft, both in terms of risks and information on how individuals may avoid victimisation. It is a major contributor to identity theft because of the environment of anonymity and the opportunities it provides offenders with to obtain basic components of other people's identities.

Marshall and Stephens (2008) describe how people are required to present some kind of 'trusted token' either to validate their identity or to confirm that they have the authorisation to complete the action they are attempting. In offline contexts, this can include a credit card or identification card, such as a passport. In online contexts, such physical 'trusted tokens' are less frequently used. More frequently used 'trusted tokens' online involve passwords. The interactions that are most vulnerable to identity theft and fraud online tend to require more trusted tokens than those that are not. For example, for most email accounts, a user requires only their email address and a single password to access the information. However, for online banking it is common that three or four trusted tokens are required (such as an account number, date of birth and a password). Use of credit cards online can require even more information – the credit card number, cardholder's name, expiration date and Card Code Verification (CCV) number are normally the minimum information required, but other trusted tokens, such as the cardholder's address and a verification password, may also be required. Identity theft often involves the fraudulent presentation of such trusted tokens.

Because of the use of such trusted tokens, online identity thieves target many types of information. These can include names, user names, passwords, social security numbers, credit card numbers, bank account numbers, birth dates, mothers' maiden names and pet names, although other types of information may also be useful. With certain combinations of this information, identity thieves can access an individual's account, or can create new accounts.

Victims of online identity theft

Kirwan and Power (2013) examined the psychology of identity theft and online fraud. They posit a variety of reasons why individuals may be at risk of these crimes, including cognitive psychological processes such as decision-making behaviours, while also considering the effects of victimisation.

The study of victims first emerged in the 1940s and 1950s when Mendelsohn examined the interactions of victims and offenders and stressed the shared responsibility of crime. Mendelsohn's research (1963) found evidence that certain individuals who suffered damage and loss due to a crime might share some degree of responsibility with the offenders. Mendelsohn (1963) viewed the victim as one of many factors in any criminal case. This research led him to theorise that victims had an 'unconscious aptitude for being victimised'. This suggestion is the subject of wide criticism, and unfortunately variations on this theory have been used by lawyers in the defence of many criminals. While it is doubtless that some individuals may leave themselves more vulnerable to victimisation through their actions or lifestyle (for example, leaving a front door unlocked, hence making themselves more vulnerable to burglaries), many victims could not have reasonably prevented the crime.

Similarly, Benner et al. (2000) suggest that the reason identity theft is not always reported lies in the idea that an individual whose identity has been stolen is not always viewed as a 'victim'. According to Villiers (2009), authorities may argue that victims of an online identity theft have only themselves to blame. Society views victims as responsible for their own fate as this allows non-victims to maintain their own sense of invulnerability, safety and justice (Lerner, 1980).

Availability of identifiable information online

The Internet provides numerous opportunities for identity theft to occur. Internet users can now shop, bank, network with friends and family and study/work online. In order to do any of these tasks, users must sign up to several websites and provide social and legal identity information. Social networking websites in particular have encouraged users to provide as much detailed personal information as possible.

The majority of social networking websites share common or core features such as a main profile (a representation of the user), social networks/groups, mail and comments. Many of the characteristics that make Facebook so popular among users also put them in danger of a variety of identity-theft-related crimes (Next Advisor, 2009). The information people provide on social networking websites can make stealing of identities a much easier task. In a study of Facebook users in Carnegie Mellon University in Pittsburgh, Gross and Acquisti (2005) found that Facebook users provided a great amount of personal and legal identity information on their Facebook profiles. Such information included photographs (90.8 per cent of profiles), birth dates (87.8 per cent), phone numbers (39.9 per cent) and current residence (50.8 per cent). The majority of users also displayed their sexuality, political and religious views, and various interests.

Users also provide considerable amounts of information when shopping online. They sign up to a service by inputting contact details, passwords and security questions, and also use credit/debit cards or finance accounts. Online shoppers are vulnerable to identity theft for three reasons: the data on any computer can be compromised when online; the data transfer to an online business can be compromised; and the data stored by businesses may be compromised. Online identity thieves can also hack directly into company databases and steal both personal and financial information such as social security numbers and credit card details. Online consumers are very vulnerable targets of identity theft but are even more vulnerable when they also bank online.

Rachwald (2008) has stated that the main risks of online banking are the following. With online banking, customers' information is accessible by anyone in the world, not just in the customers' physical area. Online security is a central concern when customers are choosing who to bank with. However, for users who do not have much experience using the Internet, it can be hard to differentiate between good and bad online security practices. With the rapid growth of online banking systems, many of the common concerns have been alleviated. However, identity thieves have found new ways to resource information from customers: phishing attacks. Phishing attacks involve a thief who attempts to fraudulently acquire sensitive information from a victim. The attacker generally impersonates a trustworthy third party such as a banking corporation or university. The attacker will send an email appearing to be from the trusted third party stating that the victim should send information to the attacker. Sometimes, the attacker will add that there is a penalty if the information is not sent.

Anxiety online

Anxiety is a psychological and physiological state that is characterised by cognitive, emotional, behavioural and somatic components. These components combine to create unpleasant feelings such as uneasiness, fear or worry (Seligman *et al.*, 2001). Tyler and Rasinski (1984) found that victims of crime experienced anxiety about future victimisation that was associated with what the individuals learned from the experience of crime – for example, what the victim learned about how to protect themselves and also the emotional reactions experienced such as anger, shock, sadness and anxiety. It is not only victims of crime that experience worry and anxiety. Non-victims can experience worry when they can imagine themselves becoming victims. Victimisation has an indirect effect on anyone who has heard about a crime or knows others who have been victimised (Skogan and Maxfield, 1981).

Some research suggests that indirect experiences of crime may cause more anxiety than the direct experience of being victimised (Hale, 1996). Indirect victimisation may account for the higher levels of fear with regard to a type of crime such as identity theft. This indirect victimisation can be caused by word of mouth, which may inflate, deflate or garble the picture. It can also be caused by media influence (Skogan, 1986). The same crime can have different physical and emotional effects from one individual to another (Gabriel and Greve, 2003).

Two key features of fear of crime are sensitivity to the impact of victimisation and control over its occurrence (Ferraro, 1995; Tulloch, 2003). Whitson (2005) suggests that online crimes such as identity theft have become a locus for insecurity and anxiety. Victims of online identity theft may experience higher levels of anxiety online and offline as it can take months and even years to regain financial control and restore their good credit history after the theft occurs (Hammond, 2003).

Precautions

There is research to suggest that individuals who are most worried and anxious about crime take more precautions to make themselves feel less at risk and safer (Jackson and Gray, 2008). This is known as functional fear, and when it does not affect the individual's quality of life it can be beneficial to Internet users (Farrall and Lee, 2008). There are precautions to combat online identity theft. Online fraud and identity theft have reached a level of prevalence where many resources have been developed for both personal and corporate users advising them on how to improve their security (see, for example: Archer et al., 2012; Mintz, 2012).

The importance of choosing strong passwords should also be considered, as users tend to engage in bad password-management behaviours because of the 'convenience-security tradeoff' (Tam et al., 2009). It is easier to remember a simple password, and to use the same password for multiple online accounts, than to engage in safer behaviours such as choosing different complex passwords for each account.

Davinson and Sillence (2010) evaluated a training programme, 'Anti-Phishing Phil', in order to determine its effectiveness at improving safe online behaviours. This programme adapted a model used in health psychology to encourage healthier behaviours in individuals. The programme increased users' intentions to protect themselves online, with an increase of secure behaviour noted at a seven-day follow-up. However, Davinson and Sillence note that these changes occurred regardless of information type or training provided, and suggest that the improved security may be due simply to providing warning information, thus raising awareness of the risks. This suggests that a complex intervention strategy, targeted to individual users, may not be required in order to change user behaviour.

The present study

Although there is some research to support the assertion that people are fearful of online identity theft and experience some anxiety because of this fear, there is limited research to highlight the anxiety experienced by actual victims of online identity theft. The present study will address this issue by focusing on two groups of individuals – online identity theft victims and non-victims – and the anxiety that both groups experience online.

There are ways in which individuals can reduce the risk of becoming online identity theft victims. The present study will determine whether previous victims of online identity theft take stronger precautions and security measures when shopping and banking online. The present study will also reveal whether there is a difference in the amount of information that victims of online identity theft and non-victims provide online.

Research by Gross and Acquisti (2005) suggest that the vast amount of information individuals provide on social networking websites can make them vulnerable to online identity theft. This study will examine the amount of information individuals provide on these websites to identify how vulnerable the social networking community is to online identity theft.

The current study seeks to determine if social networking users provide sufficient information on profiles to make it possible to identify the individuals concerned. The primary hypothesis states that victims of online identity theft experience higher levels of anxiety than non-victims when shopping/banking online. The secondary hypothesis states that victims of online identity theft take stronger precautions/measures when shopping and banking online. A further hypothesis states that there is a difference between the amount of information provided by victims and non-victims online.

Study 1

A content analysis of profiles on the social networking website 'Facebook' was conducted.

Participants

Sixty participants (thirty males and thirty females) took part in Study 1. The participants were required to have an account on Facebook to take part in the study. All participants were aged between 18 and 34, with a mean age of 26.

Procedure

A pilot study was completed in order to identity any unforeseen complications or difficulties within the research. On completion of the pilot study, the main data collection commenced. Each participant consented to take part in the study prior to participating. Before the study began, the participants were fully briefed on the purpose of the study and how the study would be conducted. The researcher stated that withdrawal from the study was permitted at any stage during the study. Once all participants had provided consent, the researcher began a content analysis of the participants' profiles. When the content analysis was completed, the participants were debriefed.

A list of sixteen codes for the content analysis of the Facebook profiles was devised. The coding scheme was developed from creating a new Facebook profile and determining the information that was required and the information that was optional. The presence or absence of information in each category was noted. The codes used were: gender; hometown; date of birth; social security number; email address; mobile/house phone number; address; website; relationship status; school/ university; employer; work title; screen names; favourite things; pet name; former addresses; and information included as a response to the 'interested in . . .' prompt.

Results

Sixty Facebook profiles were analysed to determine the type and quantity of information that participants openly and freely displayed. The content analysis revealed that no participants provided all sixteen items from the coding sheet on their Facebook profiles. However, forty-two participants revealed more than half of the sixteen items on Facebook with an average of 8.8 items per participant. The information provided is depicted in Figure 10.1.

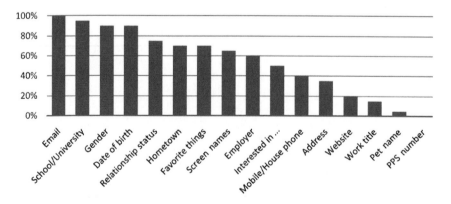

FIGURE 10.1 Information provided on Facebook

The items that appeared most often on the participants' Facebook profiles were: email (100 per cent); school/university (95 per cent); gender (80 per cent); date of birth (80 per cent); relationship status (75 per cent); hometown (70 per cent); and favourite things (70 per cent).

Study 2

An online survey to gauge participants' knowledge of online identity theft and the difference in precautions and anxiety levels of victims and non-victims was conducted.

Participants

Eighty-five participants completed Study 2. All participants were over the age of 18 and were required to currently either shop or bank online. Thirty-three participants (39 per cent) were in the 18–25 age group, twenty-three (27 per cent) were in the 26–35 age group, ten (12 per cent) were in the 36–45 age group, eleven (13 per cent) were in the age group 46–55 and five (6 per cent) were in the 56+ age group. Forty-six female participants (52 per cent) took part in the study along with 39 male participants (48 per cent). Thirty-two participants (38 per cent) self-rated as beginner or intermediate computer users and the remaining fifty-three participants (62 per cent) were advanced computer users.

Materials

Previous research and documentation was used to aid in creating the online identity theft questionnaire. The online survey scripts consisted of questions relating to online identity, attitudes and knowledge. It asked about: the user's understanding of the term 'identity theft'; whether they had obtained a copy of their credit report during the previous year; their use of sensitive information (such as date of birth or mother's maiden name) as passwords; their checking of bills for errors; logging out behaviours; use of online revenue services; prior victimisation of identity theft; and online behaviours (such as shopping using credit/debit cards or online bill payment services).

Beck's Anxiety Inventory (BAI) was also used to analyse the amount of anxiety experienced by different levels of computer users, online identity theft victims and non-victims. The inventory consists of twenty-one items, each of which describes a common symptom of anxiety such as feeling nervous, shaky, scared or faint. The participants rated how much they had experienced each symptom over the past week on a four-point scale. The BAI is a reliable and valid scale for measuring anxiety (reliability −.60, validity −.48).

Results

Knowledge and experience of identity theft

The majority (88 per cent) of participants reported that they understood what the term 'identity theft' meant, and 12 per cent revealed that they somewhat understood the term 'identity theft'. No participants indicated that they did not understand the term. Seventeen participants (21 per cent) had had personal identity information stolen or used. Eighteen participants (22.2 per cent) had had credit or debit cards stolen. One participant (1.2 per cent) had had their social security number stolen and twenty-two participants (26.7 per cent) had found unauthorised charges on bank statements.

Participants who had previously experienced one or more incidents of identity theft had higher anxiety scores ($M = 11.6$, $SD = 10.30$) than those participants who had never experienced any form of identity theft ($M = 4.1$, $SD = 2.21$). This result was found to be significant ($t = 4.929$, $df = 83$, $p < .001$).

The 21 per cent of participants who had had their personal identity information stolen had higher levels of anxiety ($M = 18$, $SD = 11.20$) than participants who had experienced any of the other three types of identity theft and participants who had not experienced any form of identity theft ($M = 5$, $SD = 3.46$). This result was found to be significant ($t = 8.234$, $df = 83$; $p < .001$).

There was no significant difference ($t = .033$, $df = 83$; $p = .213$) between age ranges with regard to online anxiety. There was also no significant difference in anxiety levels between beginner/intermediate ($M = 8.0$, $SD = 9.13$) and advanced ($M = 8.9$, $SD = 6.93$) computer users ($t = .664$, $df = 77$; $p = .189$).

Internet usage and victimisation

Sixty-eight participants (87.2 per cent) indicated that they shopped online using credit cards, and forty participants (51.3 per cent) shopped online using debit cards. Fifty-two participants (66.7 per cent) used online bill payment services and thirty-four participants (43.6 per cent) provided information on social networking websites.

There was no significant difference between victims of credit card theft/debit card theft and non-victims with regard to using credit cards: $- \chi^2$ (1, $N = 85$) = .012, $p = .913$) – or debit cards – χ^2 (1, $N = 85$) = .171, $p = .679$) – to shop and bank online. There was also no difference between victims of social security number theft and non-victims in providing social security numbers online: χ^2 (1, $N = 80$) = 1.852, $p = .174$). There was no difference in participants' usage of online bill payment services: χ^2 (1, $N = 85$) = 1.855, $p = .173$). There was no significance in the amount of information participants provided on social networking websites: χ^2 (1, $N = 85$) = 1.156, $p = .282$).

However, a chi-square test of independence revealed that participants who had previously experienced personal identity information theft, in particular, were less likely to use credit cards to shop and bank online, with this result approaching significance: χ^2 (1, N = 85) = 3.107, p = .078). There was no significant difference between victims of personal identity information theft and non-victims with regard to using debit cards to shop and bank online: χ^2 (1, N = 85) = 2.656, p = .103).

A chi-square test of independence revealed that participants who had previously experienced personal identity information theft, in particular, were less likely to use online bill payment services: χ^2 (1, N = 85) = 9.028, p = .003).

Precautions and measures online

Sixty participants (71 per cent) reported that they had not ordered a copy of their credit report in the last year. Twenty-two participants (26 per cent) had ordered a copy of their credit report in the last year. Just 3 per cent indicated that this question did not apply to them. No significant relationship was found between victimisation of identity theft and ordering of a credit report: χ^2 (1, N = 82) = .109, p = .741.

Thirty-six participants (43 per cent) had used personal information such as mother's maiden name or date of birth when creating online passwords. A chi-square test of independence was performed to examine whether victims of online identity theft were less likely than non-victims to use personal information such as pet names, mother's maiden name and date of birth when creating online passwords. The relations between these variables was significant: χ^2 (1, N = 83) = 5.793, p = .016. Victims were less likely to use this personal information when creating passwords than non-victims were.

Fifty-five participants (65 per cent) in this study found out what their personal information was going to be used for before providing information online. Thirty participants (35 per cent) did not check what their information was going to be used for. No significant relationship was found between victimisation and finding out what information would be used for: χ^2 (1, N = 85) = 1.545, p = .214.

Forty-two participants (51 per cent) never checked billing statements for mistakes. Only fifteen participants (18 per cent) always checked billing statements for mistakes, and twenty-five participants (31 per cent) sometimes checked. A chi-square test of independence was performed to examine whether victims of online identity theft were more likely to check their billing statements each month than non-victims. No significant relationship was found between the variables: χ^2 (2, N = 82) = 2.366, p = .306.

Forty-nine participants (61 per cent) had never provided their social security number online. Thirty-one (39 per cent) had at some point provided their social security number online. A chi-square test of independence was performed to examine whether victims of online identity theft were less likely to provide their social security numbers online than non-victims. No significant relationship was found between the variables: χ^2 (1, N = 80) = 1.852, p = .174. However, those who had specifically been the victims of personal identity information theft were less likely to provide social security numbers online: χ^2 (1, N = 80) = 4.050, p = .044.

A chi-square test of independence was performed to examine whether victims of online identity theft were more likely to sign out of their email accounts than non-victims. No significant relationship was found between the variables: χ^2 (2, $N = 81$) = .295, $p = .863$.

Discussion

The purpose of the present study was three fold: to determine whether victims of online identity theft experience higher levels of anxiety online than non-victims; to reveal if there is a difference in the amount of information that victims and non-victims provide online; and to determine whether victims of online identity theft take stronger precautions when shopping and banking online.

There was a significant difference between victims' and non-victims' levels of anxiety when shopping and banking online, with victims experiencing higher levels of anxiety: thus the primary hypothesis was supported. This confirms Hammond's (2003) research that suggested that victims of online identity theft experience more anxiety online. This also supports the findings of Tyler and Rasinski (1984), who suggested that victims of crime experienced anxiety about future victimisation.

There was no significant difference found in victims' and non-victims' precautions when shopping and banking online. Victims of online identity theft were no more likely to determine what personal information was going to be used for, to sign out of email accounts, to check billing statements or to order credit reports. Victims were also no less likely to provide their social security number online. There was, however, a significant difference between victims' and non-victims' usage of personal information when creating online passwords. Victims of online identity theft were less likely to use personal information such as pets' names, mother's maiden name and date of birth when creating online passwords. Thus the secondary hypothesis was partially supported. The findings from the present study do not correspond with Jackson and Gray's (2008) finding that individuals who are most worried and anxious about crime take more precautions to make themselves feel less at risk and safer.

The third hypothesis stated that victims of online identity theft would provide less information than non-victims when shopping and banking online. On examining the results of the amount of information victims and non-victims provide online, no significant difference was found. Victims of online identity theft were no less likely to use credit and debit cards online. Victims were as likely to use online banking and online bill payment services. There was also no significant difference in the amount of information that victims and non-victims provided on social networking websites.

Although there was no significant difference in the amount of information victims of online identity theft and non-victims provide online, a significant difference was discovered between victims of personal identity information theft, in particular, and non-victims/victims of other online identity theft. Victims of personal identity information theft were less likely to use credit cards to shop online. Personal identity information theft victims were also less likely to provide social security numbers online and were less likely to use online bill payment services. Gabriel and Greve (2003) suggest that different crimes can have different emotional and physical effects from one individual to another. Personal identity information theft may cause more emotional strain and anxiety than the other types of information theft such as credit/debit card theft, and this may account for personal identity information victims providing less information online.

The research question queried whether social networking users provided enough information on profiles to make it possible to identify the individuals concerned. The results of the content analysis of Facebook profiles are adjacent to those of Gross and Acquisti (2005), who identified that the amount of information provided on social networking websites was considerable. In the present study, the majority of participants provided email addresses, gender, date of birth, relationship status, hometown and school on the Facebook profiles.

Conclusion

This study has implications for many sections of society. In this study alone, more than 70 per cent of participants had experienced some form of identity theft. As a significant relationship was disclosed between victims of online identity theft and higher levels of anxiety, online banks, retailers and companies should acknowledge this problem and consider addressing this anxiety by creating safer websites and more visible security features and information. The findings of the present study show that victims of online identity theft do not take stronger precautions when shopping and banking online. Not only was there no significant difference between the two groups but a high number of participants used personal information to create passwords, with 31 per cent of participants using their mother's maiden name in passwords. The majority of participants did not order credit reports or check billing statements. The lack of precautions taken by both victims and non-victims on the Internet may result in online identity theft becoming even more prevalent than it already is. The results of the content analysis of social networking site users illustrate how much information individuals provide to strangers online. Social networking websites have become major sources of information for identity thieves. Individuals who choose to join social networking websites should be made aware of what their information might be used for and also policies for adding and removing friends from their network.

References

Archer, N., Sproule, S., Yuan, Y., Guo, K. and Xiang, J. (2012). *Identity Theft and Fraud: Evaluating and managing risk*. Ottawa: University of Ottawa Press.

Benner, J., Mierzwinski, E. and Givens, B. (2000). Nowhere to turn: Victims speak out on identity theft. California Public Interest Research Group and the Privacy Rights Clearinghouse. Retrieved from: www.privacyrights.org/ar/idtheft2000.htm.

Burr, V. (2003) *Social Constructionism*. Hove: Routledge.

Davinson, N. and Sillence, E. (2010). It won't happen to me: Promoting secure behaviour among Internet users. *Computers in Human Behaviour*, 26, 1739–1747.

Farrall, S. and Lee, M. (2008). *Fear of Crime: Critical voices in an age of anxiety*. Oxford: Routledge.

Ferraro, K.F. (1995). *Fear of Crime: Interpreting victimization risk*. New York: Suny Press.

Finch, E. (2007). The problem of stolen identity and the Internet. In Y. Jewkes (ed.) *Crime Online: Committing, policing and regulating cybercrime*. London: Willan.

Gabriel, U. and Greve, W. (2003). The psychology of fear of crime: Conceptual and methodological perspectives. *British Journal of Criminology*, 43, 600–614.

Gonzales, A.R. and Majoras, D.P. (2007). *Identity Theft Task Force Comprehensive Strategic Plan*. Retrieved from: www.usdoj.gov/archive/ag/speeches/2007/ag_speech_0704231. html.

Gross, R. and Acquisti, A. (2005). Information revelation and privacy in online social networks (The Facebook case). Pre-proceedings version. *ACM Workshop on Privacy in the Electronic Society (WPES)*.

Hale, C. (1996). Fear of crime: A review of the literature. *International Review of Victimology*, 4, 79–150.

Hammond, R.J. (2003). *Identity Theft: How to protect your most valuable asset*. North Chelmsford, MA: Bookmart Press.

Jackson, J. and Gray, E. (2008). *Functional Fear: Adaptational features of worry about crime*. Working Paper. London: LSE.

Kirwan, G. and Power, A. (2013). *Cybercrime: The psychology of online offenders*. Cambridge: Cambridge University Press.

Lerner, M.J. (1980). *The Belief in a Just World: A fundamental delusion*. New York: Plenum.

Locke, J. (1690). *Essays on Human Understanding, Book II*. Retrieved from: http://humanum. arts.cuhk.edu.hk/Philosophy/Locke/echu/.

Marshall, A. and Stephens, P. (2008). Identity and identity theft. In R. Bryant (ed.) *Investigating Digital Crime* (pp. 179–193). Chichester: John Wiley & Sons.

Maxfield, M. and Clarke, R. (eds) (2004). Understanding and preventing auto theft. Crime Prevention Studies. *Criminal Justice Press*, 17.

Mendelsohn, B. (1963). The origin of the doctrine of victimology. *Excerpta Criminologica*, 3, 30.

Mintz, A. (2012). *Web of Deceit: Misinformation and manipulation in the age of social media*. Medford, NJ: Information Today.

Newman, G. and Clarke, R. (2003). *Superhighway Robbery: Preventing e-commerce crime*. London: Willan.

Next Advisor (2009) *Facebook Identity Theft Protection Guide*. Retrieved from: www.next advisor.com/identity_theft_protection_services/facebook_identity_theft_protection_ guide.php.

Rachwald, R. (2008) Is banking online safer than banking on the corner? *Computer Fraud and Security*, 11–12.

Seligman, M.E.P., Walker, E.F. and Rosenhan, D.L. (2001). *Abnormal Psychology*, 4th edn. New York: W.W. Norton & Company.

Skogan, W. (1986) Fear of crime and neighborhood change. *Crime and Justice*, 8, 203–229.

Skogan, W. and Maxfield, M. (1981) *Coping with Crime*. Beverly Hills, CA: Sage.

Smith, R.G. (2010). Identity theft and fraud. In Y. Jewkes and M. Yar (eds) *Handbook of Internet Crime* (pp. 173–301). Cullompton: Willan.

Tam, L., Glassman, M. and Vandenwauver, M. (2009). The psychology of password management: A tradeoff between security and convenience. *Behaviour & Information Technology*, 29, 233–244.

Torpey, J. (2000). *The Invention of the Passport: Surveillance, citizenship and the state*. Cambridge: Cambridge University Press.

Tulloch, M. (2003). Combining classificatory and discursive methods: Consistency and variability in responses to the threat of crime. *British Journal of Social Psychology*, 42 (3), 461–476.

Tyler, T. and Rasinski, K. (1984). Comparing psychological images of the social perceiver: Role of perceived informativeness, memorability, and affect in mediating the impact of crime victimisation. *Journal of Personality and Social Psychology*, 46 (2), 308–329.

Villiers, P. (2009). *Police and Policing: An introduction*. Hook: Waterside Press.

Whitson, J.R. (2005). (In)security and technology: Identity theft. Paper presented at the annual meeting of the American Society of Criminology, Royal York, Toronto. Abstract retrieved from: http://citation.allacademic.com/meta/p_mla_apa_research_citation/0/4/2/9/3/p42938_index.html?phpsessid=9bdec6ad1f9cdf8c8b30d329bf8c61ba.

11

PERSONALITY CAUGHT IN THE SOCIAL NET

Facebook phishing

Kelly Price and Gráinne Kirwan

Chapter summary

Phishing is a well-documented social phenomenon whereby an individual or group poses as a trustworthy source to lure an unsuspecting user to give up sensitive, personal details willingly; this data is deceitfully utilised in identity theft, cash transfer and fraudulent credit card transactions. This study focuses on the correlation of phishing and Facebook users' personality traits. Participants were asked to complete questionnaires measuring conscientiousness, impulsivity and trust in online firms; additionally they were asked to rate the legitimacy of Facebook email and web login page stimuli where some samples were genuine and others were phish. The findings indicate that: individuals who score highly in cognitive instability, a subscale of impulsivity, log in more frequently and identify fewer phishing stimuli than those who score low in cognitive instability; not all users identify all trust factors (present or missing) in Facebook emails and websites; and individuals mistake authentic Facebook emails and web pages as phish.

Introduction

Phishing is a well-documented social phenomenon (Anandpara *et al.*, 2007) whereby an individual poses as a trustworthy source to lure an unsuspecting user to willingly give up sensitive, personal details (Soghoian and Jakobsson, 2009). Although there is much discussion of social media phishing in Internet magazines, forums and intelligence reports (Krebs, 2009; Symantec, 2012), most of it is about the scams themselves or the technicalities of how the scams are executed (Bergholz *et al.*, 2010; Petre, 2010). Some literature has been completed about why some people fall prey to online attacks, such as inherent phishing properties unawareness (Chandrasekaran *et al.*, 2006; Vishwanath *et al.*, 2011; Workman, 2008). There may be aspects of personality that may lead an individual to be more susceptible to phishing, as identified in a framework by Parrish *et al.* (2009). Parrish *et al.* provided an investigative model for future research that recommended four phishing and personality relationship considerations: personal, experiential, personality profile and phishing susceptibility. This study focuses on identifying who is most vulnerable to Facebook phishing by examining personality (conscientiousness, impulsivity and trust in Facebook as an online firm) and experiential (Facebook login frequency and duration) factors.

Personality is commonly categorised into five domains: extraversion, neuroticism, openness to experiences, conscientiousness and agreeableness. Conscientiousness, the focal personality trait in this study, echoes a level of meticulousness, organisation and precision of an individual. Previous research indicates that Facebook users do not rate as highly on conscientiousness as non-Facebook users (Ryan and Xenos, 2011) and those who score lower on conscientiousness spend more time on Facebook (Gosling *et al.*, 2011; Ryan and Xenos, 2011). However, it is purported that individuals who scored high on conscientiousness had a higher number of Facebook friends and uploaded fewer pictures (Amichai-Hamburger and Vinitzky, 2010). While research exists regarding relationships between personality, Internet use and social networking sites, gaps in literature exist between these elements and phishing susceptibility. In terms of conscientiousness and victimisation, research suggests there is a positive correlation between high levels of conscientiousness and less victimisation in adolescents (Jensen-Campbell and Malcolm, 2007).

According to Evenden (1999), impulsivity is a sub-set of all personality traits, regardless of any theoretical approach, and McCrae and John (1992) categorised impulsivity as one of the six facets of neuroticism. Although there is discrepancy in what defines impulsivity, most researchers find that impulsivity relates to an individual's ability to behave without complete forethought or the realisation of what is usually a negative consequence. Barnard (2009) examined the participants in fraudulent Ponzi schemes and found that most victims who invested in these schemes were men who rated high in risk and impulsivity and were susceptible to gambling. Lastly, researchers examining self-control and online victimisation conducted an online experiment involving 295 university students (mean age = 40) and purported that self-control was positively related with online harassment from strangers and non-strangers and negatively related with person-based cybercrime victimisation, where the user was a specific target (Ngo and Paternoster, 2011). Additionally, the researchers noted that they did not find any significance to phishing, but stated that anyone, regardless of self-control, is a potential phishing victim.

McCrae and John (1992) categorised trust as one of the six facets of agreeableness. Trust represents a level of security felt towards another individual (McKnight *et al.*, 2002). Phishers have learned quickly they are more successful at retrieving personal data when they impersonate a trusted entity such as a bank, Internet Service Provider (ISP) or government agency (Feigelson and Calman, 2010). Due to routine interactions between people who share common interests, Facebook provides the environment for a level of trust to develop; people trust others who are perceived to be real (Amin *et al.*, 2010). Additionally, it is found that trusting behaviour is determined by former trusting experiences, as well as by the level of social relationships (Glaeser *et al.*, 2000). Workman (2008) found that those who were more trusting were more susceptible to social engineering than those who were not as trusting.

Petre (2010) demonstrated the ease with which a phisher could enter a circle of friends by setting up a Facebook account, joining groups to acquire friends and sending the new Facebook friends an illegitimate link. Of the new Facebook friends 24 per cent followed this link even though they did not know who it was really from or where the link was going. Petre and the new Facebook friends had never met in real life, which demonstrates the power of online trust purely from social connections.

Trust research has been completed in online firms (Bhattacherjee, 2002; McKnight *et al.*, 2002), and it has been found that trust and familiarity is directly related to whether a user interacts with the company (Bhattacherjee, 2002). Trust online is the security that neither the e-commerce company nor the customer will take advantage of the other's vulnerabilities (Bhattacherjee, 2002). It is noted by Bhattacherjee (2002) and McKnight *et al.* (2002) that consumers base trust in online merchants according to the merchant's ability (competence), benevolence and integrity. Bhattacherjee defines: ability as the proficiency and knowledge of the vendor to perform an expected transaction; benevolence as a company's expression of good faith and certainty; and integrity as the credibility in which a seller conducts transactions, defines (and upholds) policies and handles consumer data.

As discussed, conscientiousness is associated with meticulousness and self-discipline. According to Ryan and Xenos (2011) and Gosling *et al.* (2011), those who score highly on conscientiousness spend less time on Facebook, which may result in decreased opportunities for Facebook-related phishing. Research on adolescents also suggests a lower rate of victimisation in those who score highly in conscientiousness (Jensen-Campbell and Malcolm, 2007). Barnard (2009) found that men who fell for Ponzi schemes had impulsive characteristics. Ngo and Paternoster (2011) reported that low self-control was a target indicator to cybercrime and that there was no significance between self-control and phishing. Regarding issues of trust, Facebook regularly receives phishing and massive malware attacks (Amin *et al.*, 2010; Bonneau *et al.*, 2009), contains obscure auto-email and link syntaxes (Bonneau *et al.*, 2009) and provides the environment for a level of trust to develop (Petre, 2010).

The aim of this study was to examine whether there is a correlation between personality and susceptibility to Facebook phishing. It was hypothesised that participants who score highly in conscientiousness are less susceptible to Facebook phishing than participants who have low scores in conscientiousness. It was also hypothesised that participants who score highly in impulsivity are more susceptible to Facebook phishing than participants who have low scores in impulsivity, and that participants who score highly in trust in Facebook as an online company are more susceptible to Facebook phishing.

Method

This study was experimental in design. A questionnaire measured the independent variables of demographic characteristics, Facebook behaviour, Facebook trust, personality and impulsivity data. Facebook email and login web page screenshots measured the dependent variables of detection of phishing stimuli and rating figures.

Participants

This study was open to participants 18 years and older. Participant prerequisites included being Facebook account holders with no prior computer security training or a computer science degree completed within the last fifteen years. This exclusion was due to the potential understanding of phishing, an insight advantageous over other groups and not a true reflection of the majority of Facebook users. Participants were recruited by convenience sampling among college students and professionals.

Nineteen participants completed the study: twelve females (63 per cent) and seven males (37 per cent). Participant ages ranged between 18 and 60 years; however, there were no participants in the 36–42 age group, and 47 per cent of the participants were in the 18–26 age group.

Materials

Each participant completed a four-section questionnaire before the phishing screenshots section took place. The questionnaire consisted of brief participant demographics and Facebook behaviour queries and three extensively used scales: the Big Five Inventory 44 (John and Srivastava, 1999), the Barratt Impulsiveness Scale (BIS-11, Patton et al., 1995) and the Individual Trust in Online Firms Scale (Bhattacherjee, 2002).

The Big Five Inventory 44 (John and Srivastava, 1999) measured neuroticism, extraversion, openness to experiences, conscientiousness and agreeableness personality factors among participants. This test is known to be a reliable scale; John and Srivastava provide alpha reliability ranges on this scale that range from .75 to .90 in the US and Canada; three-month test-retest reliabilities range from .80 to .90, with a mean of .85.

The Barratt Impulsiveness Scale (Patton et al., 1995) is a widely used self-reporting mechanism to ascertain impulsivity; this scale consists of several second order and first order factors. Patton et al. demonstrate this test to be a valid, reliable scale and report alpha coefficient ranges from .79 to .83. This scale contains thirty questions.

The Individual Trust in Online Firms Scale (Bhattacherjee, 2002) was selected to establish participants' trust in Facebook as an online company. This scale investigates the trustee's ability, benevolence and integrity. Reliability and validity (convergent, discriminant and nomological) for this scale were tested and accepted; Cronbach alphas ranged between .83 and .89. This scale contains ten items.

The second stage incorporated visual stimuli presented within four screenshots: one each to represent an authentic email, phish email, authentic web login and phish web login. The HTML screenshots contained between six and twelve stimuli; each screen included live links to facilitate hovering and link destination views. All examples were modelled on legitimate email and login pages; however, the researcher manipulated genuine data to create counterfeit examples. Screenshot cues (both authentic and spurious) include email sender name, email address, subject line text, body content, logo, URL, greeting, language selection, footer, copyright and links with active destinations. All screen sizes were 1071 × 605 pixels and 72 dots per inch (dpi).

Screenshot ratings and stimuli identification were recorded on a mirrored screenshot datasheet. Each stimulus (for counterfeit and genuine examples) was numbered with a rating checkbox.

The interviews held during the screenshot section of the study were audio recorded for verification purposes. The experiment was conducted on a laptop computer; the same computer and stimuli were used for all participants. A mouse was provided for participants unfamiliar with a touchpad.

Procedure

The research was conducted on a one-to-one basis to encourage participants to 'think out loud'. Verbal precondition assessments of computer security training, computer science degree and Facebook account status took place for each participant before performing the experiment. Each experiment took approximately twenty minutes to complete, and consent was given before initiating the testing.

Screenshots were preloaded in four separate tabs within a web browser. Once the questionnaire was completed, the participant was asked if they were familiar with the mouse and touchpad; it was important not to lead the participant to use the mouse or touchpad, but to let them know it was available. The audio recording was switched on, and the participants were told they would be shown four Facebook email and login page examples. They were asked to examine the pages to determine if the examples genuinely belonged to Facebook or were phish. Participants were asked to verbalise their observations.

As participants spoke about their observations, each identified cue was check-marked on a hard copy by the researcher. The researcher also documented other observations, such as scrolling, hovering and clicking in field notes. Internet connection was not necessary for this study; clicking on links (genuine and illegitimate) led the participant to a generic landing page, where they were asked to click the 'back page' arrow icon.

After reviewing each example, participants were asked to rate the examples as certainly phishing, probably phishing, unsure, probably not phishing or certainly not phishing. If not already disclosed, the participant was asked which features inspired confidence or generated suspicion in authenticity. A debrief page was provided at the completion of the experiment.

Results

Conscientiousness

While conscientiousness was not correlated with the rating number results for the phishing email ($rs = -.131$, $p = .617$), rating of the phishing web login page approached significance ($rs = -.461$, $p = .063$). This indicates that participants with lower levels of conscientiousness may fail to identify the phishing web login correctly. Conversely, when looking at conscientiousness and incorrectly rated phish, those who rated lowly in conscientiousness made more rating errors than participants who rated highly in conscientiousness. When considering conscientiousness and the number of stimuli identified on the phishing email ($rs = -.078$, $p = .766$) and web login page ($rs = .176$, $p = .499$), there are no significant correlation findings.

Impulsivity

When focusing on participant impulsivity levels and correctly identifying both phishing screenshots as phish, 35 per cent of the users who had a high level of impulsivity answered correctly and 65 per cent of users who had a low level of impulsivity answered correctly. Additionally, 70 per cent of the users who incorrectly rated phishing as genuine scored highly in impulsivity. In other words, those users who score low in impulsivity are better at correctly rating phish and make fewer mistakes in rating a genuine example as phish.

Cognitive instability, a sub-scale of impulsivity, was negatively correlated ($rs = -.591$, $p < .05$) with identifying phishing stimuli in a Facebook phishing email; this indicates that participants who scored highly on this measure were less likely to identify phishing components on a bogus email. Participants with high ratings of cognitive instability also logged in more frequently on Facebook ($rs = .594$, $p < .05$).

Trust in Facebook

Individuals who had higher trust in Facebook correctly identified phish more often than users who had lower trust in Facebook, although there were no significant correlation results. Conversely, there were no differences in low versus high trust ratings when incorrectly rating phish. Those who had low trust in Facebook erroneously identified components on a real Facebook email page as phish; likewise, as trust in Facebook became stronger, the number of stimuli identified in the genuine email as phishing elements decreased ($rs = -.640$, $p < .01$).

Discussion

Results indicate there were some correlations between personality and a suscept-ibility to Facebook phishing. There were no significant results for conscientiousness and Facebook phishing vulnerabilities, although outcomes for cognitive instability contain insights into possible Facebook phishing susceptibility high-risk groups. Users with high trust in Facebook correctly rated phish more often than users with low trust in Facebook; as trust in Facebook became stronger, the number of stimuli identified in the genuine email as phishing elements decreased.

Conscientiousness

Most of those who rated the website correctly scored highly on conscientiousness, which was marginally correlated. This indicates that participants with lower levels of conscientiousness may fail to identify the phishing web login correctly. When considering both elements of phishing examples, those who did not rate as highly in conscientiousness made more rating errors than participants who rated highly in conscientiousness.

Of all the participants, 89 per cent correctly identified the email example as phish. The participants who scored high in conscientiousness and low in agreeableness answered correctly. In the phishing website rating, 58 per cent of participants answered incorrectly. In this group, individuals scored low on conscientiousness and high on neuroticism. There were no significant correlations for conscientiousness and the phishing email or web login in terms of the number of stimuli identified.

There were no findings to support Ryan and Xenos (2011) and Gosling et al. (2011), who found that those who score highly on conscientiousness spend less time on Facebook. The results of this research also did not support a previous observation of a lower rate of victimisation in those who score highly in conscientiousness (Jensen-Campbell and Malcolm, 2007). The non-correlated result in this case may possibly relate to the fact that the research performed by Jensen-Campbell and Malcolm was with adolescents and not adults.

Impulsivity

The second hypothesis purported that participants who score highly in impulsivity are more susceptible to Facebook phishing than participants who score low in impulsivity. Based on the results presented in both ratings and the number of stimuli presented, this hypothesis is supported.

Participant impulsivity levels indicate that 35 per cent of the users who had a high level of impulsivity correctly identified both examples of phish, and 65 per cent of users who had a low level of impulsivity also answered correctly. Therefore, users who rate low in impulsivity correctly rate phish more than those who rate higher in impulsivity. Related with this finding, those who incorrectly rated phishing as genuine scored high in impulsivity. To summarise, those users who score low in impulsivity are better at correctly rating phish and make fewer mistakes in rating a genuine example as phish.

Trust in Facebook

The final hypothesis proposed that participants who score high in trust in Facebook as an online company are more susceptible to Facebook phishing than participants who score lowly in trust in Facebook as an online company. Analysis indicates that users with high trust in Facebook correctly rated phish more often than users with low trust in Facebook, and thus the hypothesis is not supported.

Based on count rate, individuals who had higher trust in Facebook correctly identified phish more often than users who had lower trust in Facebook, although there were no significant correlations to support this. Those who had low trust in Facebook erroneously identified components on a real Facebook email page as phish; likewise, as trust in Facebook became stronger, the number of stimuli identified in the genuine email as phishing elements decreased. Additionally, younger participants were more likely to trust Facebook as an online company than older participants were. Users who had low trust in Facebook were most likely sceptical, thus incorrectly identifying phishing elements on the genuine email.

Existing literature suggests that Facebook is vulnerable to phishing attacks (Amin *et al.*, 2010; Bonneau *et al.*, 2009), uses complicated syntaxes (Bonneau *et al.*, 2009) and facilitates an environment for trust to develop (Petre, 2010). It would appear these factors would aid phishing, however it is possible that users who trust Facebook are familiar with Facebook and recognise its genuine trust elements.

Limitations

Because the experiment was conducted on a one-to-one basis and the researcher was present, there was a probable Hawthorne effect (Landsberger, 1958). Users were asked to make any comments in relation to the study, and several stated that they would not normally take such care in their observations and decisions relating to Facebook emails and web login pages.

The appearance of email examples may have affected user rating and stimuli responses due to formatting differences between email clients. In other words, a user who was used to seeing his Facebook emails using a particular email client might have been fooled into thinking the Facebook email examples were phish just because they looked different to what they normally saw.

Lastly, some participants used their mobile handsets as their only method for accessing Facebook and were not familiar with the email and web login layouts on a laptop. The participants' answers may have been based on a cognitive bias, the representativeness heuristic, where a decision is made based on information in memory (Tversky and Kahneman, 1974).

Future research

It may be beneficial for future research to examine the way in which mobile users may be vulnerable to Facebook phish, especially since there are not as many verification methods (such as link hovering) to determine an email or web login authenticity. There is a need for research to examine who is susceptible to phishing within Facebook. Some phishing occurs via third party applications (such as games) and is often spread to other account users. Research would also be beneficial in the area of Facebook phishing victimisation, to supplement the studies conducted by Sharp *et al.* (2004). Lastly, research around Facebook phishing and cognitive load (Miller, 1956) may provide interesting results.

References

Amichai-Hamburger, Y. and Vinitzky, G. (2010). Social network use and personality. *Computers in Human Behaviour*, 26 (6), 1289–1295.

Amin, T., Okhiria, O., Lu, L. and An, J. (2010). Facebook: A comprehensive analysis of phishing on a social system. Retrieved from: http://courses.ece.ubc.ca/412/term_project/reports/2010/facebook.pdf.

Anandpara, V., Dingman, A., Jakobsson, M., Liu, D. and Roinestad, H. (2007). Phishing IQ tests measure fear, not ability. In *Proceedings from FC '07/USEC '07: 11th International Conference on Financial Cryptography and 1st International Conference on Usable Security* (pp. 362–366). Berlin: Heidelberg.

Barnard, J. (2009). Why men fall prey to ponzi schemes. Conference papers. *Law & Society*, 1.

Bergholz, A., De Beer, J., Glahn, S., Moens, M., Paaß, G., and Strobel, S. (2010). New filtering approaches for phishing email. *Journal of Computer Security*, 18, 7–35.

Bhattacherjee, A. (2002). Individual trust in online firms: Scale development and initial test. *Journal of Management Information Systems*, 19 (1), 211–241.

Bonneau, J., Anderson, J. and Danezis, G. (2009). Prying data out of a social network. Proceedings from 2009 International Conference on Advances in Social Network Analysis and Mining, Athens, Greece, pp. 249–254. Retrieved from: http://ieeexplore.ieee.org/xpl/login.jsp?tp=&arnumber=5231875&url=http%3A%2F%2Fieeexplore.ieee.org%2Fstamp%2Fstamp.jsp%3Ftp%3D%26arnumber%3D5231875.

Chandrasekaran, M., Narayanan, K. and Upadhyaya, S. (2006). Phishing email detection based on structural properties. Proceedings of the NYS Cyber Security Conference, New York.

Evenden, J.L. (1999). Varieties of impulsivity. *Psychopharmacology*, 146 (4), 348.

Feigelson, J. and Calman, C. (2010). Liability for the costs of phishing and information theft. *Journal of Internet Law*, 13, 1–26.

Glaeser, E.L., Laibson, D.I., Scheinkman, J.A. and Soutter, C.L. (2000). Measuring trust. *Quarterly Journal of Economics*, 115 (3), 811–846.

Gosling, S.D., Augustine, A.A., Vazire, S., Holtzman, N. and Gaddis, S. (2011). Manifestations of personality in online social networks: Self-reported Facebook-related behaviours and observable profile information. *Cyberpsychology, Behaviour & Social Networking*, 14 (9), 483–488.

Jensen-Campbell, L.A. and Malcolm, K.T. (2007). The importance of conscientiousness in adolescent interpersonal relationships. *Personality and Social Psychology Bulletin*, 33 (3), 368–383.

John, O.P. and Srivastava, S. (1999). The Big Five Trait taxonomy: History, measurement, and theoretical perspectives. In L.A. Pervin and O.P. John (eds) *Handbook of Personality: Theory and research*, 2nd edn (pp. 102–138). New York: Guilford Press.

Krebs, B. (2009). Spike in social media malware, phishing attacks. Retrieved from: http://voices.washingtonpost.com/securityfix/2009/11/spike_in_social_media_malware.html.

Landsberger, H. (1958). *Hawthorne Revisited: Management and the worker, its critics, and developments in human relations in industry.* Ithaca, NY: Cornell University.

McCrae, R.R. and John, O.P. (1992). An introduction to the five-factor model and its applications. *Journal of Personality*, 60 (2), 175–215.

McKnight, D.H., Choudhury, V. and Kacmar, C. (2002). Developing and validating trust measures for e-commerce: An integrative typology. *Information Systems Research*, 13 (3), 334–359.

Miller, G. (1956). The magical number seven plus or minus two: Some limits on our capacity for processing information. *Psychological Review*, 63 (2), 81–97.

Ngo, F. and Paternoster, R. (2011). Cybercrime victimization: An examination of individual and situational level factors. *International Journal of Cyber Criminology*, 5 (1), 773–793.

Parrish, J., Bailey, J. and Courtney, J. (2009). A personality based model for determining susceptibility to phishing attacks. 2009 Southwest Decision Sciences Institute Proceedings. Oklahoma.

Patton, J.H., Stanford, M.S. and Barratt, E.S. (1995). Factor structure of the Barratt Impulsiveness Scale. *Journal of Clinical Psychology*, 51 (6), 768–774.

Petre, G. (2010). Facebook: Another breach in the wall. Presented at the MIT Spam Conference of 2010, Cambridge, MA. Retrieved from http://labs.bitdefender.com/wp-content/uploads/2011/03/FB-Another-breach-in-the-wall.pdf.

Ryan, T. and Xenos, S. (2011). Who uses Facebook? An investigation into the relationship between the big five, shyness, narcissism, loneliness, and Facebook usage. *Computers in Human Behaviour*, 27 (5), 1658–1664.

Sharp, T., Shreve-Neiger, A., Fremouw, W., Kane, J. and Hutton, S. (2004). Exploring the psychological and somatic impact of identity theft. *Journal of Forensic Sciences*, 49 (1), 131–136.

Soghoian, C. and Jakobsson, M. (2009). *Social Engineering in Phishing: Information assurance, security and privacy services.* Bingley: Emerald.

Symantec. (2012). *Symantec Intelligence Report: February 2012.* Retrieved from: www.symantec.com/content/en/us/enterprise/other_resources/b-intelligence_report_02_2012.en-us.pdf.

Tversky, A. and Kahneman, D. (1974). Judgment under uncertainty: Heuristics and biases. *Science*, 185 (4157), 1124–1131.

Vishwanath, A., Herath, T., Chen, R., Wang, J. and Rao, H.R. (2011). Why do people get phished? Testing individual differences in phishing vulnerability within an integrated, information processing model. *Decision Support Systems*, 51 (3), 576–586.

Workman, M. (2008). Wisecrackers: A theory-grounded investigation of phishing and pretext social engineering threats to information security. *Journal of the American Society for Information Science & Technology*, 59 (4), 662–674.

PART IV

Internet interventions and therapies

Media portrayal of the negative aspects of online life is common – there are regular features and reports on worrying phenomena such as cyberbullying, cybercrime and Internet addiction. While these are understandably of great concern to Internet users – and, in particular, younger users and their parents – it should also be remembered that there are many ways in which the Internet can enhance our lives. In a broad sense, these include greater communication opportunities with loved ones, increased social capital, enhanced educational opportunities, wider consumer bases for businesses and greater social diversity. This section examines other ways in which the Internet can improve our lives, such as online therapies, while also examining methods by which individuals can reduce their risks of falling prey to negative consequences of online life. Recommendations on proper use are made, and attitudes of important professionals in the fields are measured.

Chapter 12 looks at Protection Motivation Theory. There is limited understanding of how users' perception of risk changes depending on the types of online activities they engage in. This chapter explores how Internet users change their privacy and risk perceptions as they engage in the online activities of searching, social networking and online shopping. People who felt competent using technology also felt they were better able to deal with perceived problems online, while people with previous experience of information misuse felt more at risk from online threats for shopping and search, but not from social networking. Chapter 13 looks at the specific example of establishing an online counselling service for substance use. It seeks to determine whether the establishment of an online counselling service for substance use issues is feasible. Counsellor willingness and ability to engage with such services are measured and issues relating to appropriate service delivery explored. Chapter 14 addresses the growing area of cyberchondria and seeks to explain the process of 'Cyberchondria by Proxy'. The use of the Internet as a source of medical information, while having an informational benefit, also has the potential to increase anxiety when employed as a diagnostic procedure. This chapter identifies the motivation behind health-related search online. This section on Internet interventions and therapies concludes with Chapter 15, which explores attitudes to computerised psychotherapy through a study of psychotherapists.

12

PROTECTION MOTIVATION THEORY AND ONLINE ACTIVITIES

Richard O'Connell and Gráinne Kirwan

Chapter summary

There is limited understanding of how users' perception of risk changes depending on the types of online activities they engage in. In this study, Protection Motivation Theory was used to explore how Internet users change their privacy and risk perceptions as they engage in the online activities of searching, social networking and online shopping. An online survey compared risk perceptions, privacy concerns and protection behaviours of participants. Shopping was found to have the highest score for perceived likelihood of financial risk but the lowest scores for perceived likelihood of information risk and self-efficacy. People who felt competent using technology felt they were better able to deal with perceived problems online. Finally, people with previous experience of information misuse felt more at risk from online threats for shopping and search but not from social networking.

Introduction

As privacy issues are often a limiting factor in Internet users' participation in new communities (Hann *et al.*, 2007), this study explored how Internet users change their privacy perceptions and behaviours as they engage in the online activities of searching, social networking and online shopping. In 2010 in America, Internet users spent 22.7 per cent of their time online engaged in social networking, 3.5 per cent of their time searching and between 3 per cent and 34 per cent of their time shopping (Nielsen Wire, 2010). These activities provide an interesting platform for discussing data privacy concerns. For example, users may search for terms that contain highly sensitive and potentially embarrassing information, such as extramarital affairs, but they may not see potential data privacy issues. This study examined whether Internet users display contradictory behaviours and perceptions as they engage in different online activities.

Protection Motivation Theory (PMT)

Protection Motivation Theory (PMT; Rogers, 1975) was first introduced as a model for discussing health attitudes and behaviours. It identifies the cognitive processes that are used by an individual when they feel threatened, and puts forward a model for how people respond to these threats. PMT proposes that a person bases their assessment of threats on severity and vulnerability. Once the threat has been assessed, they base their evaluation of the perceived usefulness of potential responses to reduce the threat, on their perception of how successful the response would be and how much faith they have in their ability to carry out the responses. If actions are available that do not remove the threat (maladaptive responses) – such as ignoring the situation instead of taking corrective action – these are also evaluated and weighted, based on perceived rewards (Anderson and Agarwal, 2010; Lee et al., 2008; Maddux and Rogers, 1983). The theory was later extended to include social norms and prior experience as factors in predicting behaviours (Tanner et al., 1991). Over the last thirty-seven years PMT has been applied to health promotion, disease prevention, politics, environmental issues, food safety, nuclear war, child protection, computer viruses and data privacy (Floyd et al., 2000; Lee et al., 2008).

Data privacy concerns

With regard to data privacy, the more a user is concerned about how their data is collected and used, the more likely they are to adopt privacy protection behaviours such as submitting false information on online forms (LaRose and Rifon, 2007; Rifon et al., 2005). Interestingly, the same users ignored all warnings about potential dangers if they felt themselves to be highly effective at minimising the negative effects of privacy breaches. This may mean that individual measures of privacy concerns are of little value when taken in isolation. Johnston and Warkentin (2010) found that self-efficacy had a positive effect on end-user intentions to adopt recommended individual computer security actions, that social influence had a positive effect on end-user intentions to adopt recommended individual computer security actions, and that perceptions of threat severity negatively influenced perceptions of self-efficacy. These findings are also supported by subsequent studies (Cromer, 2011). In opposition to PMT, the Johnston and Warkentin study did not find any relationship between perceptions of threat susceptibility and response efficacy or self-efficacy. They surmised that this might be due to the possibility that individuals perceive themselves to be less exposed to risks than their peers (Schmidt and Arnett, 2005). They also noted that it might be due to research with a sample population that had little prior experience of information misuse.

In relation to coping behaviours, Umeh (2004) noted that people used their past behaviours as an estimate for how they would behave in the future. Their study also found that threat or coping appraisal behaviours could not be used to predict behaviours, but fear could. This is interesting, as an emotion seems to be overriding cognitive processes.

Previous work has often focused on data privacy in terms of e-commerce (Kim et al., 2004; Kim et al., 2008) or the submission of personal data to websites for marketing purposes. These studies ignored the amount of extremely personal data that is now manipulated in online systems. Examples of this are the advertisements in email services that programmatically 'read' a user's email and provide personalised advertisements based on their content. Researchers have also noted that the rise of social networking may have changed privacy norms for a large proportion of certain populations (Bartel Sheehan and Grubbs Hoy, 1999) and that activities that were considered risky in the past, such as blogging, can now be seen as a positive activity for professional reasons (Milne et al., 2009).

Trust and risk perceptions

Kim et al. (2008) studied the factors that can influence user trust and perceived risk. These factors are observation-based (such as information quality), affect-based (such as recommendation systems), experience-based (such as Internet experience) and personality-based (such as trust propensity). Their findings suggested that consumer trust is heavily influenced by company reputation, website quality and baseline measures of disposition to trust. Raman and Pashupati (2004) investigated avoidance and coping behaviours of users by assessing their baseline measure of Self-Perceived level of Technological Competence (SPTC). That study proposed that users with high SPTC scores would be comfortable in performing adaptive responses to technology threats and that users with lower SPTC scores would adopt maladaptive responses. They found a clear correlation between SPTC scores and coping strategies.

Online privacy

Brown and Muchira (2004) found that privacy concerns can be grouped into: specific concerns about companies collecting too much data; companies using private data where permission has not been given; companies deleting or modifying personal data; users not knowing who accesses their information; and being sent unwanted communications. In the online arena, people become concerned about privacy when they do not know who collects data about them, how the data is obtained or why that data is collected (Lanier and Saini, 2008). Youn (2009) found that when young adolescents are more concerned about online privacy they are more likely to engage in privacy protection behaviours such as fabricating personal information, seeking support and advice from adults, and refraining from providing their information. These findings are backed up by a previous study by Youn (2005) that used PMT to explore how willing teens were to provide personal information online.

Hypotheses

The study used Protection Motivation Theory (PMT; Rogers, 1975) to investigate how a user's perceived severity of online threat and perceived likelihood of online threat related to response/self-efficacy and whether the relationship changes were based on the online activity that they engage in. The control variables used with the study participants included their trust propensity, which might affect their disclosure during the survey (Culnan and Bies, 2003), and their personal experience with information abuse, which might affect their decision to disclose information (Emerson, 1990; Homans, 1974).

The vast majority of the studies to date have applied Protection Motivation Theory to a single online activity without examining how user perceptions and behaviours change as they engage in different online activities. This study sought to address that gap by exploring how user perceptions change as they engage in different behaviours online. Specifically perceived threat severity, perceived vulnerability, perceived response efficacy and perceived self-efficacy were used to explore perception changes as the user shops, searches and uses social networking. For this study it was expected that, as previous studies have shown, people would be concerned about their financial information (Forsythe and Shi, 2003) and understand the privacy risks of social networking (Dwyer et al., 2007). It was also proposed that users would not be aware that Internet search can be a risky activity.

As shopping online requires some form of online payment, users are more likely to perceive some form of threat or financial risk when shopping that they may not associate with search or social networking (Forsythe and Shi, 2003). As shopping is an online activity that is controlled by online retailers, users may not feel as if they have the relatively high level of control offered by search or social networks, where users have been shown to have a high level of awareness of the privacy controls offered (Acquisti and Gross, 2006).

The following hypotheses were proposed:

H1 Shopping online will have higher scores than Search or Social Networking for perceived likelihood of financial loss.
H2 Shopping online will have lower scores than Search or Social Networking for self-efficacy.
H3 Searching online will have lower scores than Shopping or Social Networking for perceived likelihood of online data threats.

Hui et al. (2007) showed that people with previous experience of information misuse were less likely to engage in similar behaviours again. The current study investigated whether people's risk perception of these activities had also changed or whether their response was purely behavioural in nature.

H4 For all online activities, people with previous experience of information misuse will have higher scores for perceived likelihood of online threats.

Previous studies have shown that users with low scores for SPTC are more anxious with regard to their online privacy (Raman and Pashupati, 2004). Users with high scores for SPTC have been shown to engage in less risky behaviours online, but this study examined whether users felt more confident about performing corrective actions (as measured by self-efficacy) or whether they engaged only in risk avoidance.

H5   For all online activities, people with high self-perceived levels of technological competence (SPTC) scores will have higher scores for self-efficacy.

Method

Design

The research approach for this study was primarily quantitative and its strategy of inquiry was a survey. The survey collected some baseline data on participants using established psychological scales. The survey collected scores for an individual's trust propensity. This gave a measure of how trusting a participant is in general, with a higher score meaning that an individual is more trusting of others (Hui *et al.*, 2007). Second, the survey identified which participants had previous experience of the misuse of their private data (Hui *et al.*, 2007). Third, the survey collected a baseline measure of self-perceived level of technological competence (Raman and Pashupati, 2004). This measure served as an interesting control variable by investigating the link between SPTC and self-efficacy.

Participants

As the study was interested in the behaviour of all Internet users, it did not target specific segments or user populations, and advertised to get the greatest number of responses. To minimise ethical issues, only responses from individuals aged 18 or older were considered. Participants were sent a link to the survey via email or social networking sites. A total of 104 survey responses were collected. Over 78 per cent of respondents were between the ages of 26 and 45. With regard to gender, 60.2 per cent of respondents were male and 39.8 per cent were female.

Materials

The data was collected using a survey instrument. The survey used was a modified version of surveys which were previously used by Milne *et al.* (2009) and whose work is directly relatable to this research. That study contained questions relating to perceived threats (reliability $\alpha = .93$), perceived likelihoods of threats occurring (reliability $\alpha = .96$) and the self-efficacy of participants (reliability $\alpha = .89$). The majority of responses were recorded using five-point Likert scales. Sample questions included: 'I am concerned about losing my data privacy while shopping online'; 'How likely is it for one's financial information to be stolen while shopping online'; and 'I am skilled at avoiding dangers while shopping online'. Milne's study solely focused on online shopping, so this study modified the questions for use with multiple online activities.

This study also used modified versions of questions from Raman and Pashupati (2004), which provide a rating for a participant's self-perceived technological competence. This allows people to rate how comfortable they are with technology tools and processes. From Hui *et al.* (2007) this study used the questions relating to the participants' trust propensity ('I feel that people are generally trustworthy') and questions regarding previous experience of information misuse.

Procedure

Participants were asked to complete the study online, and the survey contained full instructions to enable participants to complete it. Contact information for the researchers was also provided for people to ask questions. A pilot study was conducted with a small group of participants. As a result of the pilot study, the survey was shortened to remove unnecessary or confusing questions, and certain survey questions were clarified.

Results

The majority of people ($n = 84$; 86.6 per cent) believed that people are, in general, to be trusted. Approximately one-third ($n = 33$; 33.7 per cent) had previous experience of personal information being misused somehow. Two-thirds ($n = 69$; 70.4 per cent) had experience shopping online; almost all participants had experience searching online ($n = 96$; 98.0 per cent). Seventy-seven participants had social networking experience (79.4 per cent).

Perceived likelihood of financial loss

A Friedman test was conducted to evaluate differences in means between the perceived likelihood of financial loss while shopping (mean rank = 2.28), searching (mean rank = 1.92) and social networking (mean rank = 1.79). Confidence varied significantly across the three assessment points: χ^2 (2, $N = 51$) = 15.124, $p < .001$.

Self-efficacy

A Friedman test was conducted to evaluate differences in means among the perceived self-efficacy in performing adaptive responses while shopping (mean rank = 1.79), searching (mean rank = 2.14), or social networking (mean rank = 2.07). Confidence varied significantly across the three assessment points: χ^2 (2, $N = 53$) = 7.019, $p < .03$.

Perceived likelihood of online data threats

A Friedman test was conducted to evaluate differences in means among the perceived likelihood of online threats occurring while shopping (mean rank = 1.76), searching (mean rank = 1.78), or social networking (mean rank = 2.46). Confidence varied significantly across the three assessment points: χ^2 (2, N = 50) = 25.206, p < .0005.

Information misuse

An independent-samples t-test was performed to examine the relationship between previous experience of information misuse and perceived risks during online activities. For shopping there was no significant difference between the conditions (t = −1.108, df = 65, p = .136, one-tailed), although people who had experience of information misuse (M = 3.2857, SD = 1.10195) reported slightly higher risk concerns then those without previous experience (M = 3.0000, SD = .91894). For searching there was a significant difference between the conditions (t = −3.450, df = 91, p = .005, one-tailed), with people who had experience of information misuse (M = 3.5667, SD = .89763) reporting higher risk concerns then those without previous experience (M = 2.8413, SD = .97064). For social networking there was no significant difference between the conditions (t = .092, df = 70, p = .464, one-tailed).

Self-Perceived level of Technological Competence (SPTC)

An independent-samples t-test was performed to examine the relationship between SPTC scores and perceived self-efficacy. For shopping there was a significant difference between the conditions (t = −2.090, df = 66, p = .020, one-tailed), with people who had higher SPTC scores (M = 3.6538, SD = .73790) reporting greater perceived ability to protect themselves online than those with lower SPTC scores (M = 3.1875, SD = .91894). For searching there was a significant difference between the conditions (t = -2.101, df = 92, p = .019, one-tailed), with people who had higher SPTC scores (M = 3.8750, SD = .71083) reporting greater perceived ability to protect themselves online than those with lower SPTC scores (M = 3.5000, SD = .80178). For social networking there was a significant difference between the conditions (t = −2.309, df = 73, p = .012, one-tailed), with people who had higher SPTC scores (M = 3.7193, SD = .92107) reporting greater perceived ability to protect themselves online than those with lower SPTC scores (M = 3.1111, SD = 1.13183).

Discussion

As expected, and in accordance with previous studies (Forsythe and Shi, 2003), shopping online seems to be the activity that users perceive as having the highest risk of financial loss. It is interesting that searching has the next highest perceived risk as users do not enter any credit card information while searching. This may be related to the fact that the majority of respondents (55.3 per cent) did not know that you can shop and transfer money on social networking sites or that people see searching as part of the shopping experience.

The fact that shopping had the lowest scores for perceived self-efficacy seems to indicate that users do not feel confident in protecting themselves while shopping. The group that felt they had the ability to protect themselves while shopping online described the techniques they used to protect themselves as use of neutral payment systems, use of credit cards and not laser cards, checking for SSL icons and only shopping on trusted sites.

Shopping online was also the activity that users rated as having the lowest security risk. This disagrees with several previous studies on the perception of risk for online shopping (Forsythe and Shi, 2003), but supports the previous research on social networking as users are aware of the risks involved (Dwyer et al., 2007).

The psychological concept of 'ownership' may influence some of these results as it has been shown that when 'an individual invests more time and energy performing activities requiring the Internet and actively associating with others via the Internet, she is likely to experience an increased sense of psychological ownership' (Anderson and Agarwal, 2010). This may encourage a bias based on the amount of time a user spends performing different activities online (e.g. 'I feel shopping is a safe activity online because I spend lots of time shopping online').

The perceived likelihood of online threats was higher for shopping and search than for social networking. This hypothesis was therefore rejected. This appears to conflict with Dwyer et al. (2007), who found that users of social networks had significant privacy concerns. Overall, as previous studies have shown, people were concerned about their financial information while shopping (Forsythe and Shi, 2003) and they understood the privacy risks of social networking (Dwyer et al., 2007), but they were aware of the financial and data privacy risks involved in searching online.

The implication for online retailers is that customers may still be afraid to shop online. Over 40 per cent of respondents showed some indication that they are concerned about their financial details, and 30 per cent of participants did not regularly shop online. Retailers should invest in educating users on how to better protect themselves or provide more details on the benefits of shopping online. It is also interesting that people felt better able to protect themselves on social networks than shopping sites, as social networks are a relatively new phenomenon compared to online shopping. This may be due to the level of control offered by social networks.

The study data suggests that users do not fully trust social networking sites to protect their data. In order to allay these fears, social networking sites could provide more information to their users on how to protect their own data and how the sites use their data. In agreement with the previous work by Raman and Pashupati (2004), there appears to be a strong relationship between SPTC scores and self-efficacy. Perhaps social networking sites could look to increase the SPTC scores for their users by increasing their users' confidence in performing specific actions. They could do this by offering training, relating these actions to previous user experience or providing ratings of task difficulty for users.

Conclusion

This study compared risk perceptions, privacy concerns and protection behaviours of participants for shopping, searching and social networking. Shopping was found to have the highest score for perceived likelihood of financial risk but the lowest scores for perceived likelihood of information risk and self-efficacy. People with a high self-perceived level of technological competence score felt they were better able to deal with perceived problems online. Finally, people with previous experience of information misuse had higher scores for perceived likelihood of online threats for shopping and search but not for social networking.

References

Acquisti, A. and Gross, R. (2006). Imagined communities: Awareness, information sharing, and privacy on the Facebook. *Privacy Enhancing Technologies*, 4258, 36–58.

Anderson, C.L. and Agarwal, R. (2010). Practicing safe computing: A multimethod empirical examination of home computer user security behavioural intentions. *MIS Quarterly*, 34 (3), 613-A15.

Bartel Sheehan, K. and Grubbs Hoy, M. (1999). Flaming, complaining, abstaining: How online users respond to privacy concerns. *Journal of Advertising*, 28 (3), 37–51.

Brown, M. and Muchira, R. (2004). Investigating the relationship between Internet privacy concerns and online purchase behaviour. *Journal of Electronic Commerce Research*, 5 (1), 62–70.

Cromer, C. (2011). Understanding Web 2.0's influences on public e-services. *Innovation: Management, Policy and Practice*. Retrieved from www.innovation-enterprise.com/archives/vol/12/issue/2/article/3710/understanding-web-20s-influences-on-public.

Culnan, M.J. and Bies, R.J. (2003). Consumer privacy: Balancing economic and justice considerations. *Journal of Social Issues*, 59 (2), 323–342.

Dwyer, C., Hiltz, S.R. and Passerini, K. (2007). Trust and privacy concern within social networking sites: A comparison of Facebook and MySpace. *AMCIS Proceedings, Paper 339*.

Emerson, R.M. (1990). Social exchange theory. In M. Rosenberg and R.H. Turner (eds) *Social Psychology: Sociological perspectives* (pp. 30–65). Piscataway, NJ: Transaction.

Floyd, D.L., Prentice-Dunn, S. and Rogers, R.W. (2000). A meta-analysis of research on protection motivation theory. *Journal of Applied Social Psychology*, 30 (2), 407–429.

Forsythe, S.M. and Shi, B. (2003). Consumer patronage and risk perceptions in Internet shopping. *Journal of Business Research*, 56 (11), 867–875.

Hann, I.-H., Hui, K.-L., Tom Lee, S.-Y., and Png, I.P.L. (2007). Overcoming online information privacy concerns: An information-processing theory approach. *Journal of Management Information Systems*, 24 (2), 13–42.

Homans, G.C. (1974). *Social Behaviour: Its elementary forms*, revised edn. Oxford: Harcourt Brace Jovanovich.

Hui, K.-L., Teo, H.H. and Tom Lee, S.-Y. (2007). The value of privacy assurance: An exploratory field experiment. *MIS Quarterly*, 31 (1), 19–33.

Johnston, A.C. and Warkentin, M. (2010). Fear appeals and information security behaviours: An empirical study. *MIS Quarterly*, 34 (3), 549-A4.

Kim, H.-W., Xu, Y., and Koh, J. (2004). A comparison of online trust building factors between potential customers and repeat customers. *Journal of the Association for Information Systems*, 5 (10), 392–420.

Kim, D.J., Ferrin, D.L. and Rao, H.R. (2008). A trust-based consumer decision-making model in electronic commerce: The role of trust, perceived risk, and their antecedents. *Decision Support Systems*, 44 (2), 544–564.

LaRose, R. and Rifon, N. (2007). Promoting i-safety: Effects of privacy warnings and privacy seals on risk assessment and online privacy behaviour. *Journal of Consumer Affairs*, 41 (1), 127–149.

Lanier, C.D. and Saini, A. (2008). Understanding consumer privacy: A review and future directions. *Academy of Marketing Science Review*, 12 (2), 1–48.

Lee, D., Larose, R. and Rifon, N. (2008). Keeping our network safe: A model of online protection behaviour. *Behaviour and Information Technology*, 27 (5), 445–454.

Maddux, J.E. and Rogers, R.W. (1983). Protection motivation and self-efficacy: A revised theory of fear appeals and attitude change. *Journal of Experimental Social Psychology*, 19 (5), 469–479.

Milne, G.R., Labrecque, L.I. and Cromer, C. (2009). Toward an understanding of the online consumer's risky behaviour and protection practices. *Journal of Consumer Affairs*, 43 (3), 449–473.

Nielsen Wire (2010). What Americans do online: Social media and games dominate activity. Retrieved from: www.nielsen.com/us/en/newswire/2010/what-americans-do-online-social-media-and-games-dominate-activity.html.

Raman, P. and Pashupati, T.K. (2004). Online privacy: The impact of self perceived technological competence. *Enhancing Knowledge Development in Marketing*, 5.

Rifon, N.J., LaRose, R. and Choi, S.M. (2005). Your privacy is sealed: Effects of web privacy seals on trust and personal disclosures. *Journal of Consumer Affairs*, 39 (2), 339–362.

Rogers, R.W. (1975). A protection motivation theory of fear appeals and attitude change. *Journal of Psychology*, 91 (1), 93.

Schmidt, M.B. and Arnett, K.P. (2005). Spyware: A little knowledge is a wonderful thing. *Communications of the ACM*, 48 (8), 67–70.

Tanner, J.F., Hunt, J.B. and Eppright, D.R. (1991). The protection motivation model: A normative model of fear appeals. *Journal of Marketing*, 55 (3), 36–45.

Umeh, K. (2004). Cognitive appraisals, maladaptive coping, and past behaviour in protection motivation. *Psychology & Health*, 19 (6), 719–735.

Youn, S. (2005). Teenagers' perceptions of online privacy and coping behaviours: A risk–benefit appraisal approach. *Journal of Broadcasting & Electronic Media*, 49 (1), 86–110.

Youn, S. (2009). Determinants of online privacy concern and its influence on privacy protection behaviours among young adolescents. *Journal of Consumer Affairs*, 43 (3), 389–418.

13

ESTABLISHING AN ONLINE COUNSELLING SERVICE FOR SUBSTANCE USE

An exploratory study

Andy Osborn and Cliona Flood

Chapter summary

This research sought to determine whether the establishment of an online counselling service for substance use issues was feasible. Potential counsellors' attitudes towards a service of this nature were measured and compared to stress levels associated with the introduction of new technologies (technostress). Counsellor willingness and ability to engage with such services were also measured, and issues relating to appropriate service delivery were explored. Neutral to slightly positive attitudes were recorded. A significant correlation between levels of technostress and attitudes towards online counselling was found. Overall, the development of a service was deemed timely and favourable.

Introduction

There has been much debate about the appropriateness and effectiveness of providing counselling in an environment where the counsellor and the client do not share the same physical space. For many mental health professionals, the union of technology and psychotherapy has been a controversial concept (Rochlen *et al.*, 2004). Online counselling services continue to gain momentum worldwide, but the specific aim of this research was to determine whether the current conditions for developing an online counselling service for substance use issues are favourable.

Substance use counselling interventions

It is widely accepted that therapy has a major role to play in the treatment of substance use issues. The UK Department of Health Evidence Based Clinical Practice

Guidelines (2001) reported that patients in primary health care settings who received counselling showed significant improvement compared to patients receiving routine care. As only 51 per cent presenting for treatment received counselling (Reynolds et al., 2008), the issue of adequate counselling provision would appear to be an area that needs attention when addressing future developments aimed at decreasing the annual drug treatment statistics.

Numerous counselling approaches exist and have been applied to substance use issues with varying degrees of success. The more popular therapies include Psychoanalytic, Adlerian, Behavioural, Cognitive Behavioural, Existential, Family Therapy, Gestalt, Group Therapy, Motivational Interviewing, Person-Centred and Reality Therapy. Schilit and Gomberg (1991) argue that there is no empirical research that indicates that one theory or model is more effective than any other or under what conditions one theory or model may be more effective than any other.

Cognitive Behavioural Therapy (CBT), which focuses on eliminating or reducing distressing behaviour, has become a widely used form of therapy in many practices dealing with substance use issues. It has become very popular in managed health care settings, where it is considered an economical alternative to psycho-dynamic approaches, which are more concerned with alleged causes of personality changes and sometimes become an exhaustive, lengthy and costly process. However, critics of CBT suggest that this approach merely deals with symptoms and is a somewhat short-sighted process that does not recognise the individual as a whole or take the individual's feelings into account (Palmer, 2000).

Counselling and the online environment

Suler (2001) acknowledged that not every presenting problem is appropriate to the emergent online environment. Carlbring and Andersson (2006) demonstrated that the emergence of numerous and varied Internet-based therapeutic programmes have reported positive results. The potential for online counselling was highlighted by Griffiths as far back as 2001 as a means of helping people who might not otherwise seek counselling to gain confidence in its ability to assist them with their problems. The effective transfer of therapy to an online environment needs careful consideration. Trepal et al. (2007) highlighted the necessity for counsellor education to recognise that relationships in real time may be different when transposed to an online environment.

Effective counselling does not have to be conducted in an environment of facial expressions and non-verbal cues. It can be conducted through other mediums. The father of psychoanalysis, Sigmund Freud, counselled certain clients solely through the written word via exchanges of letters. Caspar and Berger (2005) argue that the lack of non-verbal cues presents an advantage for both the therapist and the client. Some clients feel pressurised in maintaining a constant positive personal impression, and the lack of non-verbal cues can eliminate this pressure. Hill, Thompson and Corbett (1992, as cited by Caspar and Berger, 2005) suggest that the quality of therapy can be increased by being unaware of negative reactions a client may be trying to conceal.

An absence of non-verbal cues in providing online counselling services has also been presented as advantageous for profoundly emotional reasons. Wellman and Haythornthwaite (2002) argue that a lack of social cues in the online environment can make it easier to communicate about issues of an emotional nature, on the basis that it can create an illusion of privacy, thus possibly decreasing a client's perception of interpersonal risk. In a small-scale study relating to clients' experiences of online counselling, Haberstroh *et al.* (2007) noted that clients presenting with topics that might cause them a degree of embarrassment felt less threatened when interacting online and also felt less pressurised to respond quickly.

The role of *transference* in psychotherapy is an issue that also warrants attention. Because of its roots in the unconscious, transference can play a significant part in the development of a psychodynamic therapeutic relationship. By acknowledging the transference relationship and exploring its significance, therapists can use client/therapist transference as a means to disclose unresolved issues that the client may have with figures from the client's past. Zelvin and Speyer (2004) note the importance of identifying and managing transference in an environment where the lack of visual cues can foster the projection of fantasies from client to therapist and idealisation of the client by the therapist. Jones and Stokes (2009) suggest that transference can be more powerful when working with the written word. Suler (2004) proposes that a lack of cues is advantageous for some clients as 'without the distraction of in person cues, they feel they can connect more directly with the mind and soul of the other person' (p. 24).

Therapy and virtual environments

Many psychotherapists, psychologists and counsellors still grapple with the efficacy of some of the more *traditional* forms of technology based counselling – email, message boards, chat and so on. In contrast, Virtual Reality (VR) environments (in which certain aspects of clinical psychology and psychotherapy have already been applied) provide more *futuristic* options. Maltby *et al.* (2002, as cited by Riva, 2005), propose VR Exposure Therapy (VRET) as 'a new medium for exposure therapy' (p. 221). The development of VRET is of particular interest for the field of addiction treatment and relapse prevention. In traditional substance use relapse prevention interventions, cue exposure therapy (CET) is considered a very useful approach (Manley, 2008).

Cues or *triggers* have long been an important focus area of relapse prevention within substance use therapy. The management of scenarios where people in recovery are exposed to these cues/triggers has been a focus area for many behavioural therapies and is seen by many practitioners as a crucial part of relapse prevention. Lee *et al.* (2007) applied CET in a VR environment (VR-CET) to eight members of an Alcoholics Anonymous group over eight sessions. The cues and contexts likely to elicit an urge to drink were selected. Levels of alcohol craving were measured before and after the study. Although the sample size is not substantial enough to report conclusive findings in supporting VR-CET as effective in reducing alcohol cravings, Lee *et al.* propose that VR-CET may be effective to those in an early stage of abstinence.

Substance use counselling and the online environment

Carroll (2008) evaluated the efficacy of a form of computer-based training in CBT (CBT4CBT) skills. Seventy-seven individuals seeking treatment for substance dependence at an outpatient community setting were randomly assigned to standard treatment or standard treatment with biweekly access to computer-based training in CBT4CBT. This appears to be the first randomised clinical control trial evaluating computer-assisted treatment for substance use issues that reports on biologically verified drug use outcomes. If computer-assisted delivery of CBT is demonstrably feasible and effective, the quality of addiction treatment could be considerably enhanced, as computer-assisted delivery makes it possible for CBT to be rolled out extensively. Participants assigned to the CBT4CBT condition submitted significantly more urine specimens that were negative for any type of drugs, and they tended to have longer continuous periods of abstinence during treatment. Carroll (2008) also found that completion of homework assignments in CBT4CBT significantly correlated with positive outcome, with homework completion also considered a significant predictor of treatment involvement.

Measuring attitudes

Young (2005) acknowledges that few studies have explored the area of attitudes towards online counselling and suggests that a better understanding of perceptions towards online counselling will help guide future Internet-based treatment. Young examined client perceptions and concerns about using online counselling and the reasons why clients sought online counselling over face-to-face counselling. From a sample of forty-six participants, anonymity (96 per cent) was cited as the most common reason for seeking online counselling. Privacy was the main concern, with 52 per cent worried that records of the chat logs could be compromised. A Norwegian study conducted by Wangberg *et al.* (2007) yielded similar results relating to attitudes. Mora *et al.* (2008) conducted similar research among practitioners in the USA and found that participants regarded online counselling as having a value in serving people with disabilities and those in rural areas. However, low levels of interest in using online counselling were found among the practitioners themselves. In comparison, psychoanalytically orientated practitioners rated online counselling lower than cognitive-behavioural orientated practitioners.

Mora *et al.* (2008) outline the need to conduct research among practitioners in other countries. The development of any service should always consider those most central to it – in this instance, clients and counsellors. This research measured and compared attitudes towards online counselling and levels of technostress (the negative psychological link between people and the introduction of new technologies) from both a client and a counsellor perspective.

Research questions and hypotheses

This study attempted to determine whether attitudes towards online counselling related to the levels of stress associated with the introduction of new technologies. It examined the following hypotheses:

H1 High levels of stress related to new technology will correlate with low degrees of value towards the utility of online counselling among the counsellor sample group.

H2 High levels of stress related to new technology will correlate with high degrees of discomfort associated with the provision of an online counselling service among the counsellor sample group.

Methodology

The study was a survey questionnaire combined with a semi-structured interview. The study's participants were counsellors working in certain offline substance use treatment centres. This sample group were accredited counsellors with experience of addiction issues, and were recruited from recognised addiction treatment centres and government funded addiction services. A total of 100 surveys were posted out randomly to counsellors. In addition, forty-eight surveys were distributed among the substance use counselling services. Of the forty-two returned surveys, two surveys were discarded from the final sample on the basis that most of the questions were unanswered. This resulted in a final sample of forty surveys, representing a 27 per cent response rate of usable surveys.

A total of forty counsellors from 16 to 65 years of age made up the final sample for this research. The age group with the largest number of counsellors (40 per cent) was the 35–49 age group. Females (58 per cent) narrowly outnumbered males (42 per cent) in the counsellor sample group.

Measures

Counsellors were required to complete a survey comprising a demographic questionnaire, the Personal TechnoStress Inventory (PTSI) and the Online Coun-selling Attitudes Scale (OCAS). The demographic questionnaire sought informa-tion on demographics, computer usage and skills. The questionnaire also sought information on the counsellor's experience in the area of substance use counselling and accreditation. Rosen and Weil's (1998) PTSI was used. Reliability and validity was confirmed by a Cronbach's alpha of .82, which indicates internal consistency. The scale includes a twenty-item measure of state anxiety and a ten-item measure of self-efficacy.

The original OCAS questionnaire is designed to test attitudes towards *receiving* online counselling. The changes in the counsellor's OCAS were made by the researchers and involve reversing the question scenarios to direct them towards counsellors' attitudes towards *delivering* online counselling. The ten-item OCAS consists of the following two five-item sub-scales: (1) The Discomfort of Online Counselling sub-scale (OCAS-D) and (2) The Value of Online Counselling sub-scale (OCAS-V). The OCAS-D sub-scale represented participants' emotional feelings and reactions regarding their ease and comfort associated with using online counselling services. The OCAS-V sub-scale represented the general feelings of participants towards the utility of online counselling, including their perceptions of how they and others would benefit from online counselling. Rochlen *et al.* (2004) found support for construct validity and strong evidence of internal consistency of scores in the OCAS that range from .77 to .90 and a test-retest score reliability of .77 to .88 over a three-week period.

Results

Counsellor groups reported considerably high levels of computer access and broadband access at home: almost all (97.5 per cent) reported having access to a computer at home while 95 per cent reported having broadband usage at home. Regular computer usage was high, all of the counsellors reporting using a computer either 'a few times a week' or 'most days of the week'.

The final question on the OCAS-V sub-scale asked whether, if online counselling were available at no charge, they would consider trying it. A majority (75 per cent) of counsellors either *agreed* or *strongly agreed* that they would try it. Counsellors were also asked what their preferred method would be. They were given the following options to rate in order of preference: (1) email; (2) instant messaging; (3) chat room; (4) audio; (5) webcam. Webcam was the highest first choice in the counsellor group, with 39.5 per cent indicating it as their first preference. Only 2.6 per cent chose the chat room option as their choice.

Computer-mediated communication skills

Counsellors were asked to rate their own ability in relation to the following computer-mediated communication skills: (1) ability to receive and reply to emails; (2) ability in communicating online using an instant messaging programme; and (3) ability in communicating online using voice software. A high proportion (92.5 per cent) of counsellors rated themselves as one of either *very good*, *good* or *average* in receiving and replying to emails, and 50 per cent rated themselves as one of *very good*, *good* or *average* at communicating online using an instant messaging programme. Fewer participants (45 per cent) rated themselves as one of *very good*, *good* or *average* at communicating online using voice software, and only 20 per cent rated themselves as one of *very good*, *good* or *average* at communicating online using a webcam.

Technostress and online counselling attitudes

Counsellors scored an average of 20.3198 on the PTSI (SD = 2.62446; with a minimum of 15 and a maximum of 26). In relation to attitudes towards online counselling, OCAS-V levels yielded a moderately high mean rating for counsellors (M = 17.20). OCAS-D levels yielded a neutral to moderately high mean rating for counsellors (M = 13.80). When the results for the two OCAS sub-scales were combined, the results appeared to suggest an overall *neutral* to *slightly positive* attitude towards online counselling. No significant correlation was found between levels of technostress and degree of value toward online counselling ($r(38)$ = −.215, p = .091, one-tailed). However, a significant positive correlation was identified between levels of technostress and levels of discomfort associated with the perceived provision of an online counselling service ($r(38)$ = .347, p = .014, one-tailed).

Discussion

No support was found for the primary hypotheses, which stated that higher levels of technostress in counsellors would correlate with low perceived utility of online counselling. However, the secondary hypothesis – that high levels of technostress would correlate with high degrees of discomfort associated with perceived provision of an online counselling service – was supported.

High levels of computer access at home were found among the counsellors. In addition, levels of broadband access at home were high. Given that the computer may be a necessary workplace tool for many counsellors, it is probably not surprising that computer usage levels were significantly high among this group. High levels of self-reported abilities relating to the use of *text-based* computer-mediated communication abilities were reported. However, comparatively lower levels of self-reported ability relating to the use of *non-text-based* computer-mediated communication abilities were reported.

In terms of measuring attitudes towards online counselling, the findings of neutral to slightly positive attitudes towards online counselling among the counsellors were comparatively similar to the neutral attitudes towards online counselling found in similar studies by Wangberg *et al.* (2007) and Mora *et al.* (2008). This research found relatively high levels of agreement among counsellors that they would be willing to try online counselling if it was available to them for free. In comparison, Mora *et al.* (2008) found low levels of willingness to try online counselling if the counsellors received appropriate training.

Implications for current practice

In exploring the development of a counselling service that relies on technology more than physical presence to connect people, technological ability and a willingness to engage with a technology-based service are two variables that will ultimately have a major bearing on the success of the service. This research has revealed high levels of computer access/usage and a widespread willingness to actually engage with and to sample an online counselling service (if it is available for free). Incorporating these findings alongside the overall *neutral* to *slightly positive* attitudes found among the counsellors augurs very well for supporting the establishment of some form of pilot scheme in this area.

There may be significance in the finding that the majority of counsellors chose 'webcam' as their preferred method of online counselling, although 60 per cent of counsellors reporting never having used a webcam before. Research exploring the correlation between reported preferred modalities of online counselling and specific computer-mediated communication skill sets among counsellors is a potential area for further research.

Conclusions

This research indicates that the conditions necessary to establish an online counselling service for substance use issues would appear to be favourable. A lack of negative attitudes towards online counselling and a willingness and ability to engage with an online counselling service remove certain significant blocks to potential service delivery. The online environment has the potential to offer many different aspects of the therapeutic/recovery process within the confines of a single service model. The development of a multi-faceted service model that incorporates various different service components within a single service model could be very effective and also groundbreaking. A service model of this nature could include weekly one-to-one synchronous counselling sessions via the client's preferred modality, regular access to an online peer support group, an online psycho-educational component relating to the nature of addiction and the wheel of change, CBT self-help programmes, asynchronous support and counselling via email and message board systems, downloadable intervention style resources for use at a time of crisis and online diaries to record and chart progress.

References

Carlbring, P. and Andersson, G. (2006). Internet and psychological treatment. How well can they be combined? *Computers in Human Behaviour*, 22, 545–553.

Carroll, K.M. (2008). Computer-assisted delivery of cognitive-behavioural therapy for addiction: A randomized trial of CBT4CBT. *The American Journal of Psychiatry*, 165, 881–888.

Caspar, F. and Berger, T. (2005). The future is bright: How can we optimize online counselling, and how can we know whether we have done so? *The Counseling Psychologist*, 33, 900–909.

Griffiths, M. (2001). Online therapy: A cause for concern? *The Psychologist*, 14, 244–248.

Haberstroh, S., Duffey, T., Evans, M., Gee, R. and Trepal, H. (2007). The experience of online counseling. *Journal of Mental Health Counseling*, 29, 269–282.

Jones, G. and Stokes, A. (2009). *Online Counselling: A handbook for practitioners*. Basingstoke: Palgrave Macmillan.

Lee, J., Kwon, H., Choi, J. and Yang, B. (2007). Cue-exposure therapy to decrease alcohol craving in virtual environment. *Cyberpsychology & Behaviour*, 10, 167–623.

Manley, D.S. (2008). Acceptability and applicability of cue exposure therapy as a relapse prevention intervention for individuals who have substance misuse and mental health problems. *Mental Health and Substance Use: Dual Diagnosis*, 1, 172–184.

Mora, L., Nevid, J. and Chaplin, W. (2008). Psychologist treatment recommendations for Internet-based therapeutic interventions. *Computers in Human Behaviour*, 24, 3052–3062.

Palmer, S. (2000). *Introduction to Counselling and Psychotherapy: The essential guide.* London: Sage.

Reynolds, S., Fanagan, S., Bellerose, D. and Long, J. (2008). *Trends in Treated Problem Drug Use in Ireland, 2001 to 2006.* HRB Trends Series 2 (ISSN No. 2009–0250). Dublin: Health Research Board.

Riva, G. (2005). Virtual reality in psychotherapy. *Cyberpsychology & Behaviour*, 8, 220–230.

Rochlen, A.B., Beretvas, S.N. and Zack, J.S. (2004). The online and face-to-face counselling attitudes scales: A validation study. *Measurement and Evaluation in Counselling and Development*, 37, 95–111.

Rochlen, A.B., Zack, J.S. and Speyer, C. (2004). Online therapy: Review of relevant definitions, debates, and current empirical support. *Journal of Clinical Psychology*, 60, 269–283.

Rosen, L. and Weil, M.M. (1998). Personal TechnoStress Inventory (PTSI). An inventory developed to establish measures of Technostress. Retrieved from: www.csudh.edu/psych/meas.htm.

Schilit, R. and Gomberg, E.S.L. (1991). *Drugs and Behaviour: A sourcebook for the helping professions.* Newbury Park, CA: Sage.

Suler, J.R. (2001). Assessing a person's suitability for online therapy. *Cyberpsychology & Behaviour*, 4, 657–679.

Suler, J.R. (2004). The psychology of text relationships. In R. Kraus, J. Zack, and G. Striker (eds) *Online Counseling: A handbook for mental health professionals* (pp. 19–50). London: Elsevier.

Trepal, H., Haberstroh, S., Duffey, T. and Evans, M. (2007). Considerations and strategies for teaching online counseling skills: Establishing relationships in cyberspace. *Counselor Education and Supervision*, 46 (4), 266–279.

UK Department of Health Evidence Based Clinical Practice Guidelines (2001). *Treatment Choice in Psychological Therapies and Counselling: Evidence based clinical practice guideline* (Product No. 23044). London: Department of Health.

Wangberg, S.C., Gammon, D. and Spitznogle, K. (2007). In the eyes of the beholder: Exploring psychologists' attitudes towards and the use of e-therapy in Norway. *Cyberpsychology & Behaviour*, 10 (3), 418–423.

Wellman, B. and Haythornthwaite, C. (2002). *The Internet in Everyday Life.* Oxford: Blackwell.

Young, K.S. (2005). An empirical examination of client attitudes towards online counselling. *Cybersychology & Behaviour*, 8, 172–177.

Zelvin, E. and Speyer, C.M. (2004). Online counselling skills, part 1. In R. Kraus, J. Zack and G. Striker (eds) *Online Counseling: A handbook for mental health professionals* (pp. 163–180). London: Elsevier.

14

THE PSYCHOLOGY OF CYBERCHONDRIA AND 'CYBERCHONDRIA BY PROXY'

Mary Aiken and Gráinne Kirwan

Chapter summary

The Internet is used by many as a source of medical information; however, the Web has the potential to increase anxiety when employed as a diagnostic procedure. This study sought to identify the motivation behind health-related search online. A new distinct cohort emerged: those who experience anxiety when conducting health-related search for others – Cyberchondria by Proxy (CbP). The research methodology consisted of focus groups and psychometric measures. Results indicated that health-related search behaviour is impacted by technology; additionally, there is a significant positive correlation between anxiety when searching for medical information about the self and searching for medical information about others. This finding is relevant for healthcare professionals, particularly regarding patient care and management.

Introduction

The Internet may appear to offer valuable medical information, and intuitive diagnostic websites can provide information regarding symptoms that are concerning the user. However, 'the Web has the potential to increase anxieties of people who have little or no medical training, especially when web search is employed as a diagnostic proceedure' (White and Horvitz, 2009, p. 23).

Cyberchondria – anxiety resulting from health-related search online – is an increasingly differentiated activity (Belling, 2006; Feldman, 2000; Fox *et al.*, 2000; Lewis, 2006; Ravdin, 2008; White and Horvitz, 2009). This chapter will explore the relationship between those who search health-related material for themselves online and those who search for others (Fox *et al.*, 2000; Lewis, 2006; White and Horvitz, 2009). There is a relationship between the somatoform disorder Munchausen's, and Munchausen's Syndrome by Proxy (MSbP) (Day and Moseley,

2010), that is, gratification resulting from medical attention obtained 'by proxy' (Criddle, 2010; Day and Moseley, 2010). This chapter examines whether there is a relationship between anxiety resulting from search for self (cyberchondria), and anxiety resulting from search for others (Cyberchondria by Proxy).

Knowledge, empowerment, support, reassurance and altruism may all be considered positive aspects of health-related search online (see, for example, Adar and Huberman, 2000; Bastian, 2003; Sillence and Briggs, 2007); however, some literature indicates that anxiety is likely to be a consequence (see, for example, Belling, 2006; Lewis, 2006; Ravdin, 2008; White and Horvitz, 2009). There is a relationship between health anxiety and hypochondria (Asmundson *et al.*, 2001; Salkovskis *et al.*, 2002). Health-related search online can lead to escalation of this activity and anxiety (White and Horvitz, 2009) and evidence of an association between anxiety, hypochondria and cyberchondria will be explored. The role of somatoform disorders (Asmundson *et al.*, 2001; Criddle, 2010; Day and Moseley, 2010), doctor-patient relationship (Belling, 2006; Lewis, 2006), technology underlying search (White and Horvitz, 2009) and self-diagnosis online (Belling, 2006; Lewis, 2006; Ravdin, 2006; White and Horvitz, 2009) will also be considered.

Health anxiety

Asmundson *et al.* (2001) describe *health anxiety* as 'fears and beliefs, based on interpretations, or perhaps more often, misinterpretations, of bodily signs and symptoms as being indicative of a serious illness' (p. 4). The highest scores on self-report measures of state anxiety have been recorded in those awaiting the results of medical tests or diagnoses (Asmundson *et al.*, 2001). Many severe cases of health anxiety meet diagnostic criteria for *hypochondriasis* as per the American Psychiatric Association's *Diagnostic and Statistical Manual* (currently in its fourth edition, text-revised, or DSM-IV-TR) or the World Health Organisation *International Classification of Disesases* (currently in its tenth edition, or ICD-10). This condition is characterised by multiple and stubbornly held complaints of physical illnesss although typically no evidence of such illness can be found (Carson *et al.*, 2000).

Patients with hypochondriasis are likely to be avid readers of magazines and books on medical topics (Carson *et al.*, 2000). The Internet provides another source of medical and pseudo-medical information, easily attainable by those who suffer from hypochondria and other potentially related phenomena such as cyberchondria, described as 'unfounded escalation of concerns about common symptomatology, based on the review of search results and literature on the Web' (White and Horvitz, 2009, p. 23). Escalation from common symptoms to serious health concerns may lead to unnecessary anxiety (White and Horvitz, 2009). 'In this age of cyberchondria ... medical consumers appear at the clinician's doorstep having researched their symptoms on the Internet ... the presence of symptoms with no medical explanation may be explained by somatisation' (Ravdin, 2008, p. 912). *Somatoform disorders* involve presentation of bodily symptoms suggestive of medical problems for which no organic basis can be found (Carson *et al.*, 2000).

One of the earliest mentions of somatoform disorders online occurred when Feldman (2000) coined the terms *Virtual Factitious Disorder* and *Munchausen by Internet*, referring to a form of factitious disorder deception online. Kanaan (in an interview with Kleeman, 2011) argues that Munchausen by Internet may, in fact, make sense; sympathy from hundreds of people online may be more powerful than sympathy from one person in a white coat. While interesting, the validity of these 'syndromes' must be questioned (for example, Smith *et al.*, 2002, found that only a minority of the so–called 'worried well' fitted the classic definition of a somatisation disorder).

Ranking algorithms

Health search technology affects information dissemination and can cause unnecessary anxiety (White and Horvitz, 2009). Currently health-related word search is a flawed diagnostic process (White and Horvitz, 2009) and is based on advertising search models. Results are ranked by frequency of search, and users have a tendency to escalate to search extreme results, thus impacting on rankings (White and Horvitz, 2009). White and Horvitz (2010) later investigated the possibility of an escalation prediction model. Nevertheless, at least one search provider (Google) has begun to utilise algorithms that recognise symptom-related health queries, providing a list of health conditions that may be associated with the specific symptom. A link below such a list directs the searcher to an information page (Google, 2012), where they are advised that the search results are not a diagnosis, and that they should seek medical advice if they have concerns.

White and Horvitz (2009) reviewed representative crawls of some 40 million web pages, processing them for medical search queries, and manually analysing 10,000 pages. Surprisingly high rates of linkage of rare diseases, for example 'brain tumour', to common symptoms, such as 'headache', were detected. White and Horvitz (2009) also carried out a survey asking who participants' health-related searches were primarily for. Results indicated that 58 per cent of search was for the self and 42 per cent of search was for others ($N = 515$). This finding is consistent with the work of Fox *et al.* (2000), and is of particular significance for the research outlined in this chapter.

Cyberchondria by Proxy (CbP)

Fox *et al.* (2000) reported that 57 per cent of online health information seekers claimed they looked for information for others. A series of interviews revealed that participants searched the Internet not just for themselves but also for relatives and friends (Lewis, 2006). Sillence and Briggs (2007) support this finding. Research to date on cyberchondria is limited, with little research into underlying motivation to diagnose others online, despite recurring reports (Fox *et al.*, 2000; Lewis, 2006; White and Horvitz, 2009). Hence there may exist a gap in the literature requiring further study. Hypothetically those searching symptomatology by proxy, could arguably be manifesting Cyberchondria by Proxy type behaviour.

Day and Moseley (2010) report similarities between Munchausen's and MSbP. In terms of gain, MSbP has been described as an 'abuse in which a caretaker . . . fabricates and/or induces illness in a child or proxy for the purpose of obtaining emotional or psychological benefit' (Day and Moseley, 2010, p. 14). The goal of this behaviour is 'to assume the sick role by proxy' (Day and Moseley, 2010, p. 14). Criddle (2010) supports this view, stating that the aim of the MSbP perpetrator 'is to draw recognition . . . an insatiable need for social and emotional gain' (p. 49). It is, however, notable that external incentives for MSbP type behaviour, such as economic gain, are absent (Day and Moseley, 2010).

Over-reporting of symptoms is an identifying trait of MSbP perpetrators; other factors may include a family history of frequent and unusual illness behaviour (Day and Moseley, 2010). This view is supported by Criddle (2010), describing MSbP as a potentially 'lifelong generational disorder' (p. 49), arguing that many MSbP victims can develop into Munchausen syndrome patients; the achieving gratification through illness behaviour may become rooted or learned. The majority of MSbP abusers are women: 'mothers and other women in a guardian role are by far the most frequent reported perpetrators' (Criddle, 2010, p. 49). Additionally, Criddle (2010) notes that MSbP abusers enjoy 'showing off their medical knowledge', escaping from 'other responsibilities' and having a purpose 'doing . . . important and interesting things' (p. 50).

Criddle (2010) argues that all parents 'present somewhere on a continuum of medical neediness' (p. 52), pointing out that many worry, are hypervigilant, misinterpret and exaggerate behaviours; however, illness fabrication lies at the extreme edge of the spectrum. Criddle (2010) describes MSbP as 'an escalating disorder' (p. 48), stating that 'the goal of the perpetrator is to create symptoms'. This raises the question as to when extensive medical search for others (CbP), symptom search, symptom cluster creation and escalation to review of serious medical content might become extreme.

Health search behaviour online

McDaid and Park (2011) report the findings of a large-scale survey ($N = 12,000$) that revealed that four out of five Australians turn to the Web for health information. Nearly half of those surveyed used the search engine Google to make a self-diagnosis.

Asmundson et al. (2001) note that concerns regarding relatives and friends can cause considerable anxiety. Health-related search for dependants and relatives (Fox et al., 2000; Lewis 2006; White and Horvitz, 2009), combined with the probability of escalated anxiety (White and Horvitz, 2009), is a cause for concern. Cyberchondria may be a maladaptive strategy to self-manage health in a changing society (Belling, 2006; Lewis, 2006; Ravdin, 2008) or an avoidance of the cost/disruption associated with formalised medical consultation.

Health information seeking online may fall in the abnormal psychology category of somatoform disorders, such as hypochondria typically characterised by primary and secondary gains (Asmundson *et al.*, 2001). However, the current DSM-5 work group reports that patients with hypochondriasis may fall into two distinct sub-groups; going forward, one group may be subsumed under a new diagnosis of *Somatic Symptom Disorder* (SSD) and the second group under *Illness Anxiety Disorder* (IAD); notably, online symptom checking has been considered (American Psychiatric Association, 2012). This recent development does, in fact, support an argument for the impact of technology on health information seeking online and associated anxiety. The question is: what is the extent and nature of that impact?

Symptom search may be facilitated by compulsive, rewarding and engaging technologies (Meerkerk *et al.*, 2009). Symptom search may also be related to protective/preventative carer instinct (Lewis, 2006). Anxiety may also be a predictive factor, or it may be an undesirable side-effect of search online (White and Horvitz, 2009).

The current research examines the relationship between cyberchondria and CbP-type behaviour. The primary hypothesis predicts that there will be a correlation between anxiety induced by medical search online for self (cyberchondria) and for others (CbP). A secondary hypothesis queries whether there is a correlation between anxiety, hypochondria and cyberchondria.

Method

This study investigated the hypotheses using focus groups. Participants also completed two psychometric measures and a survey. Four focus groups, each comprising five participants, were completed.

Participants

Twenty participants were recruited using local advertising and snowball sampling. Seven males and thirteen females took part in the study (mean age = 34.65, *SD* = 11.061, range = 19–58 years).

Measures/materials

The research tested the primary hypothesis by means of a survey questionaire, along with qualitative data collected from the focus group discussions. The research tested the secondary hypothesis by means of two measures: the Becks Anxiety Inventory and the Whiteley Index, which established anxiety and hypochondria measures respectively. A prompt script supported data collection during focus group sessions.

Procedure

Candidates were screened for severe anxiety and hypochondria by means of the Becks Inventory and the Whiteley index. No participant was found to have clinically concerning levels of anxiety or hypochondriasis. Participants then completed the survey questionnaire before taking part in the focus group. Strict ethical guidelines were observed.

Results

Search for Self (SFS) and Search for Others (SFO)

Search for health-related information for self online was undertaken by 55 per cent of participants ($n = 11$); 55 per cent of participants ($n = 11$) searched for others; 30 per cent of participants ($n = 6$) searched for information both for themselves and for others, and of that cohort the majority ($n = 5$, 83.3 per cent) searched for others who were relatives or dependants.

Search for Self (SFS) and Search for Others (SFO) were investigated by means of a chi-square test. Since the analysis showed that 75 per cent of the cells had an expected frequency of less than 5, the appropriate statistical test was Fisher's Exact Probability. The relationship between SFS and SFO was: χ^2 (1, $N = 20$) = .002, exact $p = .964$). The value of Cramer's V was .010 ($p = .964$).

Cyberchondria and Cyberchondria by Proxy

A number of questions in the survey measured levels of anxiety induced as a result of health-related search for self, and search for others online. There was a significant positive correlation between anxiety resulting from search for self online and anxiety resulting from search for others online ($r = .500$, $N = 20$, $p = .025$, two tailed); see Table 14.1 for correlation statistics.

Additionally significant correlations were noted between anxiety resulting from search for self online scores and review of serious content online ($r = .615$, $N = 20$, $p = .004$, two-tailed), anxiety resulting from search for self online scores and finding online search compulsive ($r = .564$, $N = 20$, $p = .010$, two-tailed), and anxiety resulting from search for self online scores and the Whiteley score ($r = .541$, $N = 20$, $p = .014$, two-tailed). Moreover significant correlations were noted between anxiety resulting from search for others online scores and review of serious content online ($r = .695$, $N = 20$, $p = .001$, two-tailed) and between anxiety resulting from search for others online scores and finding online search compulsive ($r = .482$, $N = 20$, $p = .031$, two-tailed).

Prediction of cyberchondria

No association was found between Becks scores and scores reporting anxiety resulting from search for self online, ($r = .211$, $N = 20$, $p = .372$, two-tailed); similarly no association was found between Becks scores and scores reporting anxiety resulting from search for others online ($r = -.306$, $N = 20$, $p = .190$, two-tailed). There was, however, a positive correlation between Whiteley scores and anxiety induced by search for self ($r = .541$, $N = 20$, $p = .014$, two-tailed).

TABLE 14.1 Anxiety and health related search online correlation matrix

		Anxiety search self online	Anxiety search others online	Review serious content online	Rate online diagnosis	Online compulsive	Online interesting	Whiteley
Anxiety search self online	Pearson correlation	1	.500*	.615**	.309	.564**	.344	.541*
	Sig. (2-tailed)		.025	.004	.185	.010	.137	.014
Anxiety search others online	Pearson correlation	.500*	1	.695**	.148	.482*	.012	.261
	Sig. (2-tailed)	.025		.001	.532	.031	.960	.267
Review serious content online	Pearson correlation	.615**	.695**	1	.535*	.531*	.385	.292
	Sig. (2-tailed)	.004	.001		.015	.016	.094	.212
Rate online diagnosis	Pearson correlation	.309	.148	.535*	1	.486*	.550*	-.026
	Sig. (2-tailed)	.185	.532	.015		.030	.012	.912
Online compulsive	Pearson correlation	.564**	.482*	.531*	.486*	1	.341	.256
	Sig. (2-tailed)	.010	.031	.016	.030		.141	.276
Online interesting	Pearson correlation	.344	.012	.385	.550*	.341	1	.446*
	Sig. (2-tailed)	.137	.960	.094	.012	.141		.049
Whiteley	Pearson correlation	.541*	.261	.292	-.026	.256	.446*	1
	Sig. (2-tailed)	.014	.267	.212	.912	.276	.049	
	N	20	20	20	20	20	20	20

Note: * Correlation is significant at the .05 level (2-tailed). ** Correlation is significant at the .01 level (2-tailed).

Becks and Whiteley measures

There was a significant positive correlation between the Becks Inventory and Whiteley scores ($r = .587$, $N = 20$, $p = .006$, two-tailed). Becks scores were in the mild anxiety category for 90 per cent of participants; 10 per cent ($n = 2$) fell in the moderate anxiety category. No participants met the official criteria for hypochondria according to the Whiteley scale.

Focus group analysis

Participants in the focus groups reported use of online search for dependants, while also reporting escalation of health concerns following medical search online for self and for dependants. Economic motives were expressed in terms of search for others – for example, avoidance of cost of medical consultations presenting a possible primary gain. Some expressed concerns regarding attempts to diagnose online, particularly concerning minors, an indication of concern regarding search by proxy. Additionally, participants reported curiosity, temptation and interest regarding medical information seeking for self and others online. Participants with a medical family background reported resisting temptation to search.

The focus group findings included some cautionary tales. For example, a focus group participant reported an incident in which her partner had been given medication by a relative who had searched online, and the dose provided had been an overdose.

Participants reported anxiety and concern regarding health-related search online, with reviewing severe conditions such as cancer reported as increasing anxiety. Participants noted that medical search online provided limited reassurance but that medical knowledge gained online could be powerful. A number of participants indicated that search/printouts could speed up diagnosis, referring to search as a 'second or third opinion'. Participants acknowledged that search could be stressful for doctors; however, negative feedback was reported regarding presentation of search to doctors, with practitioner attitudes described as 'disdainful', 'dismissive' and 'irritated'. Participants supported the use of chat rooms for medical exchange,

TABLE 14.2 Thematic analysis of focus group discussion content

Major overlapping themes	Minor overlapping themes	Subject specific themes
Availability	Reassurance	Doctor-patient relationship
Anxiety	Empowerment	Intervention
Trust		Medicating
Cost		Chat forums
		Future
Curiosity/information seeking	Escalation	Diagnostics

stating positives as altruistic shared experience. Regulation, filtering, monitoring and policing were all mentioned as key requirements of online health information services of the future.

Thematic analysis of qualitative data captured in focus group discussion sessions is reported in Table 14.2. Following analysis, themes were reported under three main headings: major overlapping themes; minor overlapping themes; and subject specific themes.

Discussion

There was a significant positive correlation between anxiety resulting from search for self online and anxiety resulting from search for others online, thus supporting the primary hypothesis. This finding is reflected in the focus group discussions where participants reported use of online search for dependents (Fox et al., 2000; Lewis, 2006; White and Horvitz, 2009). Participants also reported escalation of health concerns following medical search online for self (White and Horvitz, 2009) and for dependants.

Significant correlations were noted in a cluster of co-morbid tendencies: between anxiety resulting from search for self online scores, and review of serious content online, a feature of cyberchondria (White and Horvitz, 2009). This finding was supported in the focus group discussions. Positive correlations were found between anxiety resulting from search for self online, searching for others online and finding online search compulsive. This compulsive aspect perhaps provides insight into intermittent reinforcement aspects of search online and potential motivation to engage in this activity.

A positive correlation was found between anxiety resulting from search for self online scores and the Whiteley score consistent with current findings regarding hypochondriacal tendencies online (American Psychiatric Association, 2012). Moreover significant correlations were noted between anxiety resulting from search for others online scores and review of serious content online, potentially a characteristic of Cyberchondria by Proxy type behaviour.

Findings indicated a significant positive correlation between the Becks Anxiety Inventory and the Whiteley index; however, no association was found between Becks scores and scores reporting anxiety resulting from search for self or for others online. Therefore in terms of the second hypothesis, there would appear to be no relation between anxiety as measured by Becks, and anxiety resulting from search for self or search for others online. There was, however, a positive correlation between Whiteley scores and anxiety induced by search for self, thus indicating a possible association between hypochondria and cyberchondria, partially supporting the second hypothesis.

Participants acknowledged that search could be stressful for doctors (Belling, 2006). However, negative feedback was reported following presentation of search to doctors, a finding supported by Belling (2006) and McDaid and Park (2011).

Implications of the research

There are implications regarding these findings from a theoretical perspective. First, primary and secondary gains regarding somatoform disorders have been investigated (Asmundson *et al.*, 2001; Criddle, 2010; Day and Moseley, 2010), but little or no research has been conducted into gains associated with cyberchondriac or CbP-type behaviour, and this area requires further research. Second, findings support an association between hypochondria and cyberchondria, and further investigation of this relationship is required.

In terms of practical implications, patients are now presenting at medical practices with a quantity of information sourced online, with evidence suggesting that some practitioners are struggling to cope with this (Belling, 2006). A greater understanding of the impact of technology on human behaviour is required; in addition, the ranking algorithms that underlie search appear to compound the issue (White and Horvitz, 2009). Arguably, a substantial evidence-based study identifying the association between search presentation and consequential negative mental health impact is required. Cyberchondriac activity 'by proxy' is a cause for great concern, given the involvement of dependent and therefore vulnerable populations.

In terms of overall implications of this research, some key areas have emerged. First, underlying motives to search for health-related information online for self and for others require investigation. Second, technologically facilitated challenges to medical opinion and knowledge empowerment (Bastian, 2003) are problematic for medical practitioners (Belling, 2006). A limitation of the present study was the one-dimensional 'patient only' perspective. It would be useful to quantify the problem from a medical practitioner or frontline medical healthcare staff perspective. Finally, a much larger quantitative study is required to support the findings of this study as reported in this chapter; interesting variables such as gender, age, socio-economic status, ethnicity, culture and familial/generational influence could be explored. Criddle (2010) notes a greater female incidence of Munchausen's Syndrome by Proxy. This potential gender difference warrants further investigation.

Conclusion

This research addresses a gap in the literature in terms of identifying a cohort who search for self and search for others 'by proxy' (Fox *et al.*, 2000; Lewis, 2006; White and Horvitz, 2009) and establishing a common measurable trait, anxiety. Whereas a number of interesting motives were found regarding search for others – information seeking, availability, knowledge empowerment, economic factors and so forth – no definitive conclusions were reached in this regard, and separate research is required to specifically address motivation to search. Importantly, challenging professionals, compulsive medical information seeking, escalation and symptom checking or creation were identified in this study. Interestingly, these traits are also some of the characteristics of acute somatoform disorders. Investigation of this link-age is not within the scope of this study but may be an important component of fully understanding this phenomenon. It is probable that cyberpsychologists are well placed to undertake further research in this area, which will likely be of interest and importance to a wide audience in the applied psychology and medical practitioner communities.

References

Adar, E. and Huberman, B.A. (2000). Free riding on Gnutella. *First Monday*, 5 (10).

American Psychiatric Association (2012). *DSM-5: The Future of Psychiatric Development.* Retrieved from: www.dsm5.org/ProposedRevision/Pages/proposedrevision.aspx?rid =10#.

Asmundson, G.J., Taylor, S. and Cox, B.J. (eds) (2001). *Health Anxiety Clinical and Research Perspectives on Hypochondriasis and Related Conditions.* Chichester: John Wiley & Sons.

Bastian, H. (2003). Just how demanding can we get before we blow it? *BMJ*, 326, 1277–1278.

Belling, C. (2006). Hypochondriac hermeneutics: Medicine and the anxiety of interpretation. *Literature and Medicine*, 25, 2, 376–401.

Carson, R.C., Mineka, S. and Butcher, J.N. (2000). *Abnormal Psychology and Modern Life.* Boston, MA: Allyn & Bacon.

Criddle. R. (2010). Monsters in the closet: Munchausen syndrome by proxy. *Critical Care Nurse*, 30, 46–55.

Day, D.O. and Moseley, R.L. (2010). Munchausen by proxy syndrome. *Journal of Forensic Psychology Practice*, 10, 13–36.

Feldman, M.D. (2000). Munchausen by Internet: Detecting factitious illness and crisis on the Internet. *Southern Journal of Medicine*, 93, 669–672.

Fox, S., Rainee, L., Horrigan, J.B., Lenhart, A., Spooner, T. and Carter, C. (2000). *Trust and Privacy Online: The Internet life report.* Washington, DC: The Pew Internet and American life Project.

Google (2012). *Symptom Search.* Inside Search. Retrieved from: http://support.google.com/ websearch/bin/answer.py?hl=enandp=g_sympandanswer=2364942.

Kleeman, J. (2011). Sick note: Faking illness online. 26 February. Retrieved from: www. guardian.co.uk/lifeandstyle/2011/feb/26/faking-illness-online-munchausen.

Lewis, T. (2006). Seeking health information on the Internet: Lifestyle choice or bad attack of cyberchondria. *Media Culture Society*, 28 (4): 521–539.

McDaid, D. and Park, A. (2011). Online health: Untangling the Web. Retrieved from Bupa Health Pulse Research: www.bupa.com/media/44806/online_20health_20-_20untangling_20the_20web.pdf.

Meerkerk, G., Van Den Eijnden, R., Vermulst, A. and Garretsen, H. (2009). The Compulsive Internet Use Scale (CIUS). *CyberPsychology & Behaviour*, 12 (1), 1–6.

Ravdin, L.D. (2008). Guide for clinicians in the age of cyberchondria. *Journal of the International Neuropsychological Society*, 14, 912–916.

Salkovskis, P.M., Rimes, K.A., Warwick, H.M.C. and Clark, D.M. (2002). The Health Anxiety Inventory: Development and validation of scales for the measurement of health anxiety and hypochondriasis. *Psychological Medicine*, 32, 843–853.

Sillence, E. and Briggs, P. (2007). Examining the role of the Internet in health behaviour. In A. Joinson, K. McKenna, T. Postmes and U. Reips (eds) *The Oxford Handbook of Internet Psychology* (pp. 347–360). New York: Oxford University Press.

Smith, R.C., Gardiner, J.C., Lyles, J.S., Johnson, M., Rost, K.M., Luo, Z., Goddeeris, J., Lein, C., Given, C.W. and Given, B. (2002). Minor acute illness: A preliminary research report on the 'worried well'. *Journal of Family Practice*, 51, 24–29.

White, R. and Horvitz, E. (2009). Cyberchondria: Studies of the escalation of medical concerns in web search. *ACM Transactions on Information Systems*, 27 (4), 23:1–23:37.

White, R.W. and Horvitz, E. (2010). Web to world: Predicting transitions from self-diagnosis to the pursuit of local medical assistance in web search. *AMIA Annual Symposium proceedings/AMIA Symposium. AMIA Symposium, 2010*, 882–886. Retrieved from: www.ncbi.nlm.nih.gov/pubmed/21347105.

15

ATTITUDES TO COMPUTERISED PSYCHOTHERAPY

A survey of psychotherapists

Dean McDonnell, Brendan Rooney and Cliona Flood

Chapter summary

This study explores psychotherapists' attitudes to computerised psychotherapy. A total of 101 psychotherapists (thirty-one males and seventy females) completed an online measure of self-reported attitudes to computerised therapy, computers, the Internet and synchronous forms of communication. In addition, participants indicated their willingness to use computerised therapy, and provided some demographic information. Results revealed that generally attitudes to computerised therapy were positive. Such attitudes were significantly more positive for younger therapists and unrelated to therapeutic approach. Attitudes to computerised therapy were also positively related to intention to use such therapy, yet it was not associated with the belief that such therapy would be successful. These findings are indicative of the complex nature of self-reported attitudes and behaviour, especially in the political and cultural context of psychotherapeutic services.

Introduction

The ubiquity of scientific and technological developments has revolutionised many areas of human existence. In this context, it is perhaps unsurprising that surveyed psychotherapists believe the delivery of mental health services is likely to expand to some form of computerised delivery in the future (Norcross *et al.*, 2002). This presents health services and clients with a very exciting prospect, given a previously identified shortage of psychotherapists and long waiting list times (Haggarty *et al.*, 2012; London School of Economics, 2006). In addition, research demonstrates that clients *want* computerised therapy. A UK-based survey among potential users for self-help psychotherapies found that 91 per cent of the participants wanted access to some form of self-help computer application (Graham *et al.*, 2001; Zdziechowska *et al.*, 2012).

Currently such systems range anywhere from specifically designed software involving components of artificial intelligence to generic web-based forums. Thus it is perhaps helpful to talk of a spectrum of technology and psychotherapy: at one end, therapy is entirely computerised and involves no contact with a psychotherapist; at the other, technology merely supports communication between a psychotherapist and client. Both extreme ends of this spectrum bring with them support and criticisms from the limited number of researchers and findings exploring the area. However, given the speed at which technology is developing, research exploring the use of such technology in psychotherapy can quickly become outdated, and the artificial intelligence systems that are the subject of the currently available research are less advanced than what might be currently possible.

The use and evaluation of artificial intelligence (AI) systems in psychotherapy began with programmes such as Natural Language Programmes, designed with simple grammatical rules that would identify key words or phrases in a typed sentence and then respond based on syntactical structure. For example, if an individual was to say 'I am feeling very lonely', the program would identify that 'I am' is typically followed by a description of the current state of mind, and in turn would reply 'How long have you been feeling very lonely?'

Although these AI systems had no intrinsic intelligence and could not adapt to the flow of a conversation, they began to be used like a personal interactive diary, encouraging individuals to explore areas of thought that previously might not have been looked into and operating on the principles of free association (Turkle, 2007). However, research demonstrates that such computerised therapy programmes, involving no direct contact with a therapist, are associated with an enormous drop-out rate (Farvolden *et al.*, 2005; Marks *et al.*, 2007) when compared to face-to-face contact with a therapist. Even minimal contact during computerised therapy programmes has been shown to be successful (Anderson *et al.*, 2012).

The use of technology to merely support therapist driven sessions has also been criticised. While some research suggests that the use of Computer Mediated Communication (CMC) is superior to face-to-face (Jonassen *et al.*, 1999; Smith *et al.*, 2011), others criticise its lack of context and non-verbal cues (Liu, 2002; Rovai, 2000). Importantly, these strengths and weaknesses also vary, depending on whether the CMC is synchronous (e.g. video chat, instant messaging) or asynchronous (e.g. email, SMS).

In moving towards a resolution to the outlined debate, it is important to recognise that technology brings with it both advantages and disadvantages to therapy. Thus using both traditional and technological systems for therapy may offer a way to preserve the strengths of both styles and offset the weaknesses in each. In support of this idea, studies suggest that the most effective form of therapy is a hybrid model involving an active combination of computerised therapy and traditional face-to-face therapy (Anderson *et al.*, 2012; Barak *et al.*, 2008; Conn *et al.*, 2009; Titov *et al.*, 2008). These models allow for therapist supervision, but also they give the client the element of control over their own therapy sessions. In addition, Proudfoot (2004) demonstrates that the drop-out rate of the hybrid therapy is much the same as face-to-face therapy, and further research suggests that self-disclosure can often be easier through a computer (Veletsianos and Kimmons, 2013).

Although research before the year 2000 indicated that there was much excitement regarding the prospect of such hybrid technology-supported psychotherapy, relatively few psychotherapists use it (Howell and Muller, 2000; Werner, 1995). There are a number of potential reasons that computerised or computer supported therapy has not been fully integrated into already existing systems – for example, AI technology is still in its infancy, and thus there are numerous associated technological limitations (Marks et al., 2007; Yampolskiy, 2012), including appropriate emotion detection and response issues, which cannot be overlooked.

It is possible that the greatest resistance to the use of technology in therapy comes from therapists themselves. This resistance might be due to a reluctance to embrace a new method of therapy (Howell and Muller, 2000) or perhaps to technophobia – an aversion, dislike or suspicion of technology (Dinello, 2005; Miclea et al., 2010). It is also important to note that therapists may have strong concerns for the relatively unexplored ethical issues that come with handing over therapy to an automated process.

Attitudes of therapists

From the points above we can see that there are a number of issues that might be related to the low levels of technology-supported therapy. And it is important to note that the true barrier to the use of this new therapy is most likely a combination of several issues outlined above (Marks et al., 2009). However, research exploring these potential reasons is scarce, and little is known as to why therapists have yet to fully embrace computerised therapy.

In one of the few studies exploring this issue, Wangberg et al. (2007) measured the attitudes towards the use of asynchronous methods of communication for therapeutic purposes of 854 psychologists registered to the Norwegian Psychological Association. Their key finding was that the theoretical stance of a therapist is a high predictor of positive attitude towards various forms of computerised therapy. It was found that therapists practising psychodynamic orientated therapies were least likely to approve of computerised therapy, whereas therapists practising cognitive theoretical models were far more supportive. Wangberg et al. (2007) also report that younger therapists were more likely to have a positive attitude towards e-therapy. This is supported by Cotton and Gupta (2004), who report that individuals using technology for health-related activities are usually young, single, highly educated and female. However, Klein and Cook (2010) report no differences in demographic variables between those who prefer to use online mental health services in comparison to those who prefer traditional face-to-face mental health services.

Wangberg *et al.* (2007) report that previous experience using technology and CMC can also be positively related to attitudes to e-therapy. Osborn and Flood (2013) explored the feasibility of an online counselling service for individuals suffering from substance abuse issues. They report that counsellors' attitudes towards the use of online counselling for substance abuse were negatively correlated with technostress, which is negative feeling associated with the use of new technologies (Osborn and Flood, 2013). Thus the more technostress a counsellor experienced, the more negative their attitude to online counselling.

The current study

The current study aims to explore therapists' attitudes to computerised therapy. To this end, the current study uses an online questionnaire measuring attitudes to computerised therapy and its relationship to measures of other attitudes, such as attitude to computers, the Internet and technology-supported synchronous communication. The current study also explores how attitudes are related to various demographic variables and therapists' theoretical approach.

Hypotheses

H1 There will be a significant relationship between therapists' attitude to computerised therapy and demographic variables such as age and education

H2 There will be a significant relationship between therapists' attitude to compu-terised therapy and other measures such as attitude to computers, attitude to the Internet and attitude to synchronous forms of technology supported communication.

H3 There will be a significant relationship between therapists' attitude to computerised therapy and the self-reported likelihood that they will use such therapy.

H4 There will be a significant difference between therapist approach groups in attitude to computerised therapy and the other variables listed above.

H5 There will be a significant difference between those who think computerised therapy will work and those who do not think so, in terms of the dependent measures.

Method

Design

The current study uses a quantitative correlational design to explore the relation-ships between attitudes to online therapy, to computers, to the Internet, to synchronous and asynchronous communication and whether or not the therapists would use AI. Participants' therapeutic approach and some demographic variables are also explored.

Materials

Attitude to online therapy

An adapted version of the e-therapy scale (Wangberg *et al.*, 2007) was used to measure participants' attitudes to computerised therapy. This scale originally consisted of sixteen items – eight positive and eight negative – rated using a five-point Likert scale. The original scale was translated from Norwegian into English. The suitability of this translation was confirmed by translating the English version back into Norwegian and comparing with the original. Four questions were removed from the scale in order to preserve participants' responses to a set of open-ended qualitative questions (analysis of these data will be presented elsewhere), and a further question was removed later to increase internal consistency. Tests of internal consistency on the remaining eleven items revealed acceptable levels of reliability with the current sample (α = .68).

Attitude to computers

Participants' attitudes towards computers were measured using the Computer Attitude Scale (CAS) (Liaw, 2002). This scale comprises sixteen items that explore participants' opinions and beliefs about computers and their use. Participants were asked to indicate their level of agreement with each item on a five-point Likert scale. This scale demonstrated acceptable levels of internal consistency with the original sample (α = .91).

Attitude to the Internet

Similarly, participants' attitudes towards the Internet were measured using the Web Attitude Scale (WAS) (Liaw, 2002). This scale also comprises sixteen five-point Likert scale items that explore participants' opinions and beliefs about the Internet and its use. This scale demonstrated acceptable levels of internal consistency with the original sample (α = .93).

Attitude to synchronous communication

Participants who reported using synchronous communication, such as telephone calls, video-conferencing and instant messaging, were asked to indicate the perceived usefulness of such communication within different areas of their work (e.g. client consultation, teaching and administration). The usefulness of synchronous communication for each area was indicated on a five-point Likert scale with higher scores indicative of greater usefulness. Tests of internal consistency demonstrated adequate levels of reliability with the current sample (α = .86).

Other measures

In order to test the main research question, participants were asked whether they would be willing to use AI in therapy and whether they believed other therapists would. These items were each rated using a five-point Likert scale, with higher scores indicating more likelihood of using AI. Participants were also to indicate in a simple Yes/No response whether they believed AI in therapy 'would work'. Participants were offered the opportunity to elaborate on these responses using open-ended questions.

In addition to the measures and questions above, demographic information was collected from participants about their age, gender, qualifications and the therapeutic approach that best represents their work. The entire questionnaire was piloted with a non-therapist group so as to measure the time to complete and identify any potential communication issues. Following this it was reviewed by a therapist who offered further advice on phrasing.

Participants

Participants were recruited using the mailing lists of professional counselling and psychotherapy organisations. A total of 101 therapists (thirty-one male and seventy female) completed the questionnaire. Participants' mean age was 50.93 years (SD = 8.48 years).

Participants were asked to indicate their highest level of qualifications (see Table 15.1) and the therapeutic approach that was closest to their style of therapy, from a number of choices (e.g. Cognitive Behavioural Therapy, Behavioural, Humanistic, Psychodynamic, Psychoanalytic, Eclectic). Many participants chose more than one approach, and these responses where recoded into the 'Eclectic' category. This meant that other categories represented therapists who selected only one approach as the one that was closest to their own. Approaches that were selected very infrequently were amalgamated into a single 'other approaches' category. The resulting breakdown revealed fifty-nine therapists using an eclectic approach, twenty-three using only a humanistic approach, eight using only a cognitive behavioural therapy approach and ten using another approach (e.g. psychoanalysis or behavioural).

TABLE 15.1 Self-reported qualifications of participants

Self-reported highest level of education/qualification	Frequency
Higher certificate	5
Bachelor degree (Ordinary)	3
Bachelor degree (Honours)	41
Masters degree	46
Doctorate degree	1
Did not report	5

Procedure

Before beginning the questionnaire, potential participants were given a brief overview of the study, its purpose and other information to support informed consent. Participants were continuously reminded of the right to withdraw from the research. After participants completed the questions designed to measure attitude to online therapy, computers, the Internet, synchronous and asynchronous communication, they read a description of how AI could be used in therapy and the positive aspects to such use. Following this, participants were asked to respond to the outcome measure questions. They were thanked for their participation, debriefed and offered contact details should they have further questions.

Results

Mean attitude scores were calculated on each of the measures for each participant (see Table 15.2). When dealing with large samples, parametric analyses are robust to violations of the assumption of normality (Glass et al., 1972). Given the current sample size, parametric analysis was deemed appropriate for all dependent variables. Various descriptive statistics for demographic variables (such as age, qualifications and therapeutic approach) were reported earlier, in the Participants section of this chapter. In addition, descriptive statistics were generated for attitude and outcome measures and are displayed in Table 15.2.

Descriptive results demonstrate that mean attitudes to computers (4.25/5) and the Internet (4.29/5) were very positive, and although attitudes to online therapy were lower, they were still positive, above the midpoint (3.24/5). However, interestingly, therapists did not demonstrate the same mean positivity to synchronous forms of computer supported communication (2.16/5). In line with attitudes to online therapy, therapists indicated that they were somewhat in favour of using technology and computerised forms of therapy in their work (3.26/5), but in general perceived their peers as less likely to use such systems (2.64), yet this is an approximately neutral response. Finally, perhaps in line with these findings, 73 per cent of therapists (55/75) reported that they believed that this type

TABLE 15.2 Descriptive statistics (mean and standard deviations) for dependent variables

Variable	N	Mean	SD
Attitude to online therapy	101	3.24	.43
Attitude to computers	95	4.25	.49
Attitude to the Internet	95	4.29	.47
Attitude to synchronous communication	71	2.16	.79
Outcome: Will you use?	92	3.26	1.18
Outcome: Will others use?	94	2.64	.85

Note: all means adjust to a scale from 1 to 5 for comparison purposes; higher values indicative of more positive attitudes or positive response.

of therapy would work, whereas 27 per cent (20/75) reported that they did not believe it would work.

Hypothesis testing

Hypothesis 1 predicted that there would be a significant relationship between attitude to online therapy and demographic variables such as age and level of qualification. Two-tailed Pearson's correlations demonstrated a significant negative relationship between the therapist's age and their attitude towards online therapy ($r = -.20$, $p < .05$), demonstrating that younger therapists held a more positive attitude to online therapy than older therapists. No significant relationship was observed between attitude to online therapy and level of qualification ($r = .028$, $p > .05$).

Hypothesis 2 predicted that there would be a significant relationship between attitude to online therapy and attitude to computers, the Internet and synchronous communication. A series of one-tailed Pearson's correlations were conducted to test this hypothesis. Results revealed no significant relationship between attitude to online therapy and attitude to computers ($r = -.11$, $p > .05$) or attitude to the Internet ($r = -.14$, $p > .05$). However, attitude to online therapy was significantly positively related to attitude to synchronous communication ($r = .33$, $p < .01$).

Supporting Hypothesis 3, attitude to online therapy was also positively related to therapists' self-reported likelihood of using online forms of therapy themselves ($r = .52$, $p < .01$), and the perceived likelihood of their peers using it ($r = .29$; $p < .01$). Thus the more positive a therapist's attitude to synchronous forms of computer mediated communication, the more positive their attitude towards online therapy. Furthermore, a positive attitude to online therapy is also related to therapists' intentions to use such systems and the perceived likelihood of their peers doing so too.

In order to test Hypothesis 4, which stated that there would be a significant difference between therapists of different approaches in terms of their attitudes and perceived likeliness of adopting online therapy, one-way analysis of variance was conducted. This analysis compared therapists categorised into those that use an eclectic approach, those that use only Cognitive Behavioural Therapy (CBT), those that use a humanistic approach only, and those who only use another therapeutic approach (e.g. behavioural or psychodynamic). Results demonstrated no significant differences in therapeutic approaches in terms of their attitude to online therapy ($F(3, 96) = 1.99$, $p > .05$), attitude to computers ($F(3, 93) = .32$, $p > .05$), attitude to the Internet ($F(3, 90) = .22$, $p > .05$) or attitude to synchronous communication ($F(3, 66) = .70$, $p > .05$). In addition, there were no significant group effects for likelihood of adopting online therapy in one's own work ($F(3, 90) = .42$, $p > .05$) or perceived likelihood of peers adopting online therapy ($F(3, 92) = .57$, $p > .05$). This attitude to online therapy or the likelihood of adopting online therapeutic approaches was not significantly related to therapeutic approach.

Hypothesis 5 predicted that there would be a significant difference between those who believe online therapy would work and those who do not believe so, in terms of the dependent measures explored above. A series of independent t-tests revealed no significant group effects for attitude to online therapy ($t(73)$ $= -.08$, $p > .05$), attitude to computers ($t(69) = .86$, $p > .05$), attitude to the Internet ($t(69) = 1.01$, $p > .05$), attitude to synchronous communication ($t(47) = -.98$, $p > .05$), likelihood of adopting online therapy in one's own work ($t(66) = .91$, $p > .05$) or perceived likelihood of peers adopting online therapy ($t(68) = .69$, $p > .05$). There was also no significant difference between groups in terms of age ($t(67) = .67$, $p > .05$). Thus there is no evidence that the identified variables were related to a therapist's decision to use online therapy.

Discussion

The current study aimed to explore attitude of therapists to online therapy systems and its relationship to other attitudes, demographic variables and reported intention to use such systems. On average, attitudes to online therapy were positive, with therapists being somewhat in favour of using e-therapy in their work and almost three quarters of therapists indicating that they believed artificially intelligent therapy systems would work. However, in general, therapists were not positive about the use of synchronous forms of computer supported communication in their work, presumably preferring face-to-face sessions.

Hypothesis 1 predicted that there would be a significant relationship between attitude to online therapy and demographic variables. Analysis revealed age as the only variable significantly associated with attitude to computerised therapy. Results identified that more positive attitudes to online therapy were associated with younger age. These results are supported by some previous research showing that more positive attitudes towards computerised therapy are held by a younger age-group (Cotton and Gupta, 2004; Wangberg et al., 2007).

Hypothesis 2 predicted that there would be a significant relationship between attitude to online therapy and attitude to computers, the Internet and synchronous communication. Results revealed that a more positive attitude to online therapy was associated with a positive attitude to synchronous forms of computer mediated communication. Thus positive regard for things such as video-conferencing, Instant Message chats or Skype, was associated with a more positive attitude towards computerised therapy. This is in line with Wangberg et al.'s (2007) findings that previous experience using technology and CMC can also be positively related to attitudes to computerised therapy. Hypothesis 3 was also supported, as results revealed that therapists who held such a positive attitude also indicated higher levels of intention to use such systems and a higher level of perceived peer use of such systems.

Andersson (2010) suggests that the theoretical stance of a therapist may be used as a predictor of attitude towards computerised therapy. In line with this claim, Wangberg et al. (2007) found that therapists practising dynamic orientated therapies were least likely to approve of computerised therapy, whereas therapists practising cognitive theoretical models were far more supportive. Results of the current study (testing Hypothesis 4) revealed no effect of therapeutic approach on attitude or intention to use such systems in therapy. However, it is possible that the current study's finding is a product of the high number of therapists reporting the use of multiple therapeutic approaches.

In an effort to explore the link between such attitudes and the general perception of success of AI in e-therapy systems, Hypothesis 5 predicted that there would be a significant difference between those who believe online therapy would work and those who do not believe so, in terms of the dependent measures explored above. However, results of these analyses revealed no evidence that therapists' attitudes were related to whether a therapist thought that online therapy would work. This might explain how the current study identified high levels of positive attitude to online therapy, in spite of a reported low uptake in mental health services. However, this alone does not explain such disparity.

The context of the current findings and future research

The current study uses a self-report quantitative technique to measure attitudes to computerised therapy. While it does measure self-reported behavioural intention, it does not include a direct measure of behaviour. This is a typical limitation of self-report attitude measures. The major problem here, as even some of the earliest research in psychology demonstrates, is that attitudes do not always predict behaviour (LaPiere, 1934). Despite this potential problem, some of the most influential theories in social psychology recognise the important role attitudes play in determining behaviour (Ajzen and Fishbein, 1977). Indeed, Olson and Zanna (1993) have argued that the utility of the whole attitude concept rests on the assumption that attitudes contribute to behaviours. Regardless of such theoretical debate, the self-report measurement of attitudes is also subject to particular biases such as social desirability or acquiescence response bias. In an effort to reduce such bias, combinations of positive and negative items were used in an anonymous online questionnaire. While the use of the online questionnaire might have increased anonymity and reduced human error in responses, this also may have produced a biased sample of participants who were more comfortable with technology. Nevertheless, the current study offers valuable findings when interpreted within such a sample.

Building on the current findings, future research can introduce direct measures of behaviour, exploring how such attitudes and demographic variables relate to actual usage of such programmes. Compared with traditional therapy, the electronic nature of computerised therapy makes it more amenable to obtaining such usage data. Such behavioural measurement can also lead to the introduction of experimental techniques, manipulating therapists' experience with computers and/or taking advantage of the naturally occurring situations whereby therapists begin to use such technology. Finally, the current findings also demonstrate the need to qualitatively explore the lived experiences of therapists using such systems and their qualitative responses that add richness to the quantitative data presented here.

Conclusion

The current study aimed to explore therapists' attitudes to computerised therapy. Results revealed that while attitudes were generally positive, they were more positive for younger therapists and unrelated to therapeutic approach. In addition, the current study demonstrated that while attitudes to computerised therapy were related to attitudes to synchronous forms of communication, attitudes to synchronous communication were generally more negative than neutral. Attitudes to computerised therapy were also positively related to intention to use such therapy, yet it was not associated with the belief that it would work. These findings demonstrate the complex nature of the attitude and behavioural components at play, and the rapidly evolving context in which they operate. Thus we recognise the need for qualitative exploration of therapists' experiences with (and without) such systems.

References

Anderson, R.E.E., Spence, S.H., Donovan, C.L., March, S., Prosser, S. and Kenardy, J. (2012). Working alliance in online cognitive behaviour therapy for anxiety disorders in youth: Comparison with clinic delivery and its role in predicting outcome. *Journal of Medical Internet Research*, 14 (3): 88.

Andersson, G. (2010). The promise and pitfalls of the Internet for cognitive behavioural therapy. *BMC Medicine*, 8 (82). doi:10.1186/1741-7015-8-82.

Ajzen, I. and Fishbein, M. (1977). Attitude-behaviour relations: A theoretical analysis and review of empirical research. *Psychological Bulletin*, 84, 888–918.

Barak, A., Hen, L., Boniel-Nissim, M. and Shapira, N. (2008). A comprehensive review and a meta-analysis of the effectiveness of Internet-based psychotherapeutic interventions. *Journal of Technology in Human Services*, 26, 109–160.

Conn, S.R., Roberts, R.L. and Powell, B.M. (2009). Attitudes and satisfaction with a hybrid model of counselling supervision. *Educational Technology & Society*, 12 (2), 298–306.

Cotton, S.R. and Gupta, S.S. (2004). Characteristics of online and off-line health information seekers and factors that discriminate between them. *Social Science & Medicine*, 59, 1795–1806.

Dinello, D. (2005). *Technophobia!: Science fiction visions of posthuman technology*. Austin, TX: University of Texas Press.

Farvolden, P., Denissof, E., Selby, P., Bagby, R.M. and Rudy, L. (2005). Usage and longitudinal effectiveness of a web-based self-help CBT behavioural therapy program for panic disorder. *Journal of Medical Internet Research*, 7 (1), e7.

Glass, G.V., Peckham, P.D. and Sanders, J.R. (1972). Consequences of failure to meet assumptions underlying the fixed effects analyses of variance and covariance. *Review of Educational Research*, 42 (3), 237–288.

Graham, C., Franses, A., Kenwright, M. and Marks, I. (2001). Problem severity in people using alternative therapies for anxiety difficulties. *Psychiatry Bulletin*, 25, 12–14.

Haggarty, J.M., Jarva, J.A., Cernovsky, Z., Karioja, K. and Martin, L. (2012). Wait time impact of co-located primary care mental health services: The effect of adding collaborative care in northern Ontario. *Canadian Journal of Psychiatry Revue Canadienne De Psychiatrie*, 57 (1), 29–33.

Howell, S.R. and Muller, R. (2000). *Computers in Psychotherapy: A new prescription*. Hamilton, Ontario: McMaster University.

Jonassen, D., Prevish, T., Christy, D. and Stavulaki, E. (1999). Learning to solve problems on the Web: Aggregate planning in a business management course. *Distance Education*, 20 (1), 49–63.

Klein, B. and Cook, S. (2010). Preferences for e-mental health services amongst an online Australian Sample. *e-Journal of Applied Psychology*, 6 (1), 27–39.

LaPiere, R.T. (1934). Attitudes vs actions. *Social Forces*, 13, 230–237.

Liaw, S.S. (2002). An Internet survey for perceptions of computers and the World Wide Web. *Computers in Human Behaviour*, 18, 17–35.

Liu, Y. (2002). What does research say about the nature of computer-mediated communication? Task-orientated, social-emotion-orientated, or both? *Electronic Journal of Sociology*, 6 (1), A1.

London School of Economics (2006). *The Depression Report: A new deal for depression and anxiety disorders*. The Centre for Economic Performance's Mental Health Policy Group. London: London School of Economics.

Marks, I., Cavanagh, K. and Gega, L. (2007). *Hands-on Help: Computer-aided psychotherapy*. Florence, NY: Taylor & Francis.

Marks, I., Cuijpers, P., Cavanagh, K., van Straten, A., Gega, L. and Andersson, G. (2009). Meta-analysis of computer-aided psychotherapy: Problems and partial solutions. *Cognitive Behaviour Therapy*, 38 (2), 83–90.

Miclea, M., Miclea, S., Ciuca, A.M. and Budau, O. (2010). Computer-mediated psychotherapy, present and prospects: A developer perspective. *Cognition, Brain, Behaviour: An Interdisciplinary Journal*, 14 (3), 185–208.

Norcross, J.C., Hedges, M. and Prochaska, J.O. (2002). The face of 2010: A delphi poll on the future of psychotherapy. *Professional Psychology, Research and Practice*, 33, 316–322.

Olson, J.M. and Zanna, M.P. (1993). Attitudes and attitude change. *Annual Review of Psychology*, 44, 117–154.

Osborn, A. and Flood, C. (2014). Establishing an online counselling service for substance use: An exploratory study. In A. Power and G. Kirwan (eds) *Cyberpsychology and New Media*. Hove: Psychology Press.

Proudfoot, J. (2004). Computer-based treatment for anxiety and depression: Is it feasible, is it effective? *Neuroscience Biobehavioural Review*, 28, 353–363.

Rovai, A.P. (2000). Building and sustaining community in asynchronous learning networks. *The Internet and Higher Education*, 3, 285–297.

Smith, G.G., Sorensen, C., Gump, A., Heindel, A.J., Caris, M. and Martinez, C.D. (2011). Overcoming student resistance to group work: Online versus face-to-face. *The Internet and Higher Education*, 14 (2), 121–128.

Titov, N., Andrews, G. and Schwencke, G. (2008). Shyness 2: Treating social phobia online: Replication and extension. *Australian and New Zealand Journal of Psychiatry*, 42, 595–605.

Turkle, S. (2007). Authenticity in the age of digital companions. *Interaction Studies*, 8 (3), 501–517.

Veletsianos, G. and Kimmons, R. (2013). Scholars and faculty members' lived experiences in online social networks. *The Internet and Higher Education*, 16, 43–50.

Wangberg, S.C., Gammon, D., and Spitznogle, K. (2007). In the eyes of the beholder: Exploring psychologists' attitudes towards and use of e-therapy in Norway. *CyberPsychology & Behaviour*, 10 (3), 418–423.

Werner, G. (1995). Computer applications in behavioural medicine. In J. Goreczny (ed.) *Handbook of Health and Rehabilitation Psychology*. New York: Plenum Press.

Yampolskiy, R.V. (2012). Leakproofing singularity: Artificial intelligence confinement problem. *Journal of Consciousness Studies*, 19 (2): 194–214.

Zdziechowska, K., Czyżak, I., Murawiec, S. and Prot, K. (2012). Characteristics of subjects with self-reported history of psychosis who were interested in self-assessment of their functional status via online e-diaries. *Archives of Psychiatry and Psychotherapy*, 4: 31–36.

PART V

Internet and education

The final section of this volume brings together a number of studies in the fast growing area of online education. The volume of information available, the ways in which it can be stored and displayed and the pedagogical challenges in mediating this new environment all contribute to a changing experience for teacher and student. Educational experiences are no longer limited to those with the financial means to fund their studies, nor are they limited to those who live in geographical proximity to their educational provider. Many different tools are now available to those who wish to extend their knowledge, from basic, non-interactive websites to collaborative wikis that rely on contributions from users to be effective. Nevertheless, the use of such technologies should be considered empirically – a new technology might appear exciting and engaging, but if it does not enhance learning, or if students are unwilling to utilise it, then its effectiveness is limited. This section examines the use of various educational tools, and also considers how information regarding individual differences in users might be collected and used to enhance their educational experience.

Chapter 16 looks at how using multimedia lecture captures might promote learning by comparing the impact on two groups of learners. The purpose was to investigate if multimedia lecture captures promote learning or lead to cognitive overload. Chapter 17 examines the participation, interaction and learner satisfaction when using a wiki for teachers. It looks at the contribution a wiki can make to the Continuing Professional Development (CPD) of teachers in one area of their professional practice, specifically dyslexia. Finally, Chapter 18 investigates the potential contribution of the social web to e-learning systems via the use of social bits, or pieces of data acquired from a person's online social activity. A number of significant results were found, suggesting that this relationship could be useful in intelligent and adaptive e-learning systems.

16

CAPTURING LECTURES

Using multimedia lecture captures to promote learning

Genevieve Dalton, Irene Connolly and Marion Palmer

Chapter summary

The purpose of the study is to investigate whether multimedia lecture captures promote learning or lead to cognitive overload. In a classroom-based experiment, students received a lesson consisting of a multimedia lecture capture (with audio, video and presentation) or a paper lesson (with text and graphics). The lessons used the same words and graphics in the paper-based and the multimedia-based versions to give a description of the anatomical structure of the vertebral column. On subsequent retention assessments, the paper group performed significantly better than the multimedia group. This suggests care should be taken before replacing traditional paper based learning material with multimedia lecture capture material.

Introduction

Advances in technology have led to greater diversity in the learning environment. With the magnitude of multimedia methods now available, the role of these within lectures is now under scrutiny. Does the use of technology in the classroom enhance learning or are the traditional non-technological methods outweighing the newer approach? Multimedia materials for learning includes all forms of text, streaming video, audio and multimedia lecture captures. Lecture capture allows instructors to create audio/video recordings of classroom lectures or presentations. With lecture capture, instructors can record their presentations in both auditory and visual ways, including slides used, for digital publication in the online learning arena as a podcast (EDUCAUSE360, 2008). In the education context a podcast can include a combination of rich media with a full-motion video from VGA (Video Graphic Array), along with content from DVDs, PCs, document cameras or other sources from the classroom lecture (Rossell-Aguilar, 2007). These digital technologies have produced a *new culture of learning*, where learning through the use of technology can bridge the gap between formal and informal learning (Thomas and Brown, 2011).

Adoption of lecture capture systems is being driven by both student demand and the requirement to make education more accessible (AHEAD, 2009). The Charter for Inclusive Teaching and Learning from the Association for Higher Education Access and Disability (AHEAD) highlights The National Plan for Equity of Access to Higher Education 2008–2013. This emphasises that good practice for access becomes good practice for all learners (AHEAD, 2009). The charter states that a key aspect of this is mainstreaming the access agenda in higher education, which will mean changing practices and implementing new and innovative teaching and learning practice on an institution–wide basis. The use of podcasts in education has some positive advantages (Lakhal *et al.*, 2007). With lifelong learning on the increase, podcasts give students more flexibility and choice in where and when they learn outside the classroom. This piece of research examines the use of multimedia in a lecture including the use of audio material. The students' level of comfort with technology and the level of learning achieved by students through the use of multimedia lecture captures are analysed, specifically in the context of the wider and sustained development of learning on a global basis.

Several interconnecting theories exist in relation to methods of learning via multimedia: the cognitive load theory (Sweller, 1988); Bloom's taxonomy (1956), Mayer's cognitive theory of multimedia learning (Mayer, 1994) and Paivio's dual code theory of memory (Paivio, 2006). Each of these theories provides the basis for this research.

First, the cognitive load theory (Sweller, 1988) recognises that working memory has a limited capacity as compared to the endless limitations of long-term memory (Miller, 1956). Sweller's theory concentrates on the base knowledge possessed by the learner, where the cognitive composition consists of schemas that allow a person to comprehend multiple components as a single component. Within this theory, learning requires a change in the schematic structures of long-term memory. This can be demonstrated as the novice learner moves from encountering difficulty with a task to its smooth execution. Once the learner becomes more familiar with the material, the working memory operates more effectively. Schema can become automated. Cognitive load can be of three distinct types: intrinsic cognitive load; extraneous cognitive load; and germane cognitive load. The intrinsic load serves to quantify how much of the working memory is used by the interactivity of the units of information being processed. Working memory must process this new information into advanced and more complex schema. The load this process places on working memory is called germane cognitive load. The working memory load experienced by learners as they interact with the learning materials and environment represents the extraneous cognitive load. Extraneous cognitive load does not contribute to learning. Sweller's cognitive load theory is concerned with techniques for reducing working memory load in order to facilitate the changes in long-term memory associated with schema acquisition.

Another theory is that of Bloom (1956) who identified three domains of educational activities: cognitive, affective and psychomotor. According to Bloom the cognitive domain involves knowledge and the development of intellectual skills. To this end, Bloom's taxonomy named six categories in the cognitive domain. Listed from simple to complex, the categories are: Knowledge, Comprehension, Application, Analysis, Synthesis and Evaluation. While the levels in the taxonomy were arranged from simple to complex, there was no intent within the taxonomy to imply that the simple level was less important than the more complex levels of the taxonomy (Slavin, 2009). In the classroom, focus on the simpler levels of the taxonomy is often appropriate, although not to the exclusion of the higher levels. There are many concepts and skills in which students cannot be considered proficient until they can apply, analyse or evaluate that knowledge. On the flip side, it is often equally vital that teachers make sure students are grounded in the simpler basic levels before expecting them to operate at the higher levels of the taxonomy (Slavin, 2009).

Learning outcomes are concerned with the achievements of the learner rather than the intentions of the instructor, and they can take many forms and can be broad or narrow in nature (Adam, 2004). The learning outcomes of this research examining the recall of information following the lesson are based on the remembering/knowledge category of Bloom's taxonomy (Bloom, 1956). Application of Bloom's theory to technology has produced Bloom's Digital Taxonomy (Churches, 2007) emphasising the role of collaboration, which, although not a necessity in learning, can facilitate it. Some examples of technological collaboration in the lecture are wikis, classroom blogs or learning management systems such as Blackboard or Moodle.

Mayer (1994) developed the cognitive theory of multimedia learning known as the 'multimedia principle', which states that 'people learn more deeply from words and pictures than from words alone' (Mayer, 1994, p. 47). It proposes three main assumptions in relation to multimedia learning. These include the use of both auditory and visual channels of information processing within multimedia learning, which can also be called Dual Coding theory. It also proposes that each of these channels possesses a limited capacity, which is parallel to Sweller's notion of Cognitive Load, and that although based on previous knowledge, learning is an active process of filtering, selecting, organising and integrating of information. This idea of a limited channel capacity is reflected in findings by Zacks and Tversky (2003), who noted that learning material broken into meaningful units, rather than in a continuous piece, leads to better learning outcomes. Mayer's cognitive theory of multimedia learning presents the idea that the brain does not interpret a multimedia presentation of words, pictures, and auditory information in a mutually exclusive fashion; rather, these elements are selected and organised dynamically to produce logical mental constructs. This theory would apply to the use of multimedia lecture captures, which incorporate all these elements.

A concept that is related to levels of processing theory is Paivio's dual code theory of memory (Paivio, 2006). This postulates that information is retained in long-term memory in two forms: visual and verbal (Mayer and Moreno, 1998). This theory suggests that information presented both verbally and visually is recalled better than information represented in only one way. Mayer *et al.* (2005) proposed a similar hypothesis called the dynamic media hypothesis. First, it argues that processing of multimedia requires less cognitive load than the processing of static annotated illustrations, because learners do not have to engage in cognitive processing to animate the graphics when the computer does this for them. Second, the multimedia content may be more interesting, entertaining and motivating than the paper-based illustrations and text, so the learners may exert more effort in making sense of the material – that is, learners may be motivated to engage in germane processing, which helps in new schema formation (Mayer *et al.*, 2005). Such a decrease in extraneous processing and increase in germane processing should lead to better scores on retention assessment for learners receiving multimedia content than those receiving text and illustrations (Mayer *et al.*, 2005). Research by DeLeeuw and Mayer (2008) on understanding how to measure cognitive load also found adding extra content to the lesson increased cognitive load. Mayer *et al.* (2005) provided two complementary explanations for why learning from static illustrations and printed text could lead to deeper learning than learning from animation and narration: these were less load from extraneous and intrinsic processing and more germane processing. Research by both Mayer (2009) and Rasch and Schnotz (2009) supported the assertion that multi-sensory content leads to cognitive overload.

In 2007, an examination of podcasts found the difference in test performance of a group using audio podcast learning material versus text-based material was trivial. Using podcasts provided little quantitative benefit for students over written text (Abt and Barry, 2007). This was supported by Baker *et al.* (2007) and Lakhal *et al.* (2007); however, results suggested that listening to podcasts had a positive effect on student satisfaction. Hew's (2008) review on past empirical studies using podcasts in higher education settings emphasised that the limitation of these studies is based on the methodology relying on participants' self-reported data such as interviews and questionnaires and also sample size. Only three of the eleven studies used examination, test or quiz scores (Abt and Barry, 2007; Baker *et al.*, 2007; Lakhal *et al.* 2007). Also, Lakhal *et al.* (2007) pointed out that the number of students who listened to the podcasts was much lower than those who did not (42 versus 150). Another limitation was that participants in these studies were limited mainly to disciplines such as engineering, technology, business and law, and more research addressing the use of podcasting in other disciplines was needed. This meta-analysis revealed that although participants viewed the role of podcasts positively, there was no significant difference in learning outcomes as a result of using them.

The objective of the current research was to assess the effectiveness and efficiency of multimedia lecture captures as a learning tool, and to determine whether they have a negative effect, a positive effect or no effect on the learning outcomes of the student. This study is based on a similar study carried out by Mayer *et al.* (2005), which examined the effect of narrated animations versus annotated illustrations in multimedia instruction on the promotion of active learning. This research attempts to determine whether multimedia lecture captures promote learning or lead to cognitive overload. Based on this, the hypotheses are:

H1 Learning using multimedia lecture captures compared with traditional learning material has no significant effect on learning outcomes.
H2 Participant comfort level with new technology has a significant effect on learning outcomes when learning using multimedia lecture captures.

Method

Participants

Twenty undergraduate students (twelve males and eight females) were randomly allocated to each group, with ten in each. The mean age was 20.45 years ($SD = 1.90$), with a range from 18 to 27 years. The mean age for the paper lesson group was 20.30 years ($SD = 1.16$) and the multimedia lesson group's mean age was 20.60 years ($SD = 2.50$).

Materials

For the purposes of this study, the term multimedia lesson is used to refer to the lecture capture lesson and the term paper lesson is used to refer to the traditional paper based lesson. The lesson outlined the anatomical structure of the vertebral column, chosen due to the relative obscurity of the topic. The lessons were created by an established expert in that field, with standardised presentation of words and graphics on both. Students learned about the anatomical structure of the vertebral column via a web-based multimedia lecture containing video, audio and presentation or via a paper lesson including text and illustrations.

The multimedia lesson consisted of a video of the lecturer delivering a lesson in a lecture theatre synchronised with a presentation on the lesson. The presentation contained the same illustrations as the paper based lesson and similarly had arrows and labels on each one indicating the anatomical term used for the various parts and components thereof. In the video the lecturer used a model of the spinal column as an aid to point out the various components and he spoke to each component, using the same words as in the paper based lesson to give a definition of the anatomical terms. In some cases the symptoms that may occur with various problems with these components were also outlined.

The paper lesson consisted of a two-page lesson document. It contained ten illustrations of various parts of the vertebral column with arrows and labels on each one, indicating the anatomical term used for the various parts and components thereof. Beside each illustration there was a text paragraph giving a definition of these anatomical terms and again, in some cases, the symptoms that may occur with various problems with these components. Differences between the lessons were the oral presentation in the multimedia lesson, which was not presented in the paper lesson, and also a video image of the lecturer using a model of the 'vertebral column'.

Procedure

A pilot of the experiment was carried out using two participants: one completing the paper based lesson and one completing the multimedia lesson. Because the experiment was run with two groups of students in separate locations with two experimenters, a script for the experiment informed by the pilot was developed to ensure the same tasks and procedure was carried out for both groups. The pilot also gave indicative timings for the experiment.

The paper lesson and the multimedia lesson were conducted simultaneously, with each lesson lasting for sixteen minutes. Only participants who had no prior knowledge of structures of the vertebral column participated in the research. Ross and Morrison (2004) stressed that an important component of the quasi-experiment study is the use of pre-testing or analysis of prior achievement in order to establish group equivalence. At the beginning of each research session, participants read the experiment outline document. This consisted of a brief introduction to the study, outlined the purpose, the procedure, risk and the option of voluntary participation or withdrawal at any stage and consent forms. The consent form also contained a comfort-rating question on new technology adoption. Participants rated their comfort level with new technologies, rating themselves as positive, neutral or negative. Participants scored from 1 to 5 on their comfort level, with those least comfortable with new technology scoring 1 and those most comfortable with new technology scoring 5. Once consent forms were signed the lessons began. Following the lesson, both groups completed a retention assessment, which consisted of twenty true/false questions based on the content of the lesson. The form also included three illustrations on which half of the questions were based. The questions were statements about various anatomical components of the vertebral column and symptoms of problems with them.

Results

The first hypothesis stated that learning using multimedia lecture captures rather than traditional learning material has no significant effect on learning outcomes. For the retention assessment, the participants received one point for each of the twenty true/false questions they gave the correct answer for, and their points were added together to give a total for each individual student. There was a maximum score of twenty and a minimum score of zero. Hypothesis 1 was examined using an independent-samples t-test. A comparison of the retention of material from the lessons in the multimedia lesson group and the paper lesson group found a significant difference ($t(18) = 2.19$, $p = .042$) in the scores, with the multimedia lesson group scoring higher on average ($M = 12.60$, $SD = 1.78$) than the paper lesson group (M = 14.30, SD = 1.70). This hypothesis was not supported. The trend suggests that the paper lesson group retained more information than the multimedia lesson group.

The second hypothesis examined the effect of comfort with technology with learning outcomes when learning using multimedia lecture captures. Seven out of ten in the multimedia group rated themselves as positive or neutral about new technologies. There was no difference in the scores for the positive/neutral group (M = 12.860) versus the negative group (M = 12.00). This research concludes that Hypothesis 2 is not supported.

It was noted by the experimenter that the participants in the paper based group seemed less attentive to the lesson material after the first five minutes of the experiment.

Discussion

The research concluded that a difference exists in the retention levels using multimedia lessons versus paper lessons. Those participants who undertook the paper lesson scored significantly better on the retention assessments than those who undertook the multimedia lesson. Many factors need to be examined to assess the differences in the use of these methods in the classroom.

Research by Mayer *et al.* (2005) would indicate that participants who received the paper lesson should perform the best because they are encouraged to engage in germane processing and can reduce extraneous processing. There are a number of reasons why the multimedia lesson could have had a higher cognitive load than the paper lesson. The paper lesson group was presented with a visual stream only, whereas the multimedia lesson group was presented with audio, video and presentation content streams simultaneously, which would have increased cognitive load. The paper lesson involves presentation of all the learning material at one time where the learner can easily control the pace and order of presentation, whereas with the multimedia lesson the material is presented in a sequential order where the learner has no control over the pace of the lesson. Research by Zacks and Tversky (2003) found that learning material broken into meaningful units rather than in a continuous piece leads to better learning outcomes. The paper lesson group viewed the learning material on two sheets of paper, whereas the multimedia lesson group viewed it on a computer screen, which was wide screen and of a high resolution; although it is unlikely this would have affected the results, it cannot be ruled out that it could have caused extraneous cognitive load.

Because the study focused on lowest level of learning on Bloom's taxonomy, there is no supporting evidence on the impact of multimedia lecture captures on higher order learning such as comprehension, application, analysis, synthesis and evaluation (Bloom, 1956). Bloom acknowledged that knowledge recall must be mastered before moving onto the next level. Future studies could build on this research and examine the effect of multimedia lecture captures on higher order learning. The overall comfort rating of the participants with new technology appeared to have no impact on the scores of either the multimedia lesson group or the paper lesson group. This could mean that because of their comfort with technology their preference would be to use the multimedia lesson media, but it does not mean they will retain any more information on the lesson. However, further research specifically on student motivation for learning materials would need to be completed to investigate this. It is also interesting to note that while students in the paper lesson group seemed less attentive to the learning material, they did in fact score higher on average on the retention test.

Careful consideration needs to be given to how the multimedia lesson is designed, taking into account the cognitive load of the learner while taking the lesson. The lesson should be designed so it does not exceed the processing capacity of the learner. DeLeeuw and Mayer (2008) developed a method to measure cognitive load during a multimedia lesson. This method of measurement could be used to determine the optimal design of a multimedia lesson, for example, reducing redundancy by not displaying words that are spoken.

This study also suggests that it may be premature to abandon textbooks in favour of multimedia technology just because of its popularity with students. Multimedia lecture captures may be popular, but the research does not suggest that they provide more educational value than traditional paper based learning material. Some educators believe that technology is the way of the future in education; this study suggests that caution should be used in replacing textbooks with technology. Today's generation of learners have been downloading music, videos and podcasts to their MP3 players for the last number of years and are very familiar with this type of medium (Barnett, 2005; Tyre, 2005). They may also be more highly motivated to use this type of medium because they have grown up with multimedia in their everyday life. Therefore, educators need to look at making it available as complementary material alongside traditional textbooks, giving learners the option to choose the type of material from which they wish to learn.

A limitation of this research is that it does not take into account the learning style of the participants, which may have had a significant influence on the results. Learners with different learning styles should perhaps have had the option to use the complementary material to assist with their learning. A recommendation for future research would be to examine the learning style of the individual in combination with their use of multimedia and paper based material to see if this has a significant impact on the learning outcomes. Other factors worthy of future study include researching the use of multimedia lecture captures along with looking at students' learning preferences, motivation and styles and examining higher order learning.

Conclusion

This research suggests that when they are used, multimedia lecture captures appear more effective as supplementary learning aids in conjunction with traditional material. A blended learning environment where there are options for learners with different learning styles and preferences would appear to work best. Subsequent research is needed to determine what situations would best suit the use of multimedia lecture capture as an instructional learning aid. There is a temptation to use new technology in teaching and learning with the assumption that it will improve the learning outcomes for students. However, this study and previous studies have found this not to be the case, and care should be taken in replacing traditional learning material with technology enhanced learning material.

References

Abt, G. and Barry, T. (2007). The quantitative effect of students using podcasts in a first year undergraduate exercise physiology module. *Bioscience Education eJournal*, 10.

Adam, S. (2004). *Using Learning Outcomes*. Report for United Kingdom Bologna Seminar 1–2 July, Heriot-Watt University (Edinburgh Conference Centre). Edinburgh, Scotland.

AHEAD (2009). Charter for inclusive teaching and learning. Retrieved from: www.ahead.ie/publications.php.

Baker, R., Harrison, J., Thorton, B. and Yates, R. (2007). An analysis of the effectiveness of podcasting as a supplementary instructional tool: A pilot study. Paper presented at the 2007 EABR and ETLC Conference. Ljubljana, Slovenia.

Barnett, M. (2005). Tech trends: Podcasting hits the mainstream. Retrieved from: www.usnews.com/usnews/biztech/articles/050705/5podcast.htm.

Bloom, B.S. (1956). *Taxonomy of Educational Objectives, Handbook 1: The cognitive domain*. New York: David McKay.

Churches, A. (2007). *Bloom's Digital Taxonomy*. Retrieved from www.techlearning.com/techlearning/archives/2008/04/AndrewChurches.pdf.

DeLeeuw, K.E. and Mayer, R.E. (2008). A comparison of three measures of cognitive load: Evidence for separable measures of intrinsic, extraneous, and germane load. *Journal of Educational Psychology*, 100, 223–234.

EDUCAUSE (2008). College students prefer classes with online learning. Retrieved from: www.news.wisc.edu/15640.

Hew, K.F. (2008). Use of audio podcast in K-12 and higher education: A review of research topics and methodologies. *Educational Technology Research and Development*. Boston, MA: Springer.

Lakhal, S., Khechine, H. and Pascot, D. (2007). Evaluation of the effectiveness of podcasting in teaching and learning. In G. Richards (ed.) *Proceedings of World Conference on E-Learning in Corporate, Government, Healthcare, and Higher Education, 2007* (pp. 6181–6188). Chesapeake, VA: AACE.

Mayer, R.E. (1994). Visual aids to knowledge construction: Building mental representations from pictures and words. In W. Schnotz and W. Khlhavy (eds) *Comprehension of Graphic* (pp. 125–138). Amsterdam: Elsevier science.

Mayer, R.E. (2009). *Multimedia Learning*, 2nd edn. New York: Cambridge University Press.

Mayer, R.E. and Moreno, R. (1998). A split-attention effect in multimedia learning: Evidence for dual processing systems in working memory. *Journal of Educational Psychology*, 90, 312–320.

Mayer, R.E., Hegarty, M., Mayer, S., and Campbell, J. (2005). When static media promote active learning: Annotated illustrations versus narrated animations in multimedia learning. *Journal of Experimental Psychology: Applied*, 11, 256–265.

Miller, G.A. (1956). The magical number seven, plus or minus two: Some limits on our capacity for processing information. *Psychological Review*, 63 (2): 81–97.

Paivio, A. (2006). *Mind and its Evolution: A dual coding theoretical interpretation.* Mahwah, NJ: Lawrence Erlbaum Associates.

Rasch, T. and Schnotz, W. (2009). Interactive and non-interactive pictures in multimedia learning environments: Effects on learning outcomes and learning efficiency. *Learning and Instruction,* 19 (5), 411–422.

Ross, S.M. and Morrison, G.R. (2004). Experimental research methods. In D.H. Jonassen (ed.) *Handbook of Research on Educational Communications and Technology,* 2nd edn (pp. 1021–1043). Mahwah, NJ: Lawrence Erlbaum Associates.

Rossell-Aguilar, F. (2007). Top of the pods: In search of a podcasting 'pedagogy' for language learning. *Computer Assisted Language Learning,* 20 (5), 471–492.

Slavin, R. (2009). Educational psychology: Theory and practice, 9th edn. Upper Saddle River, NJ: Pearson.

Sweller, J. (1988). Cognitive load during problem solving: Effects on learning. *Cognitive Science,* 12, 257–285.

Thomas, D. and Brown, J.S. (2011). *A New Culture of Learning: Cultivating the imagination for a world of constant change.* CreateSpace Independent Publishing Platform. Retrieved from: www.newcultureoflearning.com/newcultureoflearning.html.

Tyre, P. (2005). Professor in your pocket. Retrieved from: www.newsweek.com/id/51275.

Zacks, J.M. and Tversky, B. (2003). Structuring information interfaces for procedural learning. *Journal of Experimental Psychology: Applied,* 9, 88–100.

17

PARTICIPATION, INTERACTION AND LEARNER SATISFACTION IN A PROFESSIONAL PRACTICE WIKI FOR TEACHERS

Rory Tierney and Marion Palmer

Chapter summary

This study investigated the contribution a wiki can make to the Continuing Professional Development (CPD) of teachers in one area of their professional practice, specifically dyslexia. A case study approach examined participation, interaction and learner satisfaction of participants in a wiki over an initial three-week period. Twenty-nine teachers joined a wiki, which was facilitated by a specialist dyslexia teacher. Results indicated that teachers had the requisite technical skills to access the wiki. They indicated a preference for a constructivist learning environment but felt that the wiki fell short of their ideal. The level of participation and the interaction between participants in the wiki was limited, although a few participants were exceptions to this observation. Qualitative data suggested that the wiki succeeded in providing CPD for teachers, using a range of media within a constructivist framework.

Introduction

There is a general recognition that CPD for teachers has a positive contribution to make to education. This research examines the contribution that an innovative professional practice wiki can make to the CPD of teachers. By enabling participation and social interaction, and placing cumulative learning at its core, a wiki appears to have the potential to provide a satisfying learning experience, while addressing some of the limitations that have been identified in the current teacher CPD provision. A wiki is a socially orientated communication tool that enables online collaboration. Because wikis record in detail all of the interactions that take place in a learning transaction, they have the potential to offer insights that will inform educational practice.

The chosen subject matter of the wiki is teaching interventions for children with specific learning difficulties (dyslexia), the 'Dyslexia Interventions Wiki'. Approximately 10–15 per cent of school-age children experience dyslexia (Vellutino *et al.*, 2004). Teachers are motivated to better understand such needs, to facilitate students learning literacy skills and to work collaboratively with colleagues in developing their professional practice in this area.

The constructivist paradigm

Constructivism conceptualises learning as a process of active engagement and interaction in the construction of knowledge and understanding from experience. The constructivist perspective focuses on the learner as a person who is actively engaged in constructing knowledge from experience. This has a particular relevance for online learning. McFadzean (2001, p. 53) says that 'traditional teaching and learning skills need to change in order to gain the maximum benefit from virtual learning'. She argues that the structure and format of online learning has an inherent potential that cannot be fully utilised if a traditional instructivist learning model is used, and that conversely, a humanist or constructivist approach can tap into these possibilities.

A constructivist learning environment enables meaningful learning through supportive facilitation. It is active and manipulative, constructive and reflective, intentional, open, authentic, challenging and real-world (or simulated), and cooperative, collaborative and conversational (APA Task Force on Psychology in Education, 1993). Another important part of the constructivist picture comes from Slavin (2009), who observes that constructivist strategies are often referred to as being learner-centred. Cornelius-White (2007, p. 134) in a meta-analysis concluded that 'learner-centred teacher variables have above-average associations with positive student outcomes'. The analysis identified three aspects of learner behaviour that correlated most with a learner-centred approach and they were (in order) – participation, critical thinking and satisfaction.

Presence and a Community of Inquiry model (CoI)

Garrison and Anderson state that 'at the core of the e-learning context is a collaborative constructive transaction' (2002, p. 4). The 'Community of Inquiry' (CoI) model provides a dynamic framework that considers the process of constructing knowledge and 'defines the three constituting elements of e-learning' (Garrison and Anderson, 2002, p. xii). These include social presence, cognitive presence and teaching presence (Garrison *et al.*, 2009). Social presence is defined as 'the ability of participants to identify with the community (e.g. course of study), communicate purposefully in a trusting environment, and develop inter-personal relationships by way of projecting their individual personalities'. Cognitive presence is 'the extent to which learners are able to construct and confirm meaning through sustained reflection and discourse in a critical community of inquiry'. Finally, teaching presence is defined as 'the design, facilitation and direction of cognitive and social processes for the purpose of realising personally meaningful and educationally worthwhile learning outcomes'.

Within the CoI model, the interaction must proceed to 'purposeful and systematic discourse' and have the 'intent to influence thinking in a critical and reflective manner' (Garrison and Cleveland-Innes, 2005, pp. 134–135) and it must involve the integration of all three elements of social, cognitive and teaching.

Research interest in interaction arose out of concerns about the lack of a physical presence in an online environment. As Computer Mediated Communication (CMC) technologies have evolved, it has been recognised that online interactions can be richer and fuller, and include more affective and emotional elements than had originally been envisaged. As a consequence, social presence is now viewed as a quality of relational systems (Shin, 2002) and appears to be more complex and dynamic than had previously been considered in that it is determined by the participants involved in the interaction as well as by the medium in which it occurs.

This understanding of 'presence' has important implications for the experience of participants in an online learning environment, because social interaction is such a fundamental part of the constructivist learning process. It represents an important additional dimension to text-based online interactions and, as a result, makes 'lean media environments more productive' (Kehrwald, 2008, p. 99). In a constructivist online environment, it is important that participants are enabled to form relationships with others. The development of a learning environment based on respect, empathy and trust is a vital aspect of the process. Participants need to feel safe about being open or disclosing something about themselves that could result in criticism or praise.

Cognitive presence is an internal process that may or may not be demonstrated in communication and behaviour. Garrison et al. (2010) try to operationalise this dimension using the Practical Inquiry (PI) model, which they base on the phases of Dewey's notion of reflective thought. The four phases of the PI model are the triggering event, exploration, integration and resolution. This model has a particular relevance for the design of wikis, from the introduction of triggering events to enabling higher-level thinking. Early studies have suggested that students may not be proceeding to the integration and resolution phases (Garrison et al., 2010).

This also highlights the significance that teaching presence has within the CoI framework, where it is seen as providing the necessary facilitation and direction to learners that will encourage them to progress right through the PI model, to a point where higher-level thinking skills are employed (Garrison et al., 2010). Salmon (2005, p. 203) talks about 'good learning design', pedagogical input and sensitive handling, while Garrison (2009, p. 97) suggests that a teacher 'may be irreplaceable for meaningful and worthwhile learning'.

Development of an online community

An online community is not a static entity. Salmon (2000) very usefully focuses on initial engagement and then the development and progression of online learning experiences, constructing a practice-based model that includes five key steps or stages in an online interactive learning experience. The model, which complements the CoI model, begins with the essential prerequisites for participation (the base of the steps) and progresses to participants establishing online identities, through a process of socialisation, to sharing information, then to collaborating and the construction of knowledge and finally to achieving personal goals and reflection.

The initial stages of the model are particularly relevant to this research. Stage One of Salmon's model is referred to as 'Access and Motivation'. This first step of the process includes the participant getting online, finding the correct website, finding and following directions and logging on for the first time. Technical support is often a key component at this stage. Then, typically, participants have to learn the conventions and practices associated with a new piece of software and learning environment. Although in practice the cut-off point may not be so clear-cut, Salmon suggests that Stage One is over when participants are showing some familiarity with the online environment and postings have gone beyond the 'Help, where am I?' stage (Salmon, 2003).

Salmon refers to Stage Two of her model as 'Online Socialisation'. Here participants begin to feel more comfortable online in what will be for most a new environment and community. Some will make these adaptations more quickly than others, as they come to terms with the different social demands and the asynchronous nature of the communication. According to Salmon, the core elements of Stage Two are (1) identification with other participants and (2) an identification and/or acknowledgement of a common purpose.

As a sense of comfort in the online environment grows, participants' confidence in contributing and responding increases and this may be augmented by the facilitator acknowledging and valuing their views. Salmon views this stage as complete when 'participants share a little of themselves online' (Salmon, 2000, p. 29). 'Information Exchange' is the core of Stage Three. Salmon refers to two types of interaction at this stage – interaction with online material and interaction with the other participants. Garrison and Cleveland-Innes (2005) take a very similar view. They regard efforts to create social presence and relationships with other participants as a prelude to a higher-level learning experience.

Salmon (2007, p. 172) evaluates the five-stage model, noting that it has 'proved "blendable" in its application to notions of communities of practice'. She views the model as being useful particularly with 'small-scale low-cost online activities' such as 'encouraging wiki use among small professional communities'.

Barriers to participation and interaction

Participation and interaction in an online community tends to be variable, with personal characteristics playing a significant role. For example, some people are comfortable and experienced in using technology, while others are not; some people prefer to work in a group, while others have a preference to work individually (Neumann and Hood, 2009). Those who generally assume an observer's role are frequently referred to as 'lurkers'. Preece *et al.* (2004) found that in some online communities, 'lurking' is the norm, with only a few participants taking an active role.

Identified barriers to online learning include psychological distance, technological problems and also unmet student expectations, with the focus on timeliness of support and faculty time limits (Chang, 2004; Northrup, 2002), insufficient supportiveness and the lack of a positive learner-tutor relationship (Maushak and Ellis, 2003).

Muilenburg and Berge (2005) suggested that the most critical barriers, in order of priority, were: (1) social interaction – a lack of interaction with participants or the facilitator; (2) administrative/facilitator issues – barriers that administrators and facilitators control; (3) learner motivation; and (4) time/support for studies from family or significant others. They also identified five independent variables that impacted on the barriers, which were: (1) ability and confidence with online learning technology; (2) effectiveness of online learning; (3) online learning enjoyment; (4) online courses completed; and (5) the likelihood of taking a future online course.

Su and Beaumont (2008) also identified factors that constituted barriers to students participating in a wiki. These included difficulties accessing the wiki, lack of personalisation, concerns of possible vandalism and plagiarism and dyslexia. Students also expressed reluctance, especially during the initial stages of the process, to make comments on others' work. However, towards the latter stages, 87 per cent had made comments and confidence in giving and receiving criticism had significantly improved.

A difficulty in participating and interacting using a wiki may be related to a lack of experience of a constructivist learning environment, coupled with an embeddedness in an instructivist way of learning or teaching. In other words, a barrier exists insofar as it is difficult for participants to transition from an instructivist learning environment to a constructivist one, specifically from traditional direct instruction to a constructivist oriented wiki.

Teachers' CPD – using online resources

Teachers are members by default of a number of professional communities – in their immediate school, in the local area and in the wider community. However, teachers can be relatively isolated; they can spend most of their days working alone with groups of students. Schlager and Fusco (2003) cite a 2000 study by Riel and Becker, who found that teachers who engaged with a larger educational community were more likely to use constructivist and collaborative instructional strategies in their classrooms, while 'private-practice' teachers were more likely to use direct instruction. Where a community of teachers functions well, the focus is on student learning, colleagues are supportive, experimentation is encouraged and there is a sharing of skills and ideas. Discussion provides intellectual stimulation and affords opportunities to question values and concepts, and provide or receive constructive feedback.

In reality, many CPD programmes for teachers are disconnected from practice and the needs of students. Some of the obstacles to effective professional development lie within schools and their cultures. Duncan-Howell (2009) proposes that 'the most influential cause of change is personal motivation or perceived need . . . rather than external factors such as requirements of the employing organisation or school' (p. 603).

A balanced range of formal and informal options is required to cater for the full range of teachers' CPD needs. Because of their availability, online learning communities have the potential to make a valuable contribution: 'the types of activities they facilitate present as viable mediums for creating genuine opportunities for continued pedagogical growth for teachers' (Duncan-Howell, 2009, p. 601). In addition, they can provide valuable social and normative support to teachers who may feel relatively isolated. In a study of social workers' use of an online learning community, Thorpe and Gordon (2012) identify its potential to develop practice. Wikis have the potential to function efficiently as a cumulative, dynamic store of a community's communications, collaborations and learning.

Use of wikis

A wiki functions to allow a group of participants to access, read, edit, reorganise and manage the pages of a shared website with relative ease, when and where they choose. At a functional level, it is designed to promote engagement and interaction within a group, thus facilitating the collaborative sharing and generation of new ideas and knowledge. Because it encourages participants (teachers in this case) to assume control over content and direction, it has the flexibility to address immediate classroom and school issues and can thus have a significant and sustainable impact on student learning and achievement. In terms of outcome, a wiki encompasses individual contributions and at the same time represents, through refinement, the cumulative or shared knowledge of the group.

The 'good fit' between a wiki and its constructivist and collaborative theoretical foundations is evident when key aspects of these perspectives are considered (Leuf and Cunningham, 2001). The constructivist approach promotes the participants' active involvement in creating knowledge, as opposed to more passively absorbing it (Bruner, 1990), while Piaget (1971) identified a key element as the integration of ideas into existing frameworks and a reframing of beliefs as a result of new learning experiences.

The age and characteristics of participants appears to be important. Wikis have been successfully employed, particularly in third level and higher education (Guzdial et al., 2001), where learners may be expected to bring relevant experience and a degree of self-reliance to the process. Elgort et al. (2008, p. 195) suggest that the purpose of a wiki is important. They cite a 2006 study by Bower et al., who stress task authenticity, and a 2007 study by Choy and Ng, who argue that if there is not a requirement to work collaboratively, then the use of wikis may not be appropriate.

It has also been claimed that the success of some wikis is determined to a large degree by the measures used to evaluate them. For example, Ebner *et al.* (2008) note that evaluations of wikis often consist of qualitative analyses of teacher and learner experiences, and success is often judged more in terms of level of interaction than quantifiable improvements in learning outcome. In other words, process may be a more relevant measure than outcome. They also note that the outcomes of wiki projects may sometimes be skewed by factors that enforce or incentivise initial engagement and ongoing participation. Highlighting this possibility, they note that in their study of 287 college students over one semester, none created new articles or edited existing ones when no rewards were offered for participation. The main reasons for the students' non-participation were given as: not having time (27 per cent); problems editing articles (24 per cent); not trying (18 per cent); and no perceived benefit (12 per cent). In short, Ebner *et al.* (2008) argue that simply providing interactive and collaborative technology does not necessarily translate into student engagement on a wiki. In another study, Judd *et al.* (2010) reported considerable variation in student contribution to a wiki, with 50 per cent producing 15 per cent of the content and 10 per cent contributing over 40 per cent of the content (p. 350), with the majority of the contributions made late in the study. Jones and Preece (2006) suggest that a successful online learning community needs shared knowledge, beliefs and values – that participants should come together purposively and meaningfully.

In reality, because of the complexity of the issues, easy, ready-made solutions are not to be found. Wang and Beasley (2008, p. 80) review the use of wikis within education as part of a student's or a teacher's learning process. In practical terms, wikis are a relatively new technology that demands new understandings and ways of working for all participants. Ruth and Houghton (2009) identified some aspects of wiki pedagogy, but research is still at a stage where it is identifying all of the components and learning how they operate and relate to one another. The goal of this research project is to contribute to that process, focusing on participation, interaction and learner satisfaction.

Research question and hypothesis

The key question underlying this research is whether a wiki can provide a useful CPD experience for teachers. Taking factors such as age, teaching experience and technology skills into consideration, it examines teachers' participation, interaction and satisfaction with the wiki over an initial three-week set-up period. In this study, the teachers who join and use the wiki are referred to as learners. The person adopting the 'teaching' role is referred to as the facilitator.

This research hypothesises that learners will participate and interact with the facilitator and other learners in a constructivist facilitated wiki in order to develop their professional practice. Satisfaction with the wiki will also be explored.

Method

Research design

A case study design was adopted (Robson, 1993, p. 40). Both qualitative and quantitative data collection and analysis were employed. An ADDIE instructional systems design (ISD) model was adopted in planning and developing the Dyslexia Interventions wiki, where ADDIE (a colloquial and generic term) is short for Analyse, Design, Develop, Implement and Evaluate.

Participants

The head teachers of seven schools were contacted in person; their permission was sought to approach school staff to see if they would be willing to participate in a three-week research project, focusing on the use of wikis to develop their skills and as a useful resource in relation to dyslexia interventions. A total of thirty-eight teachers offered their email addresses, and each was invited to join the study. Of these, twenty-nine (five males and twenty-four females) successfully signed up to the wiki. The age and teaching experience of the sample are outlined in Table 17.1.

A significant number of the participants appeared to have relatively little teaching experience, insofar as 34.5 per cent ($n = 10$) reported that they had taught for less than six years. However, balancing this, the survey also indicated that 55 per cent of the participants had over sixteen years' teaching experience. It is interesting to speculate whether this balance between teaching experience and relative inexperience might act as a positive mix, in terms of encouraging collaboration, sharing knowledge, seeking and offering support.

TABLE 17.1 Demographic profile of participants in the Dyslexia Interventions wiki

Age range in years	Responses	Percentage (%)
20–29	7	24.1
30–39	5	17.2
40–49	10	34.5
50–59	6	20.7
60+ years	1	3.4
Length of teaching experience	Responses	Percentage (%)
0–5	10	34.5
6–10	3	10.3
11–15	0	0
16–20	2	6.8
21–25	4	13.8
26–30	7	24.1
31–35	3	10.3

The majority of teachers (83 per cent, $n = 24$) rated their own computer skills as being at an intermediate level, with only five viewing themselves as being at a novice level. This suggested that most participants should have the technical skills to access the wiki. No teachers rated themselves as experts in computer skills. Use of social networks such as Facebook was taken as another indicator of the teacher's level of comfort with Computer Mediated Communication (CMC). The majority of teachers (62 per cent, $n = 18$) indicated that they rarely or very rarely used social networks. However, 34 per cent of participants ($n = 10$) said that they used social networks 'very often' or 'often'. This outcome may be related to the age profile of participants. Teachers were also asked to indicate whether they had ever completed an online course, on the basis that this experience should provide good preparation for using a wiki to develop professional practice. Online courses are clearly popular, as twenty-five participants (86 per cent) had completed online courses, with 31 per cent having completed more than three online courses. However, the majority of teachers (87 per cent, $n = 25$) had never actively used any wiki before.

Materials

A range of educational materials dealing with aspects of dyslexia were added to the Dyslexia Interventions website during the three-week research period. These were selected on the basis of the facilitator's or researcher's knowledge and professional experience as potentially being interesting or stimulating for the wiki participants.

Description of the Dyslexia Interventions wiki

The homepage of the Dyslexia Interventions wiki is shown in Figure 17.1. The tabs of the menu that runs across the top of the page offer access to the main features – discussions, photo and video galleries, news, updates, droplets and members.

The items most relevant to the Dyslexia Interventions wiki were: 'Discussions', which allowed participants to go directly to all discussions in the wiki; the 'video' gallery, which gave direct access to all videos on the wiki; 'updates', which presented a chronological list of all changes to the wiki; and finally 'members', which listed all members and allowed the facilitator to contact all members collectively or individually. There was also a facility that automatically sent an email to members when a page was updated, and this was switched on by default. In effect, when a participant changed a page, they were subsequently emailed whenever that same page was updated by another participant (unless they had changed the default settings). A second menu on the top left of the screen was customisable and provided links to all available pages in the wiki. An additional 'Menu Selection' (linked text that was used to highlight specific pages or resources in the wiki) was added to the front page by the researcher.

Dyslexia Interventions

FIGURE 17.1 Home page of the Dyslexia Interventions wiki (top section)

The facilitator of the wiki was a specialist teacher of children with dyslexia, with extensive experience working with children with special needs. Her role was to engage positively with participants online, respond to posts and messages, encourage contributions, provide stimulating material and share her knowledge. In addition to this, the researcher provided administrative and technical support when requested or if it was evident by participants' postings that clarification and/ or assistance was required.

Participation and interaction

A 'type of participation' list, based on Dron (2007), was used to measure frequency and type of participation, and this is given in Table 17.2. In the analysis of inter-actions, the administrator/researcher was viewed as another facilitator.

Determining what constitutes a 'participation' and what or who is the target of any act of participation is complex. In this study, where the target could be equally another participant or the facilitator, the target of the participation is deemed to be the participant. In future research, such complexities could be considered by having more than one person making this determination and examining inter-rater

TABLE 17.2 Types of participation in the wiki

participant → facilitator	facilitator → participant
participant → content	facilitator → content
participant → participant	facilitator → facilitator
content → content, e.g. an automatically generated response	

reliability. For example, the difference between adding one word and adding twenty sentences is considerable, but in this relatively basic analysis, both are counted as one participation.

Finally, it is noted that 'participant → content' actions (and similarly 'facilitator → content' actions) refer to actions that impact primarily on the content of the wiki. These could include, for example, reformatting a table or completing an assigned task. The participation attributed to the 'participant → content' heading refers to the assigned weekly activities. Each task was counted as one act of participation.

Constructivist Online Learning Environment Survey (COLLES)

Satisfaction was measured using the Constructivist Online Learning Environment Survey (COLLES), developed by Taylor and Maor. The COLLES comes in three different versions: (1) a preferred form; (2) an actual form; and (3) a combined preferred and actual form. The combined form was used in this research as one of the set activities for Week 3. It was designed to provide a measure, within the same form, of participants' perceptions of both their preferred and their actual online learning environments (Taylor and Maor, n.d.). The combined form consists of twenty-four pairs of statements, such as 'I prefer that my learning focuses on issues that interest me' and 'I found that my learning focuses on issues that interest me'. Each pair of statements asks the participant about: (1) their preferred (or ideal) experience; and (2), in the line below, their actual experience in using the wiki. The COLLES contains a five-point Likert-type response scale. The twenty-four pairs of statements are grouped under six headings, specifically: relevance, reflection (stimulation of reflective thinking), interactivity, tutor-support, peer-support and interpretation (of each other's communications).

Procedure

This wiki was progressively developed and expanded over the three-week experimental period. At the start, the wiki included just a front page, the two activities for Week 1 (described below), a few additional pages giving some information on dyslexia and a few blank pages with just a heading. Each week participants were asked to complete two new activities.

Week 1

On the first day of the research, a standard email was sent to every teacher who had indicated an interest in joining the wiki. The email provided further details of the research, invited the teacher to join and provided instructions on how to log in to the wiki. When anyone joined the wiki, the facilitator was notified by email and she responded by sending an email to the new user, welcoming them.

The front page was divided into four quadrants. One quadrant included a picture of a girl reading. The second had a simple welcome message that stated that the wiki was 'first and foremost for teachers' and that the goal was 'to enable the sharing of information about dyslexia interventions that appear to be effective'. The third quadrant included an extra menu, designed with two aims: (1) to highlight particular pages in the wiki; and (2) to indicate the incompleteness of the wiki. This was highlighted by having some non-functioning links in the menu and others that linked to empty pages with only a heading. The initial design of the wiki attempted to find a good balance between projecting a professional image with an organised structure and giving new users the impression of informality – that the wiki was incomplete and a work-in-progress. There was a help page that included an email address for the facilitator and the administrator.

Participants were asked to complete two activities in Week 1. The first was a short demographic survey. The second activity was designed to give participants their first experience of editing a page on a wiki. Step-by-step instructions were provided, and participants were asked to make a few corrections to a nonsense definition of dyslexia.

At the end of Week 1, a final invitation was sent to anyone who had not yet responded. When any participant made a change to the wiki or added a comment or observation, the facilitator usually responded, welcoming the contribution and sometimes suggesting another page or element of the wiki that she felt might be of particular interest.

Week 2

At the start of the week, a message was sent to all participants in the wiki, thanking them for completing the two Week 1 activities. They were also informed that the Week 2 activities had been added to the wiki and they were invited to complete them.

The activities for Week 2 were designed to maintain and develop individual engagement. A true or false test of dyslexia knowledge was presented. At the end of Week 2, cumulative scores and answers were added. The intention was to provide all participants with another opportunity to engage in a common activity and to give them a sense that it was their collective, as opposed to individual, knowledge that was important. It was also designed to create a slight tension – asking a question but not providing the collective response or a full explanation. Again, this was designed to maintain interest and engagement.

The second activity for Week 2 asked participants to indicate two topics of interest in the field of dyslexia by adding their username beside any two topics. This was introduced with three purposes in mind to indicate to participants: (1) that they collectively exercised control over the direction that the wiki would take; (2) that the wiki was incomplete and they could contribute to its progress; and (3) that in attaching their names to an area of interest, they were making a small commitment to that particular aspect of dyslexia and also to the other participants who indicated a similar interest. In other words, it was envisaged that this activity was a step towards a shared identity and could form the basis of some topic-focused teamwork at a later date.

A selection of other pages was added to the wiki on a gradual basis, to provide new, stimulating material for participants and to provide a good model. Progressively, over the three weeks of the experimental phase of the wiki, a range of relevant text and multimedia resources were gradually added, such as a reading page.

Week 3

The two activities for Week 3 were added to the wiki at the beginning of the week. The first activity was to complete the combined version of COLLES, which provided a measure of each participant's satisfaction with the wiki.

The second activity, the 'Alice story', presented a relatively detailed description of an authentic problem that a student was experiencing with spellings. It included the student's perspective, the parent's perspective and the teacher's perspective on the situation. A number of people made interesting and constructive suggestions and even commented on what others had said. More than any other single aspect, this activity pointed towards the potential for collaboration in the wiki.

At the end of the three-week experimental period, a final reminder was sent to the participants who had not completed the COLLES survey. Finally, a few days after the completion of the research, the researcher sent a thank-you email to all of the participants and also placed a thank-you message on the front page of the wiki.

During the three-week experimental period, neither the facilitator nor the researcher discussed any aspect of the wiki or the research with any participants outside the wiki or emailed messages.

Results

The majority of the teachers (93 per cent, $n = 27$) reported that they found the Dyslexia Interventions wiki 'easy' or 'relatively' easy to access. Approximately 41 per cent of the people who joined the wiki ($n = 12$) participated in it between four and six times. The number of participations with the wiki is presented in Figure 17.2.

Seven different types of participation (Dron, 2007) were analysed in the wiki and the frequency of their occurrence is detailed in Table 17.3.

These figures suggest that approximately half of the participation of the learner/ participants had a social dimension, in that the action was directed towards another person. The actions that were directed from facilitator to participant included emails of welcome and prompts to have a look at new material in the wiki. The high level of participation by the facilitator was intended to convey the impression of ongoing development.

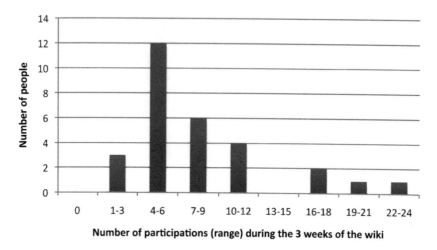

FIGURE 17.2 Number of times people participated in the wiki

TABLE 17.3 Frequency and type of participation in the wiki

Types of participation	Number	Percentage within type
Initiated by the learner (participant)		
participant → facilitator	10	5
participant → content	104	50
participant → participant	95	45
Initiated by the facilitator		
facilitator → participant	219	39
facilitator → content	339	61
facilitator → facilitator	0	0
Initiated by the wiki		
content → content	Est. 100+	100

The number of participants who completed the weekly activities is presented in Figure 17.3. Participants clearly enjoyed some of these activities in particular. For example, in the editing task, participants were asked to make five or six changes to a nonsense definition, but a number of participants made 50–60 changes, revising the whole definition. Both the quiz and the indication of interests were popular.

Only 34 per cent of participants responded to the Alice story, but in many respects those responses were the most interesting and promising. It was the first time a number of the participants had used the threaded conversations facility in the wiki.

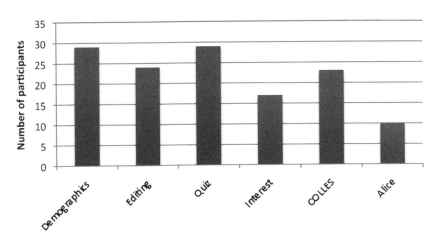

FIGURE 17.3 Number of participants who completed weekly activities in the wiki

Interactions

Interactions within the wiki form a subset of the overall level of participation. They refer to occasions where one participant seeks to communicate with another, either participant-to-participant or participant-to-facilitator or vice versa. The total number of interactions initiated by participants was 105. Approximately 31 per cent ($n = 9$) of participants did not interact at all. A further 35 per cent ($n = 10$) interacted between 1 and 3 times. These results are depicted in Figure 17.4.

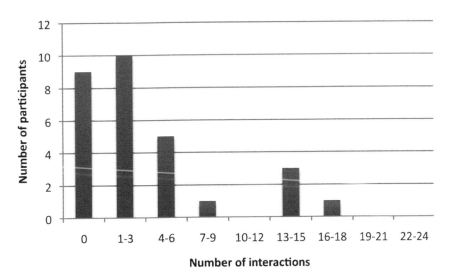

FIGURE 17.4 Number of times participants interacted in the wiki over the three-week experimental period

A number of the participants ($n = 10$) learned how to use the threaded conversations and discussions facility in the wiki. Where it was used, this appeared to prompt a more immediate conversational tone to postings. Over the course of the three weeks, twenty-five threads were started – four of these by the facilitator. The remaining twenty-one threads were started by ten different participants – mostly one or two threads each. However, two participants started four and six threads respectively. The majority (68 per cent) of the threads were started in the final week of the research.

In addition to this, many of these threads generated replies from other participants (or from the facilitator) – eight of the threads generated one reply, two generated two replies, two generated three replies, one generated four replies and two generated six replies. Nine of the participants in the wiki (other than the facilitator) contributed to these replies.

Satisfaction

Of the twenty-nine people who completed the demographic survey, twenty-three completed the final COLLES form. Participants indicated a strong preference for a social constructivist learning environment ($4.05 \pm .4$) but their rating of the actual Dyslexia Interventions wiki learning environment was significantly lower ($3.52 \pm .4$). Participants expressed the highest preference for the aspect of Facilitator Support ($4.50 \pm .1$) and the lowest preference for Interaction ($3.48 \pm .2$). The participants' rating of the intervention wiki followed a similar pattern to their preferences, with the highest actual score being for Facilitator Support ($3.95 \pm .1$) and the lowest for Interaction ($2.80 \pm .1$). The preferred and actual COLLES scores were compared using the paired t-test, and all differences were found to be statistically significant. This suggested that participants' expectations were not fulfilled or they were dissatisfied across all measured aspects and in general with the wiki. The mean results are outlined in Table 17.4.

TABLE 17.4 Comparison of preferred and actual COLLES scores across all aspects of the survey

Aspects	Preferred COLLES score mean (SD)	Actual COLLES score mean (SD)	p
Relevance	4.33 (.096)	3.80 (.141)	.0087
Reflection	3.80 (.082)	3.38 (.171)	.0109
Interaction	3.48 (.183)	2.80 (.141)	.0060
Making sense	4.43 (.191)	3.88 (.275)	.0012
Facilitator support	4.50 (.082)	3.95 (.058)	.0003
Peer support	3.74 (.250)	3.28 (.050)	.0228
Total	4.05 (.4263)	3.52 (.4446)	.0001

Discussion and conclusions

This study explored the viability and benefits of using a wiki to deliver CPD to teachers in one area of their professional practice, namely dyslexia. The results of the study suggested that many teachers had the computer and technical skills needed to access a wiki. Over the three weeks that the wiki was in operation, the teachers participated to a limited degree, and this appeared to have been facilitated by the structured learning activities and the support of the facilitator. Interaction between participants was generally quite low but increased in frequency, particularly in the final week of the wiki. Taking Salmon's five-step model into account (Salmon, 2000), it could be argued that the wiki was transitioning from the first to the second step of that process and that level of participation and interaction was consistent with what would be expected in the initial stages of a wiki. Nevertheless, it should be remembered that a small number of the participants contributed a disproportionate number of participations and interactions.

It may be tentatively concluded that teachers will participate and interact in a constructivist facilitated wiki in order to develop their professional practice, although satisfaction with the wiki seemed to be limited.

Implications

This study indicates that a wiki is not a panacea for all online learning needs or for the delivery of all CPD to teachers. However, a wiki appears to have the potential to be a really useful learning tool in both of these areas. Garrison and Anderson (2002) suggested that as our understanding of online media grows it will transform the teaching and learning experience. In particular, Garrison and Anderson refer to the integration of constructivist theory into the creation and implementation of an online learning environment, the identification of an appropriate population of learners, adding clear purpose and meaning, stimulating collaborative activities and integrating sound pedagogy.

There were a number of limitations in the current study. Dyslexia was chosen as a subject for the wiki because it is a significant issue for teachers and their pupils. However, as the topic did not originate from the teachers themselves, they did not come together purposively and meaningfully (Jones and Preece, 2006). It is likely that the participants in the wiki experienced only a limited sense of purpose and meaning.

Another significant limitation was the length and timing of the research project. The end of the project coincided with the last day of the school term before a holiday period, which may have distracted teachers from the wiki. Most wiki projects have a much longer time span. It is possible that with time, participants would connect more fully with the process, learning to collaborate and engage in the higher-order thinking that Garrison refers to in the Practical Inquiry model (Garrison *et al.*, 2009).

The wiki was very much guided by the constructivist paradigm; however, while constructivism may be one of the wikis greatest strengths, it may also be a significant weakness. Teachers, learners and facilitators may have difficulty operating effectively in a constructivist learning environment, as they may not possess all of the requisite skills needed to learn in this way. An in-depth assessment of individual learning skills and perhaps even wikis in constructivist learning might be good places to start that journey.

Many of the barriers to online learning mentioned in the research had relevance for participants in the study wiki, but some clearly did not. For example, technology did not appear to be a barrier in this study, whereas in other research over 50 per cent of participants had difficulty accessing a wiki (Su and Beaumont, 2008).

It would be interesting to complete a longer-term study of wiki use by a group of teachers to determine more clearly its future course and usefulness. In addition, the many variations of wikis could be examined, with a view to determining which are the most critical aspects with regard to functioning as constructivist learning environments.

References

APA Task Force on Psychology in Education (1993). *Learner-Centered Psychological Principles: Guidelines for school redesign and reform.* Washington, DC: American Psychological Association and Mid-continent Regional Educational Laboratory.

Bruner, J. (1990). *Acts of Meaning.* Cambridge, MA: Harvard University Press.

Chang, S. (2004). The roles of mentors in electronic learning environments. *AACE Journal,* 12 (3), 331–342.

Cornelius-White, J. (2007). Learner-centered teacher-student relationships are effective: A meta-analysis. *Review of Educational Research,* 17 (1), 113–143.

Dron, J. (2007). *Control and Constraint in e-Learning: Choosing when to choose.* Hershey, PA: Information Science Reference, imprint of IGI Publishing.

Duncan-Howell, J. (2009). Online professional communities: Understanding the effects of membership on teacher practice. *The International Journal of Learning,* 16 (5), 601–613.

Ebner, M., Kickmeier-Rust, M. and Holzinger, A. (2008). Utilizing wiki-systems in higher education classes: A chance for universal access? *Universal Access in the Information Society,* 7 (4), 199–207.

Elgort, I., Smith, A.G. and Toland, J. (2008). Is wiki an effective platform for group course work. *Australian Journal of Educational Technology,* 24 (2), 195–210.

Garrison, D.R. (2009). Implications of online learning for the conceptual development and practice of distance education. *Journal of Distance Education,* 23 (2), 93–104.

Garrison, D.R. and Anderson, T. (2002). *E-Learning in the 21st Century: A framework for research and practice.* London: Taylor & Francis.

Garrison, D.R. and Cleveland-Innes, M. (2005). Facilitating cognitive presence in online learning: Interaction is not enough. *The American Journal of Distance Education,* 19 (3), 133–148.

Garrison, D.R., Ice, P. and Akyol, Z. (2009). The Community of Inquiry Framework: A review of the research and practical implications. The 7th Annual Hawaii International Conference on Education, Honolulu. [PowerPoint slides]. Retrieved from: http://communitiesofinquiry.com/presentations.

Garrison, D.R., Anderson, T. and Archer, W. (2010). The first decade of the community of inquiry framework: A retrospective. *Internet and Higher Education,* 13, 5–9.

Guzdial, M., Rick, J. and Kehoe, C. (2001). Beyond adoption to invention: Teacher-created collaborative activities in higher education. *The Journal of the Learning Sciences*, 10, 265–279.

Jones, A. and Preece, J. (2006). Online communities for teachers and lifelong learners: A framework for comparing similarities and identifying differences in communities of practice and communities of interest. *International Journal of Learning Technology*, 2 (2–3), 112–137.

Judd, T., Kennedy, G. and Cropper, S. (2010). Using wikis for collaborative learning: Assessing collaboration through contribution. *Australian Journal of Education Technology*, 26 (3), 341–354.

Kehrwald, B. (2008). Understanding social presence in text-based online learning environments. *Distance Education*, 29 (1), 89–106.

Leuf, B. and Cunningham, W. (2001). *The Wiki Way: Collaborating and sharing on the Internet*. Upper Saddle River, NJ: Addison-Wesley.

Maushak, N.J. and Ellis, K.A. (2003). Attitudes of graduate students toward mixed-medium distance education. *Quarterly Review of Distance Education*, 4 (2), 129–141.

McFadzean, E. (2001). Supporting virtual learning groups. Part 1: A pedagogical perspective. *Team Performance Management*, 7 (3/4), 53–62.

Muilenberg, L. and Berge, Z. (2005). Student barriers to online learning. *Distance Education*, 26 (1), 29–48.

Neumann, D.L. and Hood, M. (2009). The effects of using a wiki on student engagement and learning of report writing skills in a university statistics course. *Australian Journal of Educational Technology*, 25 (3), 382–398.

Northrup, P.T. (2002). Online learner's preferences for interaction. *Quarterly Review of Distance Education*, 3 (2), 219–226.

Piaget, J. (1971). *Psychology and Epistemology*. New York: Grossman.

Preece, J., Nonnecke, B. and Andrews, D. (2004). The top 5 reasons for lurking: Improving community experiences for everyone. *Computers in Human Behaviour*, 20, 201–223.

Robson, C. (1993). *Real World Research: A resource for social scientists and practitioner-researchers*. Oxford: Blackwell.

Ruth, A. and Houghton, L. (2009). The wiki way of learning. *Australasian Journal of Educational Technology*, 25 (2), 135–152.

Salmon, G. (2000). *E-Moderating: The key to teaching and learning online*. London: Kogan Page.

Salmon, G. (2003). *E-tivities: The key to active online learning*. London: Routledge-Falmer.

Salmon, G. (2005). Flying not flapping: A strategic framework for e-learning and pedagogical innovation in higher education institutions. *ALT-J Research in Learning Technology*, 13 (3), 201–218.

Salmon, G. (2007). The tipping point. *ALT-J, Research in Learning Technology*, 15 (2), 171–172.

Schlager, M.S. and Fusco, J. (2003). Teacher professional development, technology, and communities of practice: Are we putting the cart before the horse? *The Information Society*, 19 (3), 203–220.

Shin, N. (2002). Beyond interaction: The relational construct of 'transactional presence'. *Open Learning*, 17 (2), 121–137.

Slavin, R.E. (2009). *Educational Psychology: Theory and practice*. Columbus, OH: Pearson.

Su, F. and Beaumont, C. (2008). Student perceptions of e-learning with a wiki. *SOLSTICE Conference*. Ormskirk: Edge Hill University.

Taylor, P.C. and Maor, D. (n.d.). *The Constructivist On-Line Learning Environment Survey (COLLES)*. Retrieved from Surveylearning.com: http://surveylearning.moodle.com/colles/.

Thorpe, M. and Gordon, J. (2012). Online learning in the workplace: A hybrid model of participation in networked professional learning. *Australasian Journal of Educational Technology*, 28 (8), 1267–1282.

Vellutino, F.R., Fletcher, J.M., Snowling, M.J. and Scanlon, D.M. (2004). Specific reading disability (dyslexia): What have we learned in the past four decades? *Journal of Child Psychology and Psychiatry*, 45 (1), 2–40.

Wang, L. and Beasley, W. (2008). The wiki as a web2.0 tool in education. *Journal of Technology in Teaching and Learning*, 4 (1), 78–85.

18

SOCIAL BITS

Personality and learning style profiling
via the social web

Kostas Mavropalias and Ellen Brady

Chapter summary

This study aimed to investigate the potential contribution of the social web to
e-learning systems via the use of social bits, or pieces of data acquired from a person's
online social activity. The social bits of an international sample of 121 participants
were analysed in order to examine any links between social networking site use
and personality characteristics and learning styles. A number of significant results
were found, suggesting that this relationship could be useful in intelligent and
adaptive e-learning systems. The novel methodology used and the practical
implications for online learning are discussed.

Introduction

As the popularity of online learning environments grows, one challenge presented
to e-learning systems is to respond by tailoring the learning experience towards
the personality and learning capacity of each learner. One method used for
customised learning environments is the creation of a user model, which holds a
combination of personality factors, behavioural factors and knowledge factors that
the e-learning system believes to be an accurate representation of the learner (Özpolat
and Akar, 2009). The information contained within a user model is used as the
basis for intelligent adaptation of the learning material, the user interface and other
areas of an e-learning system, depending on its capabilities. An important aspect
of information for an e-learning system is the learning style of a student (Cha
et al., 2006; Özpolat and Akar, 2009), which describes the individual process by
which a student learns, facilitating the customisation of learning material (Fatahi
and Ghasem-Aghaee, 2010; Jovanovic *et al.*, 2008).

In developing user models, two techniques have been predominantly used to
identify learning styles and personality characteristics: questionnaires and ongoing

behaviour and performance monitoring (Graf *et al.*, 2008). Both techniques have significant drawbacks, however. Questionnaires must be completed in advance of a student using an e-learning system, and they can only provide data from a single point in time, thus failing to acknowledge any change or adaptation in learning styles or user characteristics (Popescu, 2010; Villaverde *et al.*, 2006). Conversely, behaviour and performance monitoring occurs subsequent to a student beginning to use an e-learning system and continues during the learning process. This provides a non-disruptive method to profile the personality and learning style of the user, though it can be slow to produce useful results and is highly reliant on the system's capabilities to identify potential useful characteristics of the learner.

This suggests that there is a need to develop a strategy for creating an accurate user model prior to the commencement of the learning strategy that will continue to evolve along with the user and their learning capabilities. A key challenge in the development of such user models is the acquisition of relevant and accurate user data. Considering this, third-party sources that may encapsulate information such as the behavioural and learning characteristics of an individual could offer a useful method of gathering pertinent data. In particular, the Internet, and specifically the social web, could be used as a third-party source of such data.

Over the past few years, the growth of the social web has given rise to hundreds of social networking sites (SNSs) that cater to a wide range of interests and target audiences. The popularity of SNSs has attracted the interest of scholars and researchers, making the social web a thriving environment for research and study (Wilson *et al.*, 2012). The most prevalent SNS, Facebook, serves more than 845 million users who spend over 9.7 billion minutes per day on it (Facebook, 2012). As a result, the majority of psychological research on the social web has focused on Facebook, though online social activities also include websites such as Last.fm, where users can listen, share and discover music, Foursquare, which enables its users to publicise their geographical activity online, LinkedIn, a communication platform for professionals, Flickr, which allows members to share their photos online, and Twitter, which provides a platform for the exchange of short messages. The present study defines the content shared and published online by individuals as social bits: pieces of data acquired from a person's online social activity.

In order to utilise the application of SNSs to e-learning systems and user models, the link between these sites and users' personality characteristics and learning styles must be explored. While there has been limited research around the connection between SNSs and learning styles (e.g. Chen, 2011), SNSs and personality characteristics have received more attention. In line with research on other aspects of SNSs, these studies have predominately focused on Facebook (Amichai-Hamburger and Vinitzky, 2010; Ross *et al.*, 2009; Ryan and Xenos, 2011); links between Twitter use and personality traits have also been examined (Hughes *et al.*, 2012). Though these studies have resulted in some mixed findings, overall, the research appears to indicate that Facebook and Twitter use is associated with the personality of individuals. For example, an individual's neuroticism, or their level of emotional instability (Goldberg, 1990), has been shown to be related to their use of Facebook (Amichai-Hamburger and Vinitzky, 2010; Hughes *et al.*, 2012; Ross *et al.*, 2009; Ryan and Xenos, 2011), with Internet users with higher levels of neuroticism spending significantly more time on Facebook per day (Ryan and Xenos, 2011).

More specifically, however, aspects of SNS use, or social bits, have also been linked with personality characteristics. Ross *et al.* (2009) and Ryan and Xenos (2011) reported that Facebook users who scored highly on the trait of neuroticism expressed a higher preference for using the Wall feature (where users post messages and share content with other users; Facebook, 2011), than individuals who showed lower levels of neuroticism. While the rationale for this link has not been fully explored (for example, Ross *et al.*, 2009, suggest that neurotic individuals may like the level of information control offered by the wall feature), the findings indicate that the use of SNSs, and the manner of use of these sites, may provide a level of information about a user's personality. Consequently, SNSs could offer a method of data extraction that may be useful in the creation of user models for e-learning systems.

The present study was designed to explore how personality characteristics and learning styles relate to the use of multiple SNSs and whether such a relationship could be useful in intelligent and adaptive e-learning systems. Specifically, the research question posed by the study was: can personality traits and learning styles be predicted by analysing the social bits and patterns of use of SNSs by individuals? Previous studies have suggested a significant connection between personality and SNS use. However, many of these studies have used homogenous samples (Amichai-Hamburger and Vinitzky, 2010; Hughes *et al.*, 2012; Ross *et al.*, 2009) or self-report measures (Hughes *et al.*, 2012; Ryan and Xenos, 2011), or they have focused only on a single SNS (Amichai-Hamburger and Vinitzky, 2010; Ross *et al.*, 2009; Ryan and Xenos, 2011), limiting the level to which these results can be extrapolated. Furthermore, the lack of research around SNSs and learning styles makes it difficult to develop detailed and concise hypotheses for further study.

To that end, a simple exploratory hypothesis was developed: the online social networking activity of individuals as measured by their social bits has a significant correlation with personality characteristics and learning style attributes.

Method

This study used a quantitative approach that enabled the examination of relationships between social network use, personality characteristics and learning style attributes. Participants completed online measures in order to assess their personality and learning style, while a third-party application created by the first author accessed individuals' SNSs accounts with their permission and retrieved the available data for analysis.

TABLE 18.1 Age and gender of participants

	18–24 years	*25–34 years*	*35–49 years*	*50+ years*	*Total*
Male	12	27	20	1	60
Female	16	29	13	3	61
Total	28	56	33	4	121

Participants

In order to examine the research question among a diverse group of participants, an international sample of 121 people from twenty-one countries (though predominately Ireland, Greece and the United States) was recruited online using convenience and snowball sampling. The age and gender of participants is contained in Table 18.1.

Individuals known to the researchers were invited to participate and simultaneously encouraged to invite their peers to participate. The study was also promoted by mentions in relevant websites and through online advertisement. All participants were over the age of 18 and had an account on at least one of the following SNSs: Facebook, Twitter, LinkedIn, Flickr, Foursquare and Last.fm. The selection of sites was based on their popularity, niche and availability of developer tools to collect user data.

Measures

Participants completed online measures of personality characteristics and learning styles. Personality was assessed using the International English Big-Five Mini-Markers (Thompson, 2008), a forty-item questionnaire that measures five dimensions of personality: conscientiousness, extraversion, openness to experience, emotional stability or neuroticism and agreeableness. This measure was chosen because of its suitability for an international sample. Learning style was assessed via the Index of Learning Styles (Felder and Spurlin, 2005). This measure consisted of forty-four questions and assessed learning style preference on four dimensions of learning: active/reflective, sensing/intuitive, visual/verbal, sequential/global. Both measures showed acceptable levels of reliability and validity (Felder and Spurlin, 2005; Thompson, 2008).

Procedure

A website was created by the researcher in order to collect the required data from each participant. Upon entering the website, individuals were presented with a detailed information sheet explaining the purpose and nature of the research. Following this, participants provided some basic demographic information, gave the study access to their SNSs and completed the online questionnaires.

Finally, participants were offered the opportunity to share the study with other SNS users.

Ethics

This study was conducted in accordance with ethical standards. Internet-based research methods pose unique challenges in comparison to traditional laboratory research. Critical issues in online research ethics include the security of confidential data, the anonymity of participants and the storage of data (Nosek *et al.*, 2002). To address any ethical considerations, the present study provided a detailed brief to all participants with information on the privacy and anonymity of the study to enable them to provide informed consent. The participants were informed that they could withdraw from the study at any time, and were provided with a unique personal code in order to delete their data after the culmination of the research. In addition, no potentially identifying information such as names, addresses or phone numbers was collected. All the data acquired was stored in a secure password-protected directory on a reputable web hosting company, and were transferred to the researcher's personal computer using a secured connection.

Results

The data collected by the participants' online profiles, using the study's especially developed applications, along with the data from the International English Big-Five Mini-Markers (Thompson, 2008) and the Index of Learning Styles (Felder and Spurlin, 2005), were analysed using a software package for statistical analysis (SPSS).

Personality differences between users of different SNSs

In order to investigate people's use of different SNSs (Facebook, Twitter, LinkedIn, Foursquare, Flickr and Last.fm) in regard to their personality characteristics, a series of independent t-tests were carried out. The mean scores on each of the five personality factors, as measured by the International English Big-Five Mini-Markers (Thompson, 2008), for users and non-users of each of the SNSs were compared in order to reveal any significant differences between the groups. The results are reported in Table 18.2.

Looking at the results of the t-tests, openness to experience and emotional stability represent the traits that showed the highest number of significant differences between SNSs users and non-SNS users. For LinkedIn and Flickr, users of these sites reported higher levels of openness to experience than non-users. By contrast, Facebook users showed lower levels of openness to experience than non-users ($t(119) = -2.722$, $p = .007$). In addition, users of LinkedIn showed higher levels of conscientiousness than non-users ($t(119) = 2.331$, $p = .02$), and Last.fm users showed lower levels of extraversion than non-users ($t(119) = -2.825$, $p = .006$).

TABLE 18.2 Personality characteristics of SNS users and non-users

	User n	Non-user n	Conscientiousness			Extraversion			Openness to experience			Emotional stability			Agreeableness		
			User M (SD)	Non-user M (SD)	P-value	User M (SD)	Non-user M (SD)	P-value	User M (SD)	Non-user M (SD)	P-value	User M (SD)	Non-user M (SD)	P-value	User M (SD)	Non-user M (SD)	P-value
Facebook	111	10	29.31 (5.6)	31.1 (6.47)	.34	26.69 (6.3)	26.8 (7.2)	.96	30.28 (5.28)	34.90 (2.77)	.007**	24.20 (5.41)	26.8 (4.05)	.141	32.5 (4.4)	32.5 (3.5)	.99
Twitter	36	85	28.56 (4.51)	29.84 (6.1)	.26	26.75 (5.8)	26.68 (6.6)	.958	31.22 (5.5)	30.42 (5.2)	.45	25.75 (4.37)	23.82 (5.68)	.073	32.5 (3.3)	32.5 (4.7)	.95
LinkedIn	42	79	31.07 (5.34)	28.59 (5.68)	.02*	26.19 (6.3)	26.97 (6.4)	.52	32.76 (4.21)	29.54 (5.47)	.001**	25.67 (5.6)	23.75 (5.11)	.06	32.8 (3.4)	32.3 (4.8)	.55
Flickr	12	109	29.67 (5.16)	29.43 (5.7)	.89	24.75 (7.5)	26.92 (6.2)	.26	33.58 (4.19)	30.34 (5.3)	.04*	26.92 (5.13)	24.14 (5.32)	.09	34.3 (2.6)	32.3 (4.4)	.13
Foursquare	16	105	29.31 (6.4)	29.48 (5.6)	.92	26.12 (7.9)	26.79 (6.1)	.698	33.0 (5.19)	30.30 (5.22)	.057	26.38 (6.3)	24.1 (5.16)	.115	33.3 (3.6)	32.4 (4.4)	.43
Last FM	8	113	29.5 (5.8)	29.45 (5.7)	.98	20.75 (5.6)	27.12 (6.2)	.006**	34 (4.6)	30.42 (5.26)	.064	27.63 (4.81)	24.19 (5.33)	.079	33.4 (2.9)	32.5 (4.4)	.56

Note: M = mean score, SD = standard deviation, *p < .05; **p < .01.

Learning style differences between users of different SNSs

In order to examine individuals' learning styles and SNS use, an approach similar to the one used for the personality traits was followed. While all 121 participants completed the personality characteristics measures, only 107 completed the learning styles measure. A number of independent t-tests were carried out in order to compare the learning styles of users and non-users of each of the SNSs, as measured by the Index of Learning Styles (Felder and Spurlin, 2005). The results of this analysis are reported in Table 18.3.

In comparing the learning style scores of users and non-users of six different SNSs, only two significant differences were recorded. LinkedIn users scored higher than non-users on the sensing/intuitive dimension, indicating that LinkedIn users are more likely to be intuitive learners than sensing ones, compared to non-users ($t(105) = 2.051$, $p = .04$). A similar result was found for Flickr, where users of Flickr displayed higher scores on the sensing/intuitive dimension than non-users, ($t(105) = 2.489$, $p = .015$).

Personality and use patterns of Facebook, Twitter and Linkedin

During the data collection process, data from all 121 participants were collected from their social networking sites. A larger number of participants had accounts on Facebook, Twitter and LinkedIn, and the use of Foursquare, Flickr and Last.fm was low. Consequently, personality and learning style analysis in relation to individual SNSs was carried out only for Facebook, Twitter and LinkedIn.

In the case of Facebook, a large amount of data was collected. On reviewing the data, a number of variables were extracted for further analysis. Where the data collected was scale data, a series of correlations were run in order to examine relationships between Facebook variables and personality characteristics. The results of this analysis are presented in Table 18.4.

A number of significant results were found in relation to personality characteristics and Facebook use. Extraversion was found to be significantly positive correlated with the number of likes or posts on an individual's Facebook page ($r = .165$, $p = .042$). Emotional stability was negatively correlated with the number of activities included on a person's Facebook page, ($r = -.179$, $p = .03$), movies liked ($r = -.174$, $p = .03$), TV shows liked ($r = -.190$, $p = .02$), pages liked ($r = -.182$, $p = .03$), number of groups ($r = -.159$, $p < .05$) and overall number of likes ($r = -.231$, $p < .01$), though it was positively correlated with the number of check-ins ($r = .196$, $p = .02$).

Agreeableness was positively correlated with the number of posts on a person's profile page ($r = .318$, $p < .000$) and the number of Facebook affiliations ($r = .220$, $p = .01$) and negatively correlated with the number of music-related likes ($r = -.172$, $p = .035$). Regarding openness to experience, this trait was positively correlated with the number of likes of books ($r = .213$, $p = .013$) and interests ($r = .228$,

TABLE 18.3 Learning styles of SNS users and non-users

	User n	Non-user n	Active/Reflective			Sensing/Intuitive			Visual/Verbal			Sequential/Global		
			User M (SD)	Non-user M (SD)	P-value	User M (SD)	Non-user M (SD)	P-value	User M (SD)	Non-user M (SD)	P-value	User M (SD)	Non-user M (SD)	P-value
Facebook	99	8	11.93 (5.1)	13 (3.2)	.56	13.14 (5.6)	14.5 (6.57)	.517	8.66 (5.0)	8.75 (8.7)	.96	12.76 (4.6)	13.5 (5.6)	.67
Twitter	32	75	11.5 (5.52)	12.23 (4.7)	.49	13.5 (6.13)	13.13 (5.5)	.761	9.44 (5.3)	8.33 (5.2)	.322	12.25 (4.9)	13.05 (4.6)	.42
LinkedIn	38	69	11.74 (4.01)	12.16 (5.4)	.68	14.74 (6.0)	12.42 (5.37)	.43*	8.00 (5.1)	9.03 (5.3)	.335	13.16 (5.2)	12.62 (4.4)	.58
Flickr	11	96	11.18 (3.6)	12.1 (5.1)	.56	17.18 (4.04)	12.79 (5.7)	.014*	6.64 (4.8)	8.9 (5.3)	.178	14.45 (4.2)	12.62 (4.7)	.22
Foursquare	14	93	11.71 (4.7)	12.05 (5.02)	.813	15.71 (5.24)	12.87 (5.67)	.08	7.00 (4.22)	8.91 (5.37)	.206	13.00 (6.23)	12.78 (4.5)	.87
Last FM	7	100	12.43 (4.42)	11.98 (5.03)	.819	15.00 (5.03)	13.12 (5.72)	.399	5.86 (3.02)	8.86 (5.34)	.145	13.57 (4.1)	12.76 (4.7)	.66

Note: M = mean score, SD = standard deviation, $*p < .05$; $**p < .01$.

TABLE 18.4 Personality characteristics and Facebook variables

	Conscientiousness	Extraversion	Openness to experience	Emotional stability	Agreeableness
	r	r	r	r	r
Activities	−.034	.055	−.021	−.179★	−.035
Affiliations	.036	.050	.044	.146	.220★
Books	.118	−.111	.213★	−.082	.057
Interests	.110	.000	.228★★	.005	.152
Movies	.073	−.146	.052	−.174★	−.043
Music	.022	−.151	−.068	−.146	−.172★
Notes	−.177★	.078	.096	−.035	−.021
TV	.082	−.160★	.030	−.190★	−.058
Wall	−.016	.090	−.100	.145	.128
Work history	.124	.005	.083	.083	.142
Family	−.065	−.029	.118	−.062	.012
Friends	−.063	−.101	.048	−.077	.044
Pages liked	.052	−.109	−.066	−.182★	−.037
Groups	.033	−.073	−.140	−.159★	.058
Likes	.062	−.104	−.068	−.231★★	−.064
Checkins	.045	.089	−.010	.196★	−.004
Links	.087	−.121	−.003	−.094	−.023
Photo tags	−.059	.038	−.027	−.031	.089
Tags	−.077	.063	−.076	−.039	.044
Posts	.058	.070	.039	−.017	.318★★
Post likes	−.008	.165★	−.046	−.082	.092
Average post likes	−.024	.110	−.030	−.091	.080
Post comments	−.044	.118	−.207★	−.027	.040
Average post comments	−.063	.118	−.134	−.063	−.003

Note: $n = 111$, ★$p < .05$; ★★$p < .01$.

$p = .008$), and negatively correlated with the number of comments on profile page posts ($r = −.207$, $p = .015$). Higher levels of conscientiousness were positively correlated with the number of notes a participant wrote ($r = .177$, $p < .05$).

In the analysis of personality effects in regard to Twitter and LinkedIn use, a number of aspects were explored. Five pieces of data were considered for Twitter (overall number of tweets, number of followers, how many people one follows, number of favourite tweets and how many times one was listed in other people's Twitter lists), and six factors were examined in the LinkedIn data (connections with other users, work history, education history, recommendations, instant messaging accounts, websites). No significant results were observed.

Learning styles and use patterns of Facebook, Twitter and Linkedin

Of the 107 participants who fully completed the learning styles questionnaire, ninety-nine used Facebook, thirty-eight had a LinkedIn account and thirty-two used Twitter. As with the personality characteristic data, a series of correlations were carried out for selected Facebook variables. These results are reported in Table 18.5.

Individuals who appeared to be reflective learners had an increased number of activities ($r = .241$, $p = .008$), movies ($r = .180$, $p = .037$) and TV shows ($r = .232$, $p = .010$) on their Facebook profiles, while those who were more active learners rather than reflective learners had more profile posts ($r = -.220$, $p = .014$) and profile post likes ($r = -.220$, $p = .014$). More intuitive learners had higher levels of books ($r = .216$, $p = .016$), family members ($r = .185$, $p = .035$), movies

TABLE 18.5 Learning styles and Facebook variables

	Active/ Reflective	Sensing/ Intuitive	Visual/ Verbal	Sequential/ Global
	r	r	r	r
Activities	.241★★	.160	.118	−.044
Affiliations	−.116	−.066	−.173★	−.114
Books	.188★	.216★	.124	−.126
Interests	.097	.015	.000	.124
Movies	.180★	.194★	.030	−.025
Music	.113	.199★	−.025	−.034
Notes	−.058	.079	−.035	.099
TV	.232★	.126	.039	−.132
Wall	−.185★	.075	−.075	−.066
Work history	.000	.075	−.201★	−.060
Family	.138	.183★	−.018	.106
Friends	.065	.061	.043	−.138
Pages liked	−.010	.090	.155	−.011
Groups	.019	.094	−.063	.076
Likes	.087	.145	.057	−.062
Check–ins	−.032	.121	−.165	.079
Links	.139	.061	−.019	−.154
Photo tags	−.091	−.069	.027	.029
Tags	−.074	.039	.032	−.085
Posts	−.220★	−.066	−.109	−.094
Post likes	−.220★	−.014	.004	.075
Average post likes	−.219★	.001	.032	.058
Post comments	−.174★	−.032	.006	−.010
Average post comments	−.116	−.019	.115	.070

Note: $n = 99$, ★$p < .05$; ★★$p < .01$.

TABLE 18.6 Learning styles and LinkedIn variables

	Active/ Reflective	Sensing/ Intuitive	Visual/ Verbal	Sequential/ Global
	r	r	r	r
Connections	.014	.222	−.014	.043
Work history	−.116	.001	−.106	−.108
Education	−.263	−.125	−.113	−.163
Recommendations	.204	.111	.124	.100
Instant messaging	−.298★	.077	.118	−.017
Websites	.018	.324★	−.057	−.215

Note: $n = 38$, ★$p < .05$; ★★$p < .01$.

($r = .194$, $p = .027$) and music ($r = .199$, $p = .024$) on their profile, while more visual learners had higher levels of affiliations ($r = −.173$, $p = .044$) and an increased work history ($r = −.201$, $p = .023$).

No significant results were found when learning styles and Twitter use were examined; however, a number of significant results were found in relation to LinkedIn. These results are contained in Table 18.6. More active learners used the instant messaging service ($r = −.298$, $p = .039$) than reflective learners, while intuitive learners had an increased number of personal website addresses on their profiles ($r = .324$, $p = .027$).

Discussion

The present study investigated whether the SNS activity of individuals as measured by their social bits correlated significantly with their Big Five personality factor and learning styles. As previous studies have indicated, an adapted learning experience, customised to the personality, learning style and preferences of individual students, can enhance the user experience, engagement levels and, crucially, the learning outcome of students (Fatahi and Ghasem-Aghaee, 2010; Jovanovic et al., 2008). Intelligent and adaptive e-learning systems have used standardised questionnaires and performance monitoring to profile students and create sufficiently accurate user models that are used to deliver learning experiences adapted to each student. However, among other drawbacks, the use of question-naires can be disruptive to the learning process, while performance monitoring requires time to produce precise results. The purpose of the present study was to explore more efficient and effective means of developing such user models for students.

One of the main requirements of a student user model is data that describe the personality and learning style of the student. The present study identified social bits, the granular information shared and stored on the social web via a number of SNSs, as a potential resource of personal data that might be useful in user modelling. Following a base of research that linked aspects of SNS use with personality characteristics, this research aimed to investigate whether personality traits and learning styles can be predicted by analysing individuals' use of Facebook and other SNSs. Notably, an automated process that enabled the collection of comprehensive sets of data across six popular SNSs from a diverse international sample was used. The study's hypothesis stated that the online social networking activity of individuals, their social bits, has a significant correlation with personality characteristics and learning style attributes. The results support this hypothesis and suggest that many aspects of personality and learning style dimensions are significantly connected to SNS use.

The initial data analysis aimed to explore differences in personality and learning styles between members of Facebook, Twitter, LinkedIn, Last.fm, Foursquare and Flickr. Openness to experience was found to be associated with the use of three SNSs. Facebook users scored lower in that trait, while LinkedIn and Flickr users scored higher than the respective non-users of these SNSs. LinkedIn users were found to score higher in the conscientiousness scale, and Last.fm users rated significantly lower in extraversion compared to non-users.

While there are a number of interpretations that could be applied to this data (e.g. LinkedIn attracts an organised, diligent and scrupulous audience, resulting in higher conscientiousness scores among users), the crucial factor in relation to the present study is that personality characteristics and SNS use appear to be related. Similarly, investigations into learning styles and SNS use indicate some links. LinkedIn and Flickr users were more likely to fall in the intuitive side of the sensing/intuitive learning dimension. As Felder and Silverman (1988) explain, intuitive learners often prefer discovering possibilities and relationships; they like innovation and dislike repetition, and are better at grasping new concepts. Notably, LinkedIn and Flickr users were also found to be more open to experience, indicating a level of overlap between the findings of the personality test and the learning style test.

The detailed analysis of data in user profiles and overall activity within each social network revealed a significantly large number of correlations with personality traits and learning styles, supporting the study's hypothesis. In addition, much of the results are in line with previous research on the topic (Amichai-Hamburger and Vinitzky, 2010; Hughes et al., 2012; Ross et al., 2009; Ryan and Xenos, 2011). For example, the sensing/intuitive dimension was found to correlate positively with four aspects of Facebook use (activities, books, movies and music) and one of LinkedIn (websites). These results suggest that individuals open to experience and intuitive in learning are more likely to share their intellectual and artistic pursuits on Facebook and LinkedIn, supporting research from Amichai-Hamburger and Vinitzky (2010). More importantly, this indicates that an individual's SNS use is linked to their learning style and personality. In the context of the present study, this suggests that this relationship could be useful in intelligent and adaptive e-learning systems.

Overall, this study aimed to provide a detailed insight into how personality and learning styles are connected to patterns of SNS use. The online methodology used – whereby participants accessed the study by allowing researcher created applications access to retrieve granular data, or social bits, from their SNSs – is relatively novel and represents an improvement in the self-reported SNS use utilised in previous research (Hughes *et al.*, 2012; Ryan and Xenos, 2011). In addition, the international sample and the variety of SNSs included in the research attempted to incorporate an inhomogeneous dataset of individuals and websites.

The data collected from Last.fm, Flickr and Foursquare could not be analysed because of the small sample size, and thus additional research targeting a variety of sites is recommended. It may also be important to examine the changes that occur in the social profiles of individuals over time, and investigate the fluctuations of their patterns of SNS use in relation to personality and learning styles (Amichai-Hamburger and Vinitzky, 2010). Such an investigation could enable adaptive e-learning systems that utilise the social web to compensate for any changes that occur over time and adjust their user models.

Finally, the practical implications of these findings for intelligent and adaptive systems in the e-learning industry, and beyond, are highly significant. The novel methodology used and the data analysis performed have suggested a method for systems to overcome issues related to the use of questionnaires and performance monitoring by making use of the social web as a potential and effective way of creating relatively accurate user models and providing instant personalisation to their users.

References

Amichai-Hamburger, Y. and Vinitzky, G. (2010). Social network use and personality. *Computers in Human Behaviour*, 26, 1289–1295.

Cha, H.J., Kim, Y.S., Lee, J.H. and Yoon, T.B. (2006). An adaptive learning system with learning style diagnosis based on interface behaviours. *Workshop Proceedings of International Conference on E-Learning and Games, Hangzhou, China* (pp. 513–524). Retrieved from: http://cdi.skku.edu/credits/publications/EI-template_Final.pdf.

Chen, Y. (2011). Learning styles and adopting Facebook technology. *Technology Management in the Energy Smart World (PICMET), Proceedings of PICMET '11*, 1–9. Retrieved from: http://ieeexplore.ieee.org/stamp/stamp.jsp?tp=&arnumber=6017676.

Facebook (2011). Share, star and hide stories. Retrieved from: www.facebook.com/help/wall.

Facebook (2012). *Statistics of Facebook*. Palo Alto, CA: Facebook. Retrieved from: http://newsroom.fb.com/content/default.aspx?NewsAreaId=22.

Fatahi, S. and Ghasem-Aghaee, N. (2010). Design and implementation of an intelligent educational model based on personality and learner's emotion. *International Journal of Computer Science and Information Security*, 7 (3), 1–13.

Felder, R. and Silverman, L. (1988). Learning and teaching styles in engineering education. *Engineering Education*, 78, 674–681.

Felder, R.M. and Spurlin, J. (2005). Applications, reliability and validity of the Index of Learning Styles. *International Journal of Engineering Education*, 21 (1), 103–112.

Goldberg, L.R. (1990). An alternative description of personality: the big-five factor structure. *Journal of Personality and Social Psychology*, 59, 1216–1229.

Graf, S., Kinshuk, and Liu, T. C. (2008). Identifying learning styles in learning management systems by using indications from students' behaviour. In P. Diaz, Kinshuk, I. Aedo and E. Mora (eds) *Proceedings of the International Conference on Advanced Learning Technologies* (pp. 482–486). Santander: IEEE Computer Science.

Hughes, D., Rowe, M., Batey, M. and Lee, A. (2012). A tale of two sites: Twitter vs Facebook and the personality predictors of social media usage. *Computers in Human Behaviour*, 28, 561–569

Jovanovic, D.V., Milosevic, D. and Zizovic, M. (2008). INDeLER: eLearning personalization by mapping students' learning style and preference to metadata. *International Journal of Emerging Technologies in Learning (iJET)*, 3 (4), 41–50.

Nosek, B.A., Banaji, M.R. and Greenwald, A.G. (2002). E-research: Ethics, security, design, and control in psychological research on the Internet. *Journal of Social Issues*, 58 (1), 161–176.

Özpolat, E. and Akar, G.B. (2009). Automatic detection of learning styles for an e-learning system. *Computers & Education*, 53, 355–367.

Popescu, E. (2010). A unified learning style model for technology-enhanced learning: What, why and how? *International Journal of Distance Education Technologies*, 65–81.

Ross, C., Orr, E.S., Sisic, M., Arseneault, J.M., Simmering, M.G. and Orr, R.R. (2009). Personality and motivations associated with Facebook use. *Computers in Human Behaviour*, 25, 578–586.

Ryan, T. and Xenos, S. (2011). Who uses Facebook? An investigation into the relationship between the Big Five, shyness, narcissism, loneliness and Facebook usage. *Computers in Human Behaviour*, 27, 1658–1664.

Thompson, E.R. (2008). Development and validation of an international English big-five mini-markers. *Personality and Individual Differences*, 45, 542–548.

Villaverde, J.E., Godoy, D. and Amandi, A. (2006). Learning styles: Recognition in e-learning environments with feed-forward neural networks. *Journal of Computer Assisted Learning*, 22, 197–206.

Wilson, R.E., Gosling, S.D. and Graham, L.T. (2012). A review of Facebook research in the social sciences. *Perspectives on Psychological Science*, 7, 203–220.

Conclusion

19

THE FUTURE OF CYBERPSYCHOLOGY

Andrew Power and Gráinne Kirwan

Chapter summary

This final chapter reviews the cyberpsychological landscape, with particular focus on how the research described in this volume can be applied to broader contexts. It goes on to consider how cyberpsychology is developing as a result of changes in our online behaviour, and discusses the importance and relevance of such research, particularly in relation to emergent phenomena and technologies.

Reviewing the cyberpsychological landscape

Chapter 1 in this volume outlined the field of cyberpsychology, identifying some of the most commonly studied areas. These included computer mediated communication, impression management, online groups, disruptive behaviour, forensic cyberpsychology, clinical cyberpsychology, the psychology of virtual reality and the psychology of artificial intelligence. The book does not consider all of these topics, but it does identify specialised subjects within many of these areas where cyberpsychological insights and theory have practical and important applications.

The research in Part II examined online communication across a variety of media, including blogs, social networking, mobile communications, online dating and website design. By necessity, each of these chapters considers only a subset of the total body of cyberpsychological knowledge regarding these methods of communication. Much of this research has foundations in key communication theories such as Walther's (1996) description of hyperpersonal communication that, while dated, continues to inform and explain computer mediated communication today. While the research studies described here focus on specific types of online behaviour, it is likely that the findings of these studies can be extrapolated and applied to other contexts. For example, the attitudes of the adolescent females towards gender-specific science-oriented websites uncovered in Chapter 6 may be helpful in looking at the views of other groups towards media with different purposes. Such insights can be helpful in the development of any online resource aimed at encouraging or promoting specific behaviours, such as healthy living, active citizenship and education.

The research outlined in Part III also has implications far beyond the scope of the projects themselves. For example, Chapter 7 highlights how emerging technologies such as virtual assistants should be used with caution – while there may be a place for such applications in the future, it appears that not all users are ready to embrace them as yet. It would seem that there is a separate body of work to be completed in determining when a society (or a subset of that society) is open to new developments of different kinds, particularly in relation to virtual entities controlled by artificial intelligence. The study outlined in Chapter 9 can provide direction to research examining apparently altruistic online behaviour. The findings in this study may be applied by designing technology to encourage others to engage in online altruism, or to use their online presence to contribute to the offline society they live in (Power, 2011). Research outlined in Chapters 10 and 11 helps to identify those most at risk of cybercrime victimisation – extensions and variations on this research may help to identify those who can benefit most from educational strategies that aim to improve online security.

Part IV identified some ways in which psychological insights and research can be used to promote well-being. There is no shortage of journalistic articles and news stories examining the negative aspects of online life, such as problematic Internet use, cyberbullying and cybercrime. It cannot be denied that these are important topics, and research into these areas – and other harmful aspects of online life – is essential because of the negative effects that they can have on well-being. The scope and importance of these subjects are outlined in detail elsewhere (see, for example, Corcoran et al., 2012; Hinduja and Patchin, 2013; Jewkes and Yar, 2010, for cybercrime; Kirwan and Power, 2013; Kowalski et al., 2012, for cyberbullying; Kuss et al., 2013, for problematic Internet use; Quayle and Ribisi, 2012; Winkler et al., 2013; Young, 1998; Young and de Abreau, 2007). However, it is important that the opportunities for psychological benefit provided by the Internet are remembered and explored, as is outlined by the authors of Chapters 13 and 15 as they explore the potential of online therapy.

Finally, Part V examined the application of the Internet to education, identifying the use of multimedia and wikis in the educational process, as well as examining how the extensive information that is now available online about users can be utilised to develop more personalised online learning experiences. Many courses of scholarship are now available online, some leading to accreditation, some associated with major universities, some provided as an adjunct to classroom based learning, and some provided for pure interest. The research provided in this section outlines the importance of adequate evaluation of such materials, as well as indicating the educational potential provided by contemporary use of Internet applications. While the topics covered in the educational materials produced in these research studies are quite specific, the applications of the findings can be generalised to a much wider range of topics.

The research in this volume examines a variety of relevant cyberpsychological phenomena but, by necessity, cannot examine every area. Some topics, such as consumer cyberpsychology and the psychology of virtual reality, have received relatively little attention here, though a considerable body of academic literature has accumulated, which the interested reader is directed to. Other areas of research that have received relatively little psychological attention to date (such as cyber-crime victimisation and educational application of wikis) are examined in greater detail in this volume. Cyberpsychology continues to attract more attention from researchers, and the gaps in knowledge are beginning to be filled. However, as our knowledge extends, so the depth and breadth of the field also expand.

The future of cyberpsychology

Despite the increasing literature dedicated to cyberpsychological research, in many cases there are still a large number of unknowns regarding human behaviour in online settings. In some cases, academic literature finds it difficult to keep up with online developments and changes. Technological advances, feature changes and developments in popular culture all contribute to a rapidly changing spectrum of available applications. The relatively slow process of academic publishing struggles to keep up with the speed of technological advancement evident in this research area.

That is not to say that there is no benefit to cyberpsychological research – the sheer quantity of interactions and activities online in modern times indicates the necessity of a greater understanding of such behaviours. This is enhanced by a greater research focus on broader online contexts rather than specific applications. The changes in usage of the Internet over the past decade in particular, also affects online behaviour – previously anonymity and identity experimentation was common, whereas contemporary online behaviour focuses more on identification of the self, with accurate but positive self-representation (Chester and Bretherton, 2007). The lack of anonymity has led to interesting research regarding trust, privacy management and self-disclosure online (see, for example, Joinson and Paine, 2007; Joinson et al., 2010).

Changes in online behaviour set interesting questions. Could it be that eventually the distinction between cyberpsychology and offline psychology will disappear, and humans will behave in almost identical fashions in both contexts? While it is possible that online behaviour will simply become an extension of offline behaviour, this is not a certainty. In many online contexts, anonymity still exists, which in some cases leads to negative online behaviours such as flaming and trolling. Offline analogues, such as aggressive actions and language, obviously do exist, but the lowered inhibitions exhibited online do seem to play a part in the prevalence of such behaviours. Of particular interest is why individuals who would not engage in certain behaviours offline (including aggression, but also other acts such as self-disclosure and altruism) are more content and willing to do so online. The disinhibition effect noted by Suler (2004) and later explored in many research studies (see, for example, Lapidot-Lefler and Barak, 2012) is thought to contribute to this phenomenon. It would seem that while there are overlaps between online and offline behaviour, there are still important differences. It will be of interest to note if, over time, such differences remain, or vanish.

It is also important to consider emergent phenomena in cyberpsychology. Problematic Internet use is gathering increased media attention, particularly in relation to specific online behaviours such as gaming (see Chapter 1 for a more thorough exploration of this). Nevertheless, the positive aspects of such technologies are also being recognised. Gamification (solving non-game problems using game mechanics) is being applied to many contexts, including education (Domínguez *et al.*, 2013) and health promotion (Ahola *et al.*, 2013). Cyberpsychologists can provide distinctive and valuable insights into these and other emergent phenomena, providing guidance on the appropriate and beneficial use of new technologies.

Conclusion

Cyberpsychology is a fascinating area of research. Each of the studies in this volume provide insights and guidance on aspects of this field, and it is exciting to consider what new technologies and behaviours will emerge over the coming years. Our use of computers and other technology is in a constant state of flux, with some associated behaviours remaining fairly consistent but others changing at a rapid pace. Cyberpsychological research has been in existence for some time now, but it remains to be seen how much it will develop and change over the coming decades – future cyberpsychological texts may still consider the same phenomena as they apply to newer technologies, or they may explore areas that are currently beyond the scope of the field. In either case, insights from such research will remain invaluable in the explanation and application of these experiences.

References

Ahola, R., Pyky, R., Jämsa, T., Mäntysaari, M., Koskimäki, H., Ikäheimo, T.M., Huotari, M., Röning, J., Heikkinen, H.I. and Korpelainen, R. (2013). Gamified physical activation of young men: A multidisciplinary population-based randomised controlled trial (MOPO study). *BMC Public Health*, 13, 32–39.

Chester, A. and Bretherton, D. (2007). Impression management and identity online. In A. Joinson, K. McKenna, T. Postmes and U. Reips (eds) *The Oxford Handbook of Internet Psychology* (pp. 223–236). Oxford: Oxford University Press.

Corcoran, L., Connolly, I. and O'Moore, M. (2012). Cyberbullying in Irish schools: An investigation of personality and self-concept. *The Irish Journal of Psychology*, 33 (4), 153–165.

Domínguez, A., Saenz-de-Navarrete, J., de-Marcos, L., Fernández-Sanz, L, Pagés, C. and Martínez-Herráiz, J. (2013). Gamifying learning experiences: Practical implications and outcomes. *Computers & Education*, 63, 380–392.

Hinduja, S. and Patchin, J.W. (2013). Social influences on cyberbullying behaviours among middle and high school students. *Journal of Youth and Adolescence*. Published online ahead of print and retrieved from: www.ncbi.nlm.nih.gov/pubmed/23296318#.

Jewkes, Y. and Yar, M. (2010). *Handbook of Internet Crime*. Cullompton: Willan.

Joinson, A.N. and Paine, C.B. (2007). Self-disclosure, privacy and the Internet. In A. Joinson, K. McKenna, T. Postmes and U. Reips (eds) *The Oxford Handbook of Internet Psychology* (pp. 237–252). Oxford: Oxford University Press.

Joinson, A.N., Reips, U., Buchanan, T. and Paine-Schofield, C.B. (2010). Privacy, trust and self-disclosure online. *Human-Computer Interaction*, 25 (1), 1–24.

Kirwan, G. and Power, A. (2013). *Cybercrime: The psychology of online offenders*. Cambridge: Cambridge University Press.

Kowalski, R.M., Morgan, C.A. and Limber, S.P. (2012). Traditional bullying as a potential warning sign of cyberbullying. *School Psychology International*, 33 (5), 505–519.

Kuss, D.J., Griffiths, M.D. and Binder, J.F. (2013). Internet addiction in students: Prevalence and risk factors. *Computers in Human Behaviour*, 29 (3), 959–966.

Lapidot-Lefler, N. and Barak, A. (2012). Effects of anonymity, invisibility and lack of eye-contact on toxic online disinhibition. *Computers in Human Behaviour*, 28 (2), 434–443.

Power, A. (2011). Social networking: A pathway to active citizenship. Presented at the Intel European Research and Innovation Conference, Leixlip, Ireland: 12–14 October.

Quayle, E. and Ribisi, K.M. (2012). *Understanding and Preventing Online Sexual Exploitation of Children*. New York: Routledge.

Suler, J. (2004). The online disinhibition effect. *Cyberpsychology and Behaviour*, 7 (3), 321–326.

Walther, J.B. (1996). Computer-mediated communication: Impersonal, interpersonal and hyperpersonal interaction. *Communication Research*, 23 (1), 3–43.

Winkler, A., Dörsing, B., Rief, W., Shen, Y. and Glombiewski, J.A. (2013). Treatment of Internet addiction: A meta-analysis. *Clinical Psychology Review*, 33 (2), 317–329.

Young, K.S. (1998). Internet addiction: The emergence of a new clinical disorder. *Cyberpsychology and Behaviour*, 1 (3), 237–244.

Young, K.S. and de Abreu, C.N. (2007). *Internet Addiction: A handbook and guide to evaluation and treatment*. Hoboken, NJ: John Wiley & Sons.

INDEX